Nation-States and Nationalisms

Political Sociology series

Daniel Béland, *What is Social Policy?*
Understanding the Welfare State

Cedric de Leon, *Party & Society*

Nina Eliasoph, *The Politics of Volunteering*

Hank Johnston, *States & Social Movements*

Richard Lachmann, *States and Power*

Siniša Malešević, *Nation-States and Nationalisms*

Nation-States and Nationalisms: Organization, Ideology and Solidarity

Siniša Malešević

polity

First published in 2013 by Polity Press

Polity Press
65 Bridge Street
Cambridge CB2 1UR, UK

Polity Press
350 Main Street
Malden, MA 02148, USA

ISBN-13: 978–0–7456–5338–9
ISBN-13: 978–0–7456–5339–6(pb)

A catalogue record for this book is available from the British Library.

Typeset in 11 on 13 pt Sabon by
Servis Filmsetting Ltd, Stockport, Cheshire
Printed and bound in Great Britain by Clays Ltd, St Ives plc

For further information on Polity, visit our website: www.politybooks.com

For my friend, Goga Uzelac

Contents

Acknowledgements

While working on this book I have greatly benefited from the comments of and discussions with numerous colleagues and friends. In particular I would like to thank: Benedict Anderson, Michael Banton, John Breuilly, Rogers Brubaker, Miguel Centeno, John Coakley, Randall Collins, Katy Hayward, Jonathan Hearn, John Hutchinson, Richard Jenkins, Stathis Kalyvas, Krishan Kumar, Michael Mann, Lisa Moran, Niall O'Dochartaigh, Liam O'Dowd, Brendan O'Leary, Umut Özkırımlı, Kevin Ryan, Stacey Scriver, Martin Shaw, Anthony D. Smith, Gordana Uzelac and Andreas Wimmer. I am especially grateful to John A. Hall and the two anonymous reviewers for their extensive and insightful comments on the entire manuscript, and to Jonathan Skerrett at Polity, who has been an excellent editor throughout this project. I would also like to thank my colleagues in the UCD School of Sociology who were so welcoming and helpful in my transition to a new university. Most importantly this book, as is the case with all my previous works, would not have seen the light of day without the love, patience and sacrifices of my wife and colleague, Vesna, and the stimulating, affectionate and welcome distractions provided by my two boys, Luka and Alex.

1

The Salience of Nationalism

Introduction

Neil Armstrong's landing on the moon in 1969 was a momentous occasion in human history. This event signified the exceptional ingenuity and determination of humankind, whose representatives were now able to develop such advanced science, technology and organization to reach, and eventually conquer, outer space. The historic landing was seen as a tremendous success for all of humanity, and Armstrong's utterance about the 'giant leap for mankind' reflected this well. Despite intense cold war animosities, the event became a source of pride throughout the world.

Such universally shared feelings were just as evident in 2010 when thirty-three miners in Copiapo, Chile, became trapped 700 metres below the surface. Their ordeal and the struggles to save their lives quickly developed into a global event where billions around the world watched the unfolding of this potential tragedy on their TV screens and sincerely empathized with the miners' suffering and the emotional turmoil that their families went through. The eventual successful rescue of all the miners resulted in globally shared joy and pride, with human resolve and ingenuity as well as technological and organizational supremacy again celebrated all over the world.

There is no doubt that these two events had strong universalist appeal; they both symbolized the power of human perseverance and inventiveness and they both provided an emotional drama with which most human beings could easily identify. Yet behind this veil of universalism, the two events were also firmly couched in the images and language of nationalism. Once on the moon Neil Armstrong did not plant the flag of the UN or of his home town of Wapakoneta, Ohio. There was no discussion of whether it would be appropriate to erect the family crests of the Armstrongs or Aldrins, the symbols of the Apollo programme team or the flag of NASA, Armstrong's employers. Instead it was beyond any question that the only flag that must be raised was the flag of a specific nation-state: the USA. In addition, it was not accidental that the lunar landing module that took the astronauts to the moon was named *Eagle*, the American national symbol, whereas the command spacecraft that was waiting in orbit to take the astronauts back to Earth was called *Columbia*, an American symbol of liberty and justice.

Although the world's public shared Armstrong's joy, there was no doubt that the conquest of the moon was first and foremost an American victory: a sign of the technological, political, economic and ultimately *cultural* superiority of the American nation-state. This was obvious in the newspaper, radio and TV reports of the event in the USA and abroad. Since then the moon landing is commemorated in school textbooks and public ceremonies as a victory of the American people and its state: 'the US textbooks of the time never failed to depict the moon landing without [*sic*] noting that it was an American achievement' (Drori et al. 2003: 142).

For all its global human appeal, the rescue of Chilean miners was thoroughly framed in nationalist discourses. 'When the miners were discovered alive, their first spoken message to the world was the Chilean national anthem sung in unison. From that day onward, there were scantly few images of the site and the rescue process that did not include a Chilean flag' (Centeno et al. 2013: 279). The tents of miners' families in the makeshift tent city that sprang up around the site of the accident, *Campamento Esperanza* (Camp Hope), were all decorated with the Chilean flag. The families erected individual shrines for all thirty-three stranded miners that displayed thirty-two Chilean flags and one Bolivian flag, one to represent each miner. The rescue capsule was also painted in the colours of the Chilean flag. After the successful rescue, the informal leader of the miners, Luis Urzua, greeted his son and then hugged the president of Chile, Sebastian Piñera, saying: 'I've delivered to you this shift of workers, as we agreed I would.' The president replied 'I gladly receive your shift, because you completed your duty, leaving last like a good captain . . . You are not the same after this, and Chile won't be the same either' (Padget 2010). Urzua brought up the large Chilean flag that was displayed in the mine chamber during the rescue, and after all thirty-three miners were evacuated from the mine the rescuers put up a large banner reading 'Misión cumplida Chile' ('Mission accomplished Chile'). President Piñera gave a speech at the rescue site in which he praised Chile and depicted the rescue as a heroic victory of all Chileans, emphasizing that he was 'proud to be the president of all Chileans'. He also referred to the recent bicentennial celebration of Chile's sovereignty and praised the national unity of Chileans as displayed during the miners' accident.

What one can see here is how something that initially was understood to be a deeply personal, and thus universal, experience suddenly became a nationally framed and nationally experienced event. The private tragedies and joys of families, friends and neighbours were gradually infused with nation-centric discourses, and what at one point was only a local, *micro*-incident was eventually transformed into a nationalist project with global resonance. Once the accident was reframed as a national calamity it became a litmus test of Chilean national endurance. As clearly stated on the banner, the event was articulated as a national mission of Chile and for Chile, which had to be accomplished successfully. To rescue miners meant not only to save thirty-three lives but also to show to the world that the Chilean nation-state was sovereign, ordered and technologically and organizationally superior, while its citizens were unified and full of solidarity and compassion for each other. In this context, the mass media emphasized the internal solidarity of the trapped miners, who, reflecting the democratic and national character of the Chilean state, had prevented conflicts by helping each other and by adopting majority-vote decision making during their ordeal. In Urzua's own words: 'You just have to speak the truth and believe in democracy . . . everything was voted on . . . we were 33 men, so 16 plus one was a majority' (Carroll and Franklin 2010). The imagery, the rhetoric and the ritualism that accompanied the entire event successfully, and apparently unproblematically, fused the sentiments and emotions of those who were directly affected by unfolding adversity, such as miners and their families and friends, with those from the rest of Chile who had never been to Copiapo and who were unlikely ever to meet anyone from this small, remote mining outpost. This constant interplay between the personal and universal on the one hand and the national/nationalist on the other was clearly visible in Luis Urzua's affectionate embrace of a man, President Sebastian Piñera, he had never met before and who received more attention from Urzua than did some of Urzua's closest family members and friends. Furthermore, instead of first contacting his employers, the San Esteban Mining Company which owned the mine, it was the president of Chile who was addressed. The brief verbal exchange between Urzua and the president reflected the understanding that since the rescue of the miners was conceived as a national mission it was the president of the nation-state who had the ultimate authority over this operation. It is no accident that this highly hierarchical, ritual exchange of greetings between the two civilians closely resembled military discourse, as the speakers utilized soldierly and bureaucratic terms such as 'captain', 'duty' and 'delivery of tasks'. In the nation-centric articulation of the event the rescue of the miners became a heroic, national event that acquired recognizable features of a military action: a courageous, superhuman struggle against unprecedented adversity with expressed willingness to make sacrifices and perform one's duty in the name of a specific nation-state.

Although the successful rescue of so many miners and the landing on the moon are unique events, there is nothing unique in the way these events were ideologically and organizationally articulated. Despite their global and personal significance and appeal, they were quickly transformed into national events. Armstrong's moon landing was a global occasion but it stayed first and foremost an American affair. The rescue of the miners was a local incident with global ramifications, yet the event always remained a matter of the responsibility, sentiment and prestige of the Chilean nation-state. In both of these cases, as in so many others all over the world today, the personal, the local and even the global are often subsumed into the national. In the contemporary world, many tragic, heroic, dramatic or joyous happenings that affect larger groups of people tend to be framed in nation-centric or nationalist terms. Every time there is a plane crash, the first thing expected to be reported is how many of 'our co-nationals' have been killed. Olympic gold medals are won by specific, named individuals and small teams but they are habitually celebrated as national victories. Hurricanes, earthquakes and floods do not stop at the borders of nation-states, yet long-term relief efforts, long-lasting popular sympathies and protracted commitment to years of rebuilding and recovering often do. Even though the scientific discoveries, artistic accomplishments and heroic achievements of exceptional individuals are recognized all over the world, these individual successes are typically interpreted as enhancing the national prestige of specific nation-states. Why are we inclined to mourn the deaths of our 'co-nationals' much more than those of inhabitants of other nation-states? Why do we celebrate the victories of 'our' Olympians, scientists and artists and remain indifferent or hostile to the victories of others?

Despite some prevalent views that see the contemporary world as an interdependent global hub where advanced technology, communications and transport have apparently made human beings much more individualized and globalized (Bauman 2006; Beck 2006; 2002; 2000), it seems that the nation-state still remains the key organizing principle of our age. Rather than being a relic of past eras, nationalism has demonstrated a vibrancy and strength that very few, if any, contemporary ideologies could match. Although the waning, and even ultimate death, of nation-states and nationalisms has been proclaimed on numerous occasions over the past century or so, there are more nation-states in the world today than ever before and, as surveys show, more people identify in national terms at present than at any time in the past (Medrano 2009; Antonsich 2009; Smith and Kim 2006). As

Antonsich's (2009: 285) analysis of the Eurobarometer and other longitudinal surveys demonstrates, European citizens have become more not less nationalist; since the early 1980s a sense of national attachment and pride in one's nation-state 'has increased by ten percentage points'.

As our two cases show, the ascendency of nation-states and nationalisms does not stop on the surface of the globe, as the symbols of nationhood have now reached the extraterrestrial sphere and the deep interior of the Earth.

Why is nationalism such a potent and resilient ideology? How, why and when has the nation-state became the pre-eminent organizing mode of social and political life? Why do nationalist discourses still appeal to so many individuals all over the world? Why and how are nation-states often conceptualized in intimate, familial terms?

Once it becomes clear that the nation-state is, in many respects, an odd and unusual form of social organization that has been in existence for, historically speaking, a very short period of time, such questions gain in pertinence. Furthermore, once we realize that there is nothing natural and self-explanatory in feeling a strong sense of attachment to a specific nation-state, and that for 99.99 per cent of our history on this planet no individual was capable of developing such sentiments, then the present-day dominance of nationalism is even more puzzling. Where did nation-states and nationalism come from?

This book aims to provide answers to these questions. More specifically, the intention is to explore the sociological underpinnings of the historical processes involved in the formation and institutionalization of nation-states and nationalisms. To understand fully how and why the nation-state has emerged as the dominant model of polity, and nationalism as the principal source of political legitimacy in the modern era, it is necessary to take a *longue durée* view of these developments. To trace the origins of nation-states, one has to look at their organizational and ideological predecessors: hunting and gathering bands, chiefdoms, tribal confederacies, city-states and city-leagues, composite kingdoms, the early 'capstone' imperial orders and the latter-day modernizing empires. Similarly, to comprehend how nationalism came to be so ubiquitous in the modern age, it is crucial to engage with the pre-nationalist ideological doctrines and value systems that underlined the pre-modern social orders – from kinship-based descent, aristocratic myths of lineage, religious canons and the divine rights of monarchs to imperial creeds and civilizing missions. Hence, although both nation-states and nationalisms are profoundly modern phenomena, they could not have emerged without the organizational and (proto-)ideological scaffolding created by their pre-modern precursors. The fact that modern-day nation-states are nothing like 'capstone' empires, city-states or composite kingdoms, and that contemporary nationalisms bear no resemblance to the imperial, mythological and religious doctrines of yesteryear, does not mean that there is no organizational or ideological continuity here. On the contrary, one of the key arguments of this book is that the appearance of the nation-state as a pre-eminent institutional form and of nationalism as a dominant (operative) ideology of the modern era owes much to the elements of continuity. However, this is not the supposed biological continuity so dear to most nationalists, socio-biologists, evolutionary psychologists and other primordialists. Moreover, as argued in chapter 3, the link between the pre-modern and modern world is not cultural either. The arguments of more sophisticated approaches such as those of ethno-symbolists (Smith 2009; 1986; Hutchinson 2005; 1994) or perennialists (Armstrong 1982; Hastings 1997) that insist on the deep cultural foundations of modern nationhood and on the 'ethnic origins of nations' are just as unconvincing. There is a substantial degree of continuity between the pre-modern and modern world but this is neither biological nor cultural continuity. Instead it is organizational and indirectly ideological continuity that is at the heart of this historical process. More specifically in this book, I focus on the three long-term historical processes which I consider decisive in shaping the character of nation-states and nationalisms as we know them today: (1) the cumulative bureaucratization of coercion, (2) centrifugal ideologization and (3) the way these two processes envelop the hubs of micro-solidarity. The book charts in detail

7

how these three processes have helped create and maintain the world of nation-states and nationalisms.

Bureaucratization

There is no doubt that social organizations are the principal and most effective vehicles for social action.[1] Although human beings might be governed by strong and uncompromising beliefs, values and ideas, as Mann (2006a: 346–7) emphasizes, 'ideas can't do anything unless they are organized'. There is no social development, economic growth or political transformation without the existence of robust social organizations. It is organizational power that is at the heart of any significant social change. However, there are substantial differences between social organizations: they vary in size, organizational reach and capacity, in ability to control their members, territory, resources and ideology, and in many other ways. Since Weber (1968 [1921]) it has become apparent that, despite its popular association with inefficiency and heartlessness, bureaucracy has proved to be the most efficient mechanism for managing large numbers of individuals. In contrast to patrimonialism, gerontocracy, sultanism and other traditional forms of rule, the bureaucratic model of administration privileges knowledge, division of labour, merit, professionalism, consistency and transparency of rules, and the impersonality of hierarchical order. Once a version of this organizational model became a historical reality, it soon proved exceptionally potent in fulfilling specific organizational tasks. In terms of instrumental efficiency the traditional patrimonial or sultanic modes of rule could never match the capability of the bureaucratic administration. The direct consequence of this was an attempt to imitate and replicate this organizational model throughout the world. As Meyer and his collaborators (1997; 1992) have demonstrated, the isomorphic features of the bureaucratic form of organization can now be encountered all over the globe as the standardized models of governance are replicated at the level of polities, social movements and non-governmental organizations. More specifically, this includes such practices as rationalized demographic record keeping, uniformization of the constitutional forms that empha-size individual rights and state power, mass schooling developed around a standardized curriculum, development-oriented eco-nomic policies, standardized welfare provisions and population control policies, the formal equalization of the rights of citizens, and so on (Meyer et al. 1997: 152–3).

However, what is regularly overlooked by Meyer, and many others working in this research tradition, is that organizational power in general, and its bureaucratic form in particular, have a deep coercive underpinning (Malešević 2010). Since their incep-tion some 12,000 years ago, large-scale social organizations such as chiefdoms, city-states or pristine empires have emerged largely through coercive and violent means: wars, religious persecutions, massacres, slavery or *corvée* labour, to name a few. With the emergence of nation-states, able and willing to claim and estab-lish legitimately a monopoly on the use of violence over their territories, this coercive organizational power has only increased. Modern nation-states have unprecedented organizational capac-ity to fight prolonged and devastating wars that no pre-modern polity could possibly match. This external capacity is firmly rooted in a state's ability to pacify coercively the domestic realm, which remains heavily policed through a combination of direct surveillance, strict legislation and normative control. Since the bureaucratic mode of administration is popularly considered to be more legitimate and more efficient, it generally encounters little resistance. A particular political or economic system might be challenged or even successfully replaced by another, but there is no ambition to revert to the pre-organizational world of foragers. The political and economic colouring of a particular nation-state can change (e.g. liberal democracy, state socialism, military dic-tatorship etc.), but once established the nation-state acquires an organizational form that few would be willing to dismantle or change. The consequence of this is the continuous proliferation of complex social organizations in the modern era. These processes have particularly intensified since 1945 with the dramatic expan-sion in number of both governmental and non-governmental organizations (Boli and Thomas 1997; Feld 1972). This is especially visible on the global scale as there are more nation-states today than ever before in history.

Hence, as a nation-state is a particular form of bureaucratic social organization, to understand its origin, development and the impact it has in the contemporary world it is of paramount importance to understand the organizational processes that underpin the nation-state. A key feature of this process is the cumulative character of organizational power and its coercive reach. Although the form of the dominant social organizations changes through time, as chiefdoms, city-states, empires and nation-states among others replace one another, the general tendency has been a gradual and cumulative increase in organizational power. Despite occasional historical reversals and stagnation, the best examples of which were the feudal fiefdoms and *Ständestaat* of medieval Europe or state failure in modern-day Africa, the trajectory of state development, viewed *sub specie aeternitatis*, is characterized by the relatively continuous increase in states' organizational capacity. The cumulative potential that has characterized organizational power since its inception has substantially intensified with the emergence of nation-states. The increasing size of populations and the corresponding demand for goods, services and resources have further reinforced the significance of social organizations and have made individuals more dependent on the workings of organizational power. Thus nation-states are a by-product of the long-term contingent historical process that I call the *cumulative bureaucratization of coercion* (Malešević 2010: 5–7, 92–130). This open-ended historical process, which involves ever-increasing coercive organizational capacity and a simultaneous attempt at the internal pacification of a polity's social order, has been in operation for centuries. However, with the gradual ascent of the nation-state – a polity that has unparalleled infrastructural reach, territorial monopoly and societal penetration – over the last two hundred years, this process has dramatically accelerated and intensified.

Ideologization

Stating the fact that social organizations are generally built around a coercive core does not mean to suggest that they are always imposed on individuals against their will. Obviously some organizations, such as prisons, psychiatric secure units, concentration camps and the Atlantic slave trade ships, relied almost exclusively on coercive control and violence. However, most social organizations combine coercive power with normative justification. Even rudimentary forms of organizations were usually built around particular belief systems which were meant to supply a degree of legitimation. Thus social organizations in the pre-modern world generally relied on mythology, religion or imperial doctrines to justify their existence and mobilize a degree of popular support. These proto-ideologies involved such discursive frameworks as mythologies of non-human descent, doctrines of the divine origins of monarchs and nobility, or imperial civilizing missions, among others. In this sense the cumulative bureaucratization of coercion was often accompanied by the proto-ideological doctrines that helped legitimize its coercive edge. The traditional rulers had to provide some kind of justification for their military conquests, for the violent suppression of the domestic population and for their right to govern. However, since most of these political orders had pronounced 'capstone' features (see chapter 2), where there was little interaction between the rulers and the rest of the population, the legitimacy was beneficial but not an indispensable prerequisite for political action.

The arrival of modernity and the formation of nation-states have brought about a profound change. The nation-states were the first polities whose legitimacy was derived from the ideas of popular sovereignty and the equal moral worth of all their citizens. In this context, the actions of social organizations and the entire process of coercive bureaucratization became heavily dependent on the ideological justification. Whereas the Egyptian pharaohs and ancient Chinese emperors could easily start wars or order their subjects to be killed over trivial issues, the presidents and prime ministers of present-day nation-states require a great deal of public support to initiate even a small change in fiscal policy or diplomacy. These structural transformations have made modern-day citizens much more receptive to ideological bifurcations. The gradual expansion of the public sphere, together with the skyrocketing of literacy rates, the proliferation of secularized ideological discourses, mass education, an affordable press, pamphlets and books, the democratization of political life, and the expansion of civil society networks, has also fostered the greater politicization of ordinary individuals. In this cacophony of ideas and practices, ideologies have become not only the key social vehicles for the articulation of blueprints and vistas for a better social order but also powerful devices for the legitimization of social action. Moreover, once despondent peasants and the urban poor found themselves on the road to becoming full citizens of their respective nation-states they also became more amenable to accepting the key tenets of particular ideological doctrines. The organizational changes which saw empires, composite kingdoms and city-states turning gradually into nation-states were rooted not only in the cumulative bureaucratization of coercion but also in the process I term *centrifugal ideologization* (Malešević 2010: 8–11). This historical process involved a gradual ideological penetration of entire societies whereby, over time, different social strata became highly receptive not only to ideological justification of particular social and political actions, but also to ideological mobilization in the pursuit of such collective action. What in early modernity was a prerogative of a small number of cultural and political elites had developed by the twentieth century into a mass phenomenon: organized individuals and groups aware of their rights, responsibilities and armed with the shared blueprints of a better future. In this sense, the steady spread of organizational power was paralleled by the expansion of ideological power: the mass educational systems created literate and ideological citizens; the burgeoning of mass media and publishing fostered the emergence of politically aware individuals; and the democratization of the public realm was highly conducive to mass ideological mobilization.

Since nation-states are large, bureaucratic units composed of highly disparate individuals and groups with different interests and values, the central issue is how to forge a degree of cultural and political unity out of this immense diversity. All major ideologies, such as liberalism, socialism, conservatism, religious fundamentalism, anarchism or republicanism, offer potent visions of a desirable social universe and recipes to achieve ideological unity. However, instead of achieving this unity, their sharp ideological differences stimulate profound disagreements and ideological polarization. Hence, such internal discords can best be circumvented through the ideological doctrine that encompasses the entire social order: nationalism. Although, like any other ideology, nationalism is deeply grounded in utopian visions that promise to transcend social conflicts and ideological polarities, its central message of all-national unity has proved appealing to rulers and ruled alike. Once the nation-state was established as the principal unit of governance in modernity, nationalism trumped other ideological doctrines to become the dominant operative ideology of this era (Malešević 2006; and see chapter 3 below). This prevalence of nationalist ideology over its rivals was deeply rooted in the long-term historical processes that are the cumulative bureaucratization of coercion and centrifugal ideologization. These two processes were responsible for enhancing the organizational and ideological powers which initially gave birth to the nation-state and then helped reinforce its dominance. Once the nation-state was established as the pre-eminent power vessel of the modern era it provided the institutional contours for nationalism. In other words, the dominance and proliferation of nationalism in modernity stems in large part from the organizational prevalence of the nation-state, which has become the near-universal model of governance in the world today. The nation-state supplies an organizational skeleton for nationalism and nationalism remains dependent on this organizational scaffolding.

Solidarity

To argue that nation-states and nationalisms are the product of continuous bureaucratization and ideologization does not mean to suggest that they are imposed against the will of the individuals involved. As I have emphasized in previous studies (Malešević 2011a; 2011b; 2010; 2006), nationalism is not a form of false consciousness. Although its origins, expansion and present-day dominance are rooted in the *longue durée* processes of coercive bureaucratization and centrifugal ideologization, one's sense of attachment to a particular nation-state is not an artefact produced by some kind of gargantuan brainwashing. On the contrary, 'being national' today is a near-universal norm, and for an overwhelming majority of inhabitants of this planet, nationhood is understood to be the principal form of human solidarity. Although all nationalisms depend on the workings of social organizations and entail a substantial degree of ideological know-how, the ultimate success of this ideology[2] has always been dependent on its ability to penetrate the grassroots. Although nationalist ideologies address millions of individuals and articulate visions for entire countries, the resonance of their message remains dependent on their ability to permeate the micro-universe of family, friends, lovers, neighbours, peers and one's locality. Since most human beings find a sense of comfort, security and fulfilment in small, face-to-face groups rather than in anonymous, large-scale organizations, the central goal for any nationalist discourse is to blend the national successfully with the local, the macro with the micro, and the organizational with the personal.

However, the relationship between the micro- and the macro-universe is filled with tension. As the nation-state is essentially a bureaucratic unit, it is not easy to make it lovable. The nation-state like any organization is built on principles that foster the ethics of professional detachment, instrumental rationality, formality, legality and hierarchy, whereas the realm of family and friendship belongs to the world that stimulates the exact opposite: informality, emotional commitment, deep involvement, non-hierarchical relationships and love. Hence nationalism develops as an ideology which attempts to transcend the public/private dichotomy by casting social organizations in the image of kinship and friendship networks.

As Weber (1968 [1921]) demonstrated convincingly, all

bureaucratic social organizations, and the nation-state is no exception, eventually start to resemble each other. As they embrace the principles of rational calculation, control and teleological efficiency, there is a constant pull towards sameness, towards what Weber called the iron cage and 'the polar night of icy darkness'. In contrast, family life, kinship networks, friendships, peer groups and other forms of micro-solidarity stimulate difference, the unique shared experiences and the spontaneous expressions of mutual commitment. Thus, nationalism emerges as an ideological surrogate that aims to link the two contrasting realms. In this context, ideologization remains crucial, as when it is able to justify the very existence of the social organization that is the nation-state. Nationalism reconciles the deep tension between the rationality and coldness of the social organizations on the one hand, and the emotionality and warmth that are created in the hubs of micro-solidarity on the other. In other words, nationalist ideology attempts to bridge the ongoing division between the 'state' part and the 'nation' part of the nation-state by depicting the nation as a community of close friends or a giant extended family. For example, the Japanese nationalist project was particularly successful in blending the familial and the national in the imaginary of the family-state (*kazoku kokka*) and the 'conservation of the national essence' (*kokusui hozon*) interpreted through the prism of shared, family-centred ethics (Surak 2012).

Solidarity is at the heart of any nationalist project, and the nationalist ideology can only work properly when able to achieve full ideological penetration and tie the pockets of micro-solidarity around the existing bureaucratic scaffolding. In contrast to Durkheim, who differentiates between the mechanical solidarity of the pre-modern world and the organic solidarity of the modern era, it is crucial to emphasize that in some important respects all genuine solidarity is 'mechanical'. Genuine solidarity entails protracted emotional commitment and face-to-face interaction, which large-scale social organizations simply cannot provide. One can never love the bureaucratic unit that is the nation-state in the same way one loves one's children or parents. Yet when successful, nationalism is capable of projecting parental and other forms of love onto the contours of the nation-state. By invoking the images of our brothers, who are sacrificing their lives so that we can live, and our mothers and daughters who need to be protected from the merciless enemy, nationalist ideology can tap into the micro-universes of families, lovers and friends, and, in the process, make a nation-state resemble those most dear to us.

The Structure of the Book

This book offers a comparative historical and sociological analysis of the processes involved in the emergence, formation, expansion and transformation of nation-states and nationalisms. The approach articulated emphasizes the central role that the organizational and ideological powers play in this process. More precisely, I explore how the cumulative bureaucratization of coercion and centrifugal ideologization have stimulated the development of nation-states and nationalisms. Furthermore, I chart the key historical organizational and ideological transformations which fostered the ever-closer links between the intimacy of the micro-world and the cold rationalities of the bureaucratic macro-universe. I explore when, how and why nationalist macro-ideologies were able to envelop the microcosm of family, kin, residential and friendship networks. In particular, I look at the processes through which bonds of micro-solidarity have been successfully transformed into believable nationalist narratives with strong emotional resonance.

The second chapter focuses on pre-modern social organizations and group attachments. It records the changes in human collectivities by looking at the relationships between dominant forms of social organizations, the principal proto-ideological discourses and one's personal sense of belonging and solidarity during different historical epochs. The chapter explores the role of mythology, religion and imperial doctrines as sources of proto-ideological power and their congruence with specific social organizations, such as nomadic bands, complex sedentary hunting and gathering 'tribes', chiefdoms, city-states, agrarian 'capstone' empires and the latter-day modernizing empires. My analysis emphasizes the inherent lack of social solidarity and group attachments beyond one's social strata and kinship. Pre-modern social orders had neither the means to foster cultural homogeneity nor an interest in doing so, and until the early modern era there was little, if any, overlap between existing polities and cultural identities. However, this analysis also indicates that there is a significant element of organizational and, indirectly, ideological continuity between the pre-modern and modern worlds which has proved decisive for the latter-day emergence of nation-states and nationalisms.

The third chapter explores the key structural transformations that were decisive for the development and expansion of nationalist ideals and the establishment of the first nation-states. I analyse the existing theoretical accounts of these developments and engage in a brief debate with the leading theorists of nationalism. Although highly sympathetic to the modernist interpretations of nation-state formation, I contest both the rigid emphasis on historical discontinuity present in some modernist positions and the ethno-symbolic approaches that insist on the cultural continuity of the pre-modern and modern worlds. Instead, my analysis focuses on the steady increase in the organizational and ideological powers of new polities and the inherent tensions that emerge between the personal realm of micro-solidarity (family, kin, neighbourhood, friendships) and the macro-public realm (the state, the military, business corporations etc.). In particular, the chapter deals with the ideological legacies of the Enlightenment and Romanticism, the geo-political competition between European 'Great Powers', the outcomes of the French and American revolutions, and the social impact of dramatic changes in economy, science and technology. More specifically, the chapter charts how transformations in industry, capitalist economies, colonial expansion and inter-state rivalries shaped the character of modern nation-states by fostering greater cultural and linguistic homogeneity, standardized educational systems, the spread of universal literacy, mass military conscription, citizenship rights, urbanization and secularity. The chapter analyses when and why nationalist ideologies become appealing to different social strata and how different forms of nationalisms emerged in different parts of the world.

The fourth chapter analyses the relationship between nationalisms and organized violence. It aims to show how complex and contradictory this relationship is. I contest the views that see nationalism as being causally linked with violence and show that nationalist ideology is seldom a principal source of violent acts. The chapter situates such violent events as wars, revolutions, terrorism, insurgency, ethnic cleansing and genocide in the broader historical context. In contrast to approaches that see influential individuals or groups as the principal cause of violent nationalism, I highlight the role played by social organizations and ideologies. The key argument is that in most instances the mutation of nationalist ideas into violent acts is mediated by coercive bureaucratization, centrifugal ideologization and their link with the networks of micro-solidarity.

The focal point of the fifth chapter is the everyday, habitual nationalism expressed in international sporting contests, tourism, public ceremonics, cinematography, national cuisine, song contests and similar occasions. The chapter disputes the well-established dichotomy between 'hot' and 'banal' nationalisms, the prevalent orthodoxy that views the ordinary, everyday, expressions of nationalism as feeble, and the general perception that banal nationalism is largely a post-World War II Western phenomenon. Instead the chapter makes an argument that the triviality and banality associated with the routine, everyday expressions of nationalist experience have been a dominant feature of most nationalisms since the inception of this ideology in the late eighteenth and nineteenth centuries. In this sense, the ordinary and the trivial have been at the heart of organizational and ideological powers and their ability to penetrate successfully into the intimacies and solidarities of families, friends and locality. It is the habitual, taken-for-granted practices and actions that have helped establish and reinforce the organizational and ideological strengths of nation-states. Hence, rather than signalling weakness and the gradual disappearance of nationalist ideology, the expansion of the trivial forms of nationalist experience reveals its ever-increasing strength.

The sixth chapter challenges the popular and academic understandings of 'national identity', a notion which is often embraced as given and unproblematic. Although there are pronounced disagreements on whether national identities are modern or primordial, and on how best to gauge the intensity of identification with a particular nation, there is near-unanimity on the view that national identities are real and perceptible entities. In contrast to such a view, this chapter argues that not only was there no national identity before modernity but also that there is little empirical evidence for the existence of national identities in the modern age either. While it is obvious that many individuals show great affinity for their nation-states and often express sincere devotion to the 'national cause', these are not reliable indicators of the existence of a durable, continuous, stable and monolithic entity called 'national identity'. To understand fully the character of popular mobilization in modernity, it is of paramount importance to refocus our attention from the slippery and non-analytical idiom of 'identity' towards well-established sociological concepts such as 'social organizations', 'ideology' and 'solidarity'. In particular, the central object of this research becomes the processes through which large-scale social organizations successfully transform earnest micro-solidarity into an all-encompassing nationalist ideology. To illustrate this argument the chapter provides a critical analysis of representative quantitative and qualitative studies of 'national identity'.

The final chapter summarizes the key arguments developed and presented in the book and briefly engages with the state of nationalisms and nation-states in the contemporary world. It assesses the debates on the impact of globalization, new technologies, religious radicalism, neo-liberalism and terrorism on nation-states and nationalist ideologies. I argue that, ultimately, none of these social forces is likely to weaken substantially the power of the nation-state, which in most respects remains the most important organizational vehicle of modernity. In a similar vein, instead of weakening nationalism these new social developments are interpreted as contributing to the transformation and renewal of nationalist ideologies, which remain highly adaptable and resilient. Nationalism has always been, and continues to be, a protean doctrine and practice able to adjust, metamorphose and survive, no matter what.

2

Group Solidarities before the Nation-State

Introduction

The absolute dominance of the nation-state model as an organizing principle of the world order today might imply that this is a normal and natural way to categorize human societies and order social and political life. However, despite the popular, and some scholarly, tendency to project the concept of the nation-state into the past, for 99.99 per cent of our existence on this planet human beings did not live in such polities. Instead we inhabited a variety of social and political orders which were either much smaller, less centralized and less stratified or substantially bigger, more hierarchical and typified by a greater cultural diversity. In other words our predecessors populated such diverse entities as simple bands of foragers, complex sedentary hunting and gathering tribes, chiefdoms, city-states, city-leagues, composite kingdoms and empires, among others. These social and political orders were characterized by weaker organizational and ideological penetration of the micro-world. Before the age of the nation-state, rulers lacked the organizational means to break deeply into the microcosm of family, kinship, friendships or locality. Undeveloped transport, communication, division of labour and technology, with rampant illiteracy, were the key stumbling blocks to the expansion of the coercive reach of political power. In addition, unlike the nation-state, where the principal source of legitimacy is derived from nationalist principles of sovereignty, cultural homogeneity and the equal moral worth of all citizens, the pre-modern social orders tended to justify their existence through mythology, religion, imperial creeds or some kind of combination of these.

However, to understand the origins and present dominance of the nation-state model it is crucial to look far into the past and engage with the variety of pre-modern polities. Although a nation-state is a qualitatively different type of social and political order, it did not spring out of nowhere. Instead it emerged as a profoundly contingent outcome of different social processes. Among these processes the most important were the gradual and cumulative increase in organizational and ideological powers and the eventual ability of large-scale organizations to fuse pockets of micro-solidarities into a secularized system of shared beliefs and practices. This is not to say that the historical developments can be read back as a simple evolutionary tale from hunter-gatherers, chiefdoms, city-states and early kingdoms to empires and finally nation-states. The historical record is full of reversible processes, parallel existences of different types of polity and hybrid formations. Hunter-gatherers, chiefdoms and composite kingdoms are very much still in existence, although largely at the margins of the contemporary world.

This is also not to say that the nation-state is the ultimate and optimal unit for organizing social and political life or that empires, city-states or city-leagues can be confined to the dustbin of history. This chapter explores the organizational, ideological and micro-sociological underpinnings of the pre-modern social and political orders, with the aim of identifying the historical trajectories that gave birth to the nation-state.

From Nomadic to Sedentary Solidarities

Despite the popular perception, reinforced by much of traditional social science, of human beings as intrinsically gregarious creatures, as a number of recent studies show (Turner 2007; Turner and Maryanski 2005), intensive social bonding does not come naturally to humans. Evolutionary processes worked towards making monkeys much more social creatures than apes.[1] In contrast to monkeys that lived on trees with abundant food that could sustain sizeable troops, the walking apes could not survive in large group-ings. The large open areas of the African savannah, filled with shrinking forests, deadly predators and no place to hide, meant that the only way to survive was to avoid large congregations and move in very small packs.

Even this strategy could not guarantee survival and most species of apes eventually became extinct. In this context, as Turner (2007: 23) explains, natural selection provided a solution for limiting the group size of walking apes 'by wiring apes for the female transfer pattern that, in essence, breaks the group apart at puberty and by weakening ties among all adults so that they could move alone in temporary and small foraging parties in the forest canopy. Weak ties, mobility, individualism, and fluid groups were fitness enhancing in the marginal niches of the arboreal habitat.' While describing early humans as 'individualists' is certainly an overstatement, the available archaeological evidence points in the direction of weak and highly flexible social ties among archaic *Homo sapiens*. Consequently, the presence of constant external threats fostered the emergence of very small, hunting and gather-ing bands of early humans. Furthermore, this insecure and vastly challenging habitat had a profound impact on the cognitive and emotional capacities of hominids. The lack of sharp teeth, claws, horns, a strong sense of smell or speed meant that early humans had to develop alternative sources for long-term survival: social organization, eventually accompanied by a degree of shared practices and creeds, and, most importantly, intensive bonds of micro-solidarity.

The emergence of rudimentary social organizations and rela-tively coherent beliefs requires substantial cognitive abilities which gradually developed over millions of years. Hence it was most probable that all species of walking apes would have become extinct before any durable social organizations could appear. The fact that this did not happen[2] indicates that some walking apes adopted another social mechanism for long-term preserva-tion: social solidarity. As recent psychological and sociological studies demonstrate (Collins 2008; 2004; Damasio 2003; 1994), rather than being opposites, cognition and emotion often develop together and reinforce each other. Moreover, the rise in cognitive abilities often entails a substantial degree of emotional development. Since emotions are the essential ingredient of solidarity it seems plausible to argue, as Turner (2007: 41) does, that the very survival of our species is grounded in our ability to become emotionally attuned to each other: 'It is emotions – once controlled, channeled and expanded – that allowed our ancestors to survive, even with small brains that could not produce any more culture than the limited cultural repertoire of present-day chimpanzees.'

The central feature of emotional interaction is the ability to interpret the meanings behind expressed emotions in face-to-face contact. As Collins (2004: 78) puts it, 'face-to-face social interaction takes place among physiological systems, not merely among individuals as cognitive systems or bodily actors'. Close proximity is important for emotional interaction as humans recognize and understand emotions through visual cues. Hence the direct, face-to-face encounter is the most important source of emotional energy. Goffman (1961: 17–18) identified the encounter (or focused gathering) as a central micro-process of interaction involving the immediate physical presence of human beings. Although he distinguishes between face-to-face and group-interaction-based encounters, in both instances the encounter involves participants' continuous focus of attention and provides 'the communication basis for a circular flow of feeling among the participants'. The fact that early humans lived in very small groupings rarely exceeding a handful of individuals, who would often move from one micro-group to another, meant that they had to develop superior cognitive and emotional capacities to read the emotional cues of (changing) others. This long-term evolutionary process fostered the creation of a very complex and extensive range of emotions which now characterize human interaction, and these complex emotions and feelings such as shame, guilt, disgust, envy, pride etc. proved decisive for forging a strong sense of solidarity among early hunters and gatherers. Bearing in mind that for more than 99 per cent of our history as a species on this planet we have lived in very small and highly flexible collectivities often comprised of no more than thirty to fifty individuals (Service 1978; Fry 2005), the early forms of group solidarity could not expand much beyond immediate kin groups and extended families.

These very small hunting and gathering bands were the dominant form of social life for close to 1.8 million years, and until the end of the Mesolithic there were no significant alternatives to this rudimentary form of collective existence.[3] The highly flexible, mobile and non-sedentary lifestyle fostered the emergence of very small kinship-based clans and extended families where the enhanced sentiments of solidarity (including the sharing of scarce food and water, shelter, animal skins for clothing, and care for the sick, wounded, elderly and infants, as well as the shared responsibility for protection from predatory animals) developed as the principal mechanism for individual survival. Simply put, the original humans were not naturally communal creatures; it was the hostile structural conditions that made micro-level social bonding a necessity. More importantly for this study, the scope of human collective attachment for hundreds of thousands of years remained very small: an egalitarian, non-hierarchical, mobile, fluid, kinship-based, non-sedentary band. Hence, rather than being evolutionarily programmed to live in large-scale collectivities such as tribes, ethnic groups, cities, nation-states or empires, human beings are emotionally, cognitively, biologically and socially 'wired' for life in the much smaller entities: face-to-face micro-groups. In this sense bonds of actual solidarity (rather than the projection of solidarity later spawned by large social organizations), generated over hundreds of thousands of years in the African savannah, remain wedded to real physical interaction between human beings.

The transition from nomadic bands to sedentary, complex, hunting and gathering 'tribes', which occurred slowly and often involved reversibility to a nomadic lifestyle, did not automatically lead to the emergence of coherent, culturally differentiated and centralized collectivities. Instead the members of a settled 'tribe'[4] would often speak different languages, engage in distinct rituals, follow different leaders and with relative ease switch tribal allegiances or simultaneously belong to more than one tribe (Fry 2005; Fried 1975). In this sense the conventional description of tribal groupings as 'ethnic groups' is misleading since it presumes that shared social life inevitably implies a substantial degree of cultural homogeneity and even political identity. For example, socio-biological and other primordialist views of ethnic groups as stable and clearly distinct units of evolution that share genetic descent and date back long before the emergence of *Homo sapiens* (van den Berghe 1995; 1981; Gat 2006; van der Dennen 1999) are profoundly inaccurate.[5] Rather than resembling mutually exclusive monads and billiard balls, the early tribal formations were culturally and biologically highly diverse, fluid, often exogamous and structurally unstable. As recent research (Steuer 2006; Geary 2002; 1988) indicates, traditional historiographic and archaeological accounts that depicted migrations of prehistoric tribal associations were deeply influenced by the prejudices of their own times: Roman writers simplified, stereotyped and homogenized the cultural diversities of the 'barbarians' while nineteenth-century, nation-centric Romanticism and Enlightenment writers projected their imagined 'nations' into the past. Hence instead of tracing the complex dynamics of collectivity formation they often tended to assume the existence of clearly defined, culturally homogeneous and politically conscious ethnic groups (Geary 1988: 41–4).[6] For example, the same name is often used for completely different tribal groupings (Ariovistus' Suebi and Marcomanni, the Suebi of Tacitus and the Marcomanni of Maroboduus, the Suebi of the migration period in the Iberian Peninsula and the Marcomannic Wars of 166–80 CE), or tribal groupings were sharply distinguished from each other despite the fact that they did not see themselves in such terms (Steuer 2006; Geary 2002; 1988). Furthermore, much of European historiography talks about the migrations of entire peoples ('barbarians') who at some point settle and inhabit their 'present-day' homelands. Nevertheless, careful archaeological studies show that these movements of population were in fact military campaigns often involving temporary alliances of culturally diverse warrior bands. As Steuer (2006: 228) demonstrates: 'the groups called in the [Roman and, following them, nineteenth-century] sources by names such as Suebi or Langobardi were warrior bands and not neighbouring societies living in villages with families or kinship groups . . . through their concept of order, ancient writers equated the names of mobile and multi-ethnic warrior bands with inhabitants of the territories from which some of the warriors were drawn'. Geary's studies (2002; 1988) clearly show that the sharp distinctions between Germanic, Celtic, Slavic and other 'peoples' made by Roman scholars such as Tacitus and reproduced over centuries had little if anything to do with the reality of tribal life. 'The tribe was a constantly changing grouping of people bound together by shared perceptions, traditions and institutions. As these commonalities changed, tribes changed; they expanded to absorb other groups, they split apart to form new tribes, they disappeared into more powerful tribes . . . these groups were more processes than stable structures' (Geary 1988: 53).

In other words, although 'tribe' was a more organized unit of social life, it, too, just like a band, remained organizationally and ideologically too fragile to maintain the cultural homogeneity and political consciousness associated with the more durable collectivities that are known as ethnic groups and nation-states. The tribal associations were conglomerates of diverse clan and kinship groups often temporarily united by elements of shared mythology, joint military undertakings, economic interest, geopolitical realities and other structural forces. The principal sources of micro-solidarity remained highly localized around patrilineal or matrilineal kinship structures and households reinforced by face-to-face interaction and mutual interdependence in everyday life. While the exogamous character of most clans and other kinship groupings provided the central glue that, together with shared mythology and military goals, held the tribal associations together, networks of social solidarity would rarely reach beyond one's micro-group.[7] However, the tribal lifestyle contributed gradually to the deepening of social solidarity among micro-groups, whereas its rudimentary shared mythology of non-human descent (for example, totemism) and its fledgling social organization provided a stepping stone for more potent social formations such as chiefdoms or early kingdoms. This is not to say that one can observe a simple, evolutionary transition from bands to tribes and chiefdoms, as individuals would often belong to more than one collectivity. For example, there was no overlap between a tribe and a warrior band in the Merovingian world. The Germanic warrior bands (*comitatus* or *Gefolgschaft*) would regularly cross tribal lines, thus creating mutually competing sources of micro-solidarity: 'these warrior bands were destabilising groups within an already fragile tribal structure . . . [but] they were also potential nuclei around which might form new tribes' (Geary 1988: 56). Hence rather than assuming the existence of clearly defined, fixed, continuous, culturally and even politically self-conscious Celts, Goths, Avars, Suebs or Franks, it is crucial to understand that such labels were provisional, externally imposed categories, the contents of which were constantly changing.[8] Similarly, the existence of basic mythology and embryonic social institutions does not suggest possession of a durable, complex, stable and centralized social organization and society-wide shared ideology, which, in addition to the sense of micro-solidarity, are the principal ingredients of nationhood. Therefore, as nationhood cannot be built on kinship alone, there were no structural conditions for the development of nationalism in the non-sedentary and simple sedentary collectivities.

Territorial Loyalties without Nation: The City-State

Although, with the possible exception of socio-biologists, most scholars would agree that there was no room for nationhood in any form before antiquity, some (Roshwald 2006; Grosby 2006; Cohen 2000; Hastings 1997) argue that one could identify several groups such as Egyptians, Jews, Armenians, Greeks or Chinese as examples of 'ancient nations'. For instance, Roshwald (2006: 14–32) argues not only that both ancient Jews and ancient Greeks were fully fledged nations but even that one could legitimately speak about Greek and Jewish nationalism in antiquity. Through the rather imaginative interpretation of passages from the biblical texts and fairly scant archaeological artefacts,[9] Roshwald aims to show that the organizational preconditions for nations and nationalism already existed in ancient Judaea and Greece. In this understanding the ancient world was already in possession of 'means and forms of mass mobilization' such as mass media, political parties or universal education. In his own words: 'Hearing the Torah read in public every Sabbath and market day from early Second Temple times on must have created (and still does) a sense of simultaneity of experience that was more, not less, powerful than the daily ritual of reading the newspaper that Anderson refers to as the hallmark of modern imagined communities' (Roshwald 2006: 17). Leaving on one side the fact that the use of literary (biblical) texts written, and periodically altered, over many years by different authors is not much proof of mass behaviour in antiquity, the attempt to conflate a specific religious ritual with the ideology of nationalism is completely misplaced. This view makes no distinction between the enormous socio-economic, cultural and political differences between the pre-modern and the modern worlds. It wrongly conflates the small, semi-nomadic, religious groupings of ancient Judaea, who understood the world in the eschatological sense of heaven, hell and final judgement and had no concept of secularized territorial sovereignty, with the mass-scale, popular, cross-class mobilization of citizens infused with Enlightenment-inspired beliefs in the moral equality of human beings and the demotic right of self-determination of sovereign nations. As Shlomo Sand (2010: 124) convincingly shows in his study, ancient Judaea did not meet the elementary organizational conditions for the emergence of nations and nationalism: 'In an illiterate peasant society without an educational system or a standard common language, and with limited means of communication – only a few percent could read and write – a copy or two of the Torah might have been a fetish but could not have served as an ideological campfire.' To hear a sermon from the Torah in a synagogue is a profoundly different experience from reading a national newspaper: while the former inspires existential angst and religious awe, the latter conceptualizes the world in the essentially secular terms of shared political and economic interests, group belonging beyond kinship and below religion, and a sense of large-scale sovereign territoriality.

In a similar vein ancient Greeks did not constitute a nation in any sociologically meaningful sense. Cohen (2000) argues that since the polis was a small, self-governing community where inhabitants were able to know each other personally and define social status in terms of residency (being an *astos* or *aste*, a townsman or townswoman, one could legitimately talk about the 'Athenian nation'. This argument is often illustrated by the comments made by Pericles in his Funeral Oration, where he glorifies the greatness and freedom of Athens. However, despite shared cultural practices including festivals, sports, language, mythology and the pantheon of deities on Olympus, the Hellenic world was essentially not more than a common cultural universe, while political loyalties rested with the individual city-states. As Smith (2004: 130–2) points out, there were significant cultural and linguistic differences between Ionians, Dorians, Aeolians and others, and the Hellenic world never had a single centre of authority or unifying legal system. Hall (1997: 153) emphasizes that 'the language that we term Ancient Greek was in reality a collection of regionally specific (or epichoric) dialects which can be traced by identifying isoglosses'. Moreover, apart from the small number of rhetoricians influenced by Isocrates, there was no political will among the elites of city-states to forge anything beyond temporary alliances for the purpose of war. Even the largest city-states such as Athens or Sparta were too small, territorially too porous, internally too heterogeneous, politically and socially too stratified, and lacking in a unique cultural heritage and ancestral mythology to constitute nations in themselves.[10] Moreover, Greek city-states utilized a very restrictive concept of citizenship which was based on the family, clan and phratry (brotherhood), that is, on descent, and which excluded not only foreigners and slaves but also women and Greeks from other city-states: 'the blood of both parents came to be an essential requirement demonstrating that they belonged to the civil communities of the polis'. This kinship-based exclusion went so far that Athenians had no difficulty in enslaving Spartans or Ionians and vice versa: 'since all other poleis were regarded as foreign states . . . Greeks were regularly enslaved by other Greeks' (Thomas 1981: 47–50).

The vague sense of pan-Hellenic cultural similarity was occasionally reinforced by brief political alliances (against Persians and others) but it never materialized into a durable, politically conscious community. In this sense the war speeches of Pericles and other orators cannot be read at face value as a sign of shared loyalty to the entire Hellenic world. Instead they were often just rhetorical devices used in times of extreme hardship (such as war) to forge alliances and mobilize as many warriors as possible (de Romilly 1963).

Saying that there were no nations and nationalisms in ancient Judaea, Greece and other regions of antiquity does not mean that inhabitants of city-states did not have a strong sense of territorial loyalty. On the contrary, most populations of city-states throughout history tended to have a pronounced sentiment of local attachment. This comes across from the archaeological evidence even for some of the first known, Sumerian, city-states such as Babylon, Uruk, Kish, Lagash or Ur, where one can find references to a fervent shared devotion to reconstructing a destroyed city temple when the ruler Gudea 'gave direction to his city as to a single man, [and the inhabitants of the city-state of] Lagash followed him unanimously like the children of one mother' (Falkenstein 1974: 8). However, much of this attachment was religious in nature, as the majority of the population perceived their city-states through the prism of local divinities ('it was their duty to bring honour and glory to the god who gave them life and light') and the feelings of 'local patriotism [were] generated by special loyalty to the local deities' (Rhee 1981: 24).

More secular communal identification was present in the European Renaissance and post-Renaissance city-states and city-leagues of what are today Northern Italy, Northern Germany, Switzerland and the Netherlands. In particular, the thirteenth-century Apennine small city republics such as Florence, Venice, Genoa, Milan, Pisa, Brescia or Verona[11] became prosperous, well-organized and efficiently run autonomous cities. Furthermore these Renaissance cities had the most literate populations in the world, with vernacular literacy rates reaching one third of the male population. Such an audience was highly receptive to sophisticated poetry, oratory displays, theatrical performances, narratives and other artistic creations produced by city-based artists who were able to capture the sentiments of the shared popular devotion to one's city-state.[12] Being expelled from the city was deemed a particularly cruel form of punishment and the excluded citizens would often spend years of their life trying to find a way to return. For example, an exile from the city-state of Lucca, Pietro dei Faitinelli, vowed that upon his return to Lucca he would go 'licking the walls all round and every man I meet, weeping with joy' (Martines 1983: 150). Similarly, negative depictions of one's city were greeted with anger and it was expected that one would lavish compliments on the city's achievements and its citizens. Hence the prospective leader of the city (*podestà*) would in a public speech typically proclaim the superiority of the city of which he was prospective leader and the need to keep and expand this reputation further. So on one such occasion the *podestà* of Pavia spoke about the immense 'glory of this glorious city and its citizens, subjects, friends and allies', about this 'magnificent city, its noble knights and the nobility of its *popolo* . . . nobility of its beginnings, its faith and its prudence' (Martines 1983: 169).

This sense of strong local attachment also received intellectual articulation in the form of a nascent proto-ideology: the city-state as a universal political community. For Brunetto Latini, Dante's guardian and teacher, the city was 'the essential political community, the true form of civilized society'. The city-state, together with the family, was seen as the natural form of social life: 'Every man who comes into the world is first born to his father and relatives, then to his commune [i.e. city-state].' Moreover, one's city was the innate bedrock of stability and security: 'as long as Florence continues to exist, no one will ever really lack a homeland' (Viroli 1997: 28). Latini also argued that loyalty to one's city was a form of normative obligation: 'I want you to be honest and loyal to your commune and whatever happens to it, strive

31

to keep it from perishing' (Martines 1983: 156, 166). All this has led some analysts (such as Viroli 1997 and Snyder 1968) to believe that the Renaissance city-state represented a mini-nation and that these feelings of communal attachment are early forms of nationalism/patriotism.[13] Nevertheless, 'local patriotism' is not nationalism. Regardless of the emerging seeds of secularity in the Renaissance, the perceptions of one's city-state, on both elite and popular levels, were still deeply rooted in the theological frame of thinking. The ideal social order was conceptualized in the religious terms of sin, vice, virtue and chastity, and the aspiration was to model one's city-state on heavenly imagery, thus creating a 'new Jerusalem'. For example, Giacomino de Verona in one of his poems envisages an ideal polity as a 'Heavenly Jerusalem' – 'a walled-in city at peace under one ruler, Christ'. Religious morality infused the perception of cities, which were often symbolized as a 'chaste mother or woman' (Martines 1983: 153–4). All Apennine city-states were identified with a particular patron saint (e.g. St Ambrose, St Geminian, St Bassiano etc.), the daily life of citizens revolved around religious events and ceremonies, and Christianity remained the undisputed source of political legitimacy.

Furthermore, despite the rhetoric of shared values and common citizenship, nearly all pre-modern city-states were profoundly hierarchical and inegalitarian social orders. For example, in contrast to the post-Enlightenment understanding of justice as a moral equality of all human beings, the populations of the thirteenth-century city-states conceptualized justice in a traditional, early Christian sense, as a just (hierarchical) order where everybody knew their place and fulfilled their obligations. The city-states remained socially polarized entities with extensive and elaborate hierarchies of multilayered social stratification, pronounced internal divisions and limited citizenship rights. For example, in contrast to the popular perceptions of egalitarian and solidary republics, the Apennine city-states were brimful of internal conflicts: 'Each city was divided into quarters, wards and parishes, which in turn divided loyalties. Each city was full of voluntary associations such as guilds, religious fraternities and political factions. All these associations (factions in particular) cut across the "horizontal" solidarities of *popolo grasso, popolo minuto* and *plebe'* (Burke 1986: 142).

In addition, most city-states throughout history have been too small to generate a sense of popular belief in an abstract community that is the nation. Most interaction among citizens was direct, face to face, rather than mediated and imagined as in nation-states. For example, most city-states of Sumer were tiny, with Erech comprised of less than two square miles; 'Athens's centre encompassed just under one square mile; Florence's walls in the early fourteenth century enclosed about two and one half square miles' (Griffeth and Thomas 1981: 186). Although some of these polities had relatively large populations, and hence extremely high population densities, only small numbers of individuals were citizens entitled to full political rights. In most instances the peasantry living outside the city walls, who were nominally inhabitants of these polities, did not have any citizenship rights, just like 'foreigners', slaves and some other permanent residents living within the city walls. An overwhelming majority of city-states were oligarchies run by representatives of influential families. For example, all Sumerian, European Renaissance and Greek poleis, including Athens,[14] were essentially ruled by oligarchs. Even when citizenship rights had a broader application, the governing structure was ultimately in the hands of a few individuals 'related by kinship ties, heirs of the commune, members of certain guilds' (Griffeth and Thomas 1981: 187). Even though the structure and organization of the city-states have changed through time, what is striking is that nearly all of them – from the ancient Sumerian and Hellenic worlds, through Renaissance and post-Renaissance Europe, to the Hausa city-states of Western Africa – were firmly rooted in kinship ties. Whereas the Sumerian city-states emerged from kinship-based farming village communities, in Hellenic, Renaissance and post-Renaissance city-states and city-leagues family genealogies remained a crucial source of political legitimacy, while citizenship was regularly determined by patrilineal inheritance (Martines 1983; Rhee 1981; Thomas 1981; Friedrichs 1981).

Finally, rather than being completely autonomous and sovereign polities, most city-states operated under the broader umbrella (explicit or implicit protection) of larger political entities – empires. Moreover, no city-state was ever economically self-sufficient as they were all dependent on rural produce, trade and imports of goods from outside of the city walls. City-states typically emerge in a specific historical context when there is a geo-political vacuum and they are in a position to play one great power against the other (Dubrovnik/Ragusa vis-à-vis Ottoman and Venetian rule, or the existence of the Apennine republics 'in the no-man's land between empire and papacy'). In this sense they are nearly always a part of the larger, imperial world which is often reflected in the shared high culture and proto-ideology of its elite (Burke 1986). To sum up, the city-state is certainly a better organized, more territorially compact, politically and economically more advanced and culturally more complex form of polity than its historical predecessors: nomadic tribes, chiefdoms and early kingdoms. The city-states and city-leagues utilized more elaborate, kinship-based networks of micro-solidarity to forge a relatively strong sense of territorial loyalty. On top of this they were in possession of the more potent social organizations and relatively coherent proto-ideologies of political allegiance often articulated as 'local patriotism'. However, as these polities were still largely patrimonial, elite-dominated and religiously inspired entities that lacked both shared, cross-strata, egalitarian secular ethics and centralized, bureaucratic organization of rule, the city-states were not nations and the sense of shared allegiances to these polities was not nationalism.

The World of Empires

While settled tribes, chiefdoms, city-states and early kingdoms constitute important forms of organized social life, throughout history it is the empire that has proved to be the most durable form of human sedentary social organization. From the third millennium BCE, when Sargon's Akkadia became the first historically recorded imperial polity, until the second half of the twentieth century, with the gradual dismantling of the British,

French, Italian, Dutch, Portuguese and, some would argue, Soviet imperial orders, the empire was the most important configuration of political power on the planet. Furthermore, despite our late twentieth- and early twenty-first-century nation-centric view of the world, which consigns the imperial organizations to the dustbin of history, it is not self-evident that empires are only relics of yesteryear. Although, apart from Japan,[15] no contemporary state defines itself explicitly as an empire, many scholars argue that some nominal nation-states exhibit strong imperial features. Hence the USA, China, Russia and even the European Union have been described as empires or hybrid polities such as 'nation-empires', 'incoherent empires' or 'continental empires' (Burbank and Cooper 2010; Munkler 2007; Zielonka 2006; Mann 2012; 2003). More importantly, as Kumar (2010) shows, there is no natural and inevitable progression from empires to nation-states, and rather than being absolute opposites there is an important element of continuity between nation-states and empires.

Nevertheless before elaborating on the similarities and differences between the two it is important to identify and explain the different types of empire. Although there are some universal features of all imperial orders, there are also substantive differences between early empires such as the Egyptian, Roman, ancient Chinese or Aztec and later imperial incarnations such as the Ottoman, Habsburg, British or even Soviet polities.

Empires differ from tribes, chiefdoms, city-states and early kingdoms in terms of the size of their territory and population, their organizational structure, their geo-political ambitions and, in most instances, their historical durability. In principle, empires are large-scale and populous political orders with highly centralized and expansionist power structures that are often able to last for centuries. More specifically, all empires share several key characteristics. Firstly, empires are profoundly hierarchical social orders usually dominated by a single ruler and a well-established status hierarchy that is difficult to change. The imperial orders foster a vertical sense of attachment where each social stratum maintains its socio-economic and cultural difference. Hence aristocrats interact almost exclusively with, and marry only, other aristocrats regardless of whether they inhabit the same imperial polity; the peasants are just the subjects of one's rule with little substantial distinction made between the peasantry inhabiting one's empire and those outside the empire. Moreover, this is a world where the moral order rests on status descent and inherited rigid rankings of human beings.

Secondly, empires espouse universalist principles and justify their existence in universalist, cosmological or salvational terms. Unlike sedentary tribes and city-states, which centre on shared kinship or local attachments, empires invoke universal goals and operate on the assumption that they are the centre of the world. As Munkler (2007: 5) puts it: 'empires have no neighbours which they recognise as equals'. When conquistador Francisco Pizarro addressed the Incas he describes himself as a vassal of the emperor 'who is King of Spain and the universal world' (Diamond 2005: 74).

In other words, rather than ruling in the name of a particular group, empires aspire towards establishing a singular, world-wide, moral, political and economic order: from *Pax Romana* and the *sacrum imperium* of the Holy Roman Empire to the *mission civilisatrice* of French and British nineteenth-century imperialism. As Mann (2012: 21) puts it bluntly: 'Empires always develop mission statements. The Romans said they brought order and justice to the conquered, the Spanish brought the word of God, the British free trade and prosperity, the French *la mission civilisatrice*, the Americans democracy and free enterprise.'

Thirdly, imperial rule is defined by a pronounced and entrenched cultural heterogeneity. This does not mean that empires cherished cultural difference but simply that the imperial orders had no political reason or organizational means to mould culturally homogeneous populations. On the contrary, as this was a world where noble lineage and religion were the principal sources of political legitimation, any aspiration to organize polities around shared linguistic and other cultural attributes would have been a direct threat to the very foundation of the imperial order.

Fourthly, empires are multilayered entities which usually do not have fixed and permanent internal and external borders.

Internally, an empire operates through asymmetric, ad hoc and contested power arrangements whereby some constituent units exhibit more autonomy than others and where the boundaries of responsibility and power often crosscut and overlap. Externally, an empire does not ultimately recognize the legitimacy and sovereignty of other polities, and hence territorial conquest, when justified through the dominant proto-ideology of the empire, remains a legitimate political option.

Even though all empires share these four features there are substantial differences between the two general forms of imperial orders: the 'capstone' empires and the early modernizing/ nationalizing empires. The principal differences stem from the diverse degrees of organizational development and ideological penetration and the character of micro-solidarity. Let us explore these differences in more detail.

The 'Capstone' Empires

Ancient Egypt was often identified as one of the earliest empires which exhibited a strong sense of shared values: a common religious tradition with a unified belief in pharaohs as living embodiments of gods (Amun or Ra), geographical confinement to a bounded and constricted territory on the banks of the Nile, a distinct hieroglyphic written tradition, linguistic similarity, shared rituals and mythology and a powerful state structure (Mann 1986: 108–15; Trigger et al. 1983; David 1982). Anthony Smith goes so far (2005: 104) as to argue that all of these, in addition to a 'rich corpus of myths, symbols, memories and traditions, clear attachment to the fertile land of the Nile valley, and by the time of the New Kingdom a distinctive public religious culture', indicate that ancient Egypt was 'partially approximating to the ideal type of nationhood'. Moreover, for Smith (2010: 112) the latter-day Ptolemaic Egypt (305 BCE–30 CE) 'possessing its own cult, language, calendar, laws and customs' and being a part of the 'regional international system in the Near East' is nothing less than a fully fledged nation.

Nevertheless, neither the New Kingdom nor Ptolemaic Egypt

could be defined, even in a minimalist sense, as a nation. As recent archaeological and archival research (Shaw 2004: 62) points out, the older evidence, such as Manetho's *Aegyptiaca*, which was one of the key sources for early Egyptologists, has proved to be 'fatally flawed though its basic assumption that there was one long sequence of Egyptian rulers governing over the entire country'. Instead the new research demonstrates that Egypt was 'not culturally unified and politically centralised'. In addition, as in other ancient empires, there was huge cultural, political and economic discrepancy between the nobility (including priests and scribes) and the rest of the, essentially peasant and illiterate, population. Although, highly unusually among ancient empires, the nobility and the peasantry worshipped the same deities and shared many religious rituals and customs, there were still significant differences between the two strata: the peasantry 'were not credited with an afterlife, and may not have been buried' (Mann 1986: 113), and they were 'rarely allowed to penetrate beyond the temples' outer courtyards' (Shaw 2004: 129).

In a similar way the ancient Chinese, Roman and Aztec empires cultivated a sense of shared values, developing distinct cultural practices and rituals, potent military machines and a substantial degree of political centralization over vast territories. Despite investing directly and indirectly in the Romanization of the population under its control, involving teaching Latin, incorporating local cults and religions into the Roman pantheon, building amphitheatres, and spreading the Roman legal system to the outer reaches of the empire, the Roman world remained firmly split between the patricians and plebeians, with women, slaves and foreigners being completely excluded from citizenship.[16] In other words, Roman culture was a culture of the upper classes which were fully literate, and was partially open to the incorporation of local non-Roman notables as long as they were willing to assimilate fully into the Romanized empire (Mann 1986: 267–72).

The profound status inequality in the empire was determined by its very name, as the concept of *imperium* originally implied the ruler's 'power to impose executions or beatings, to draft citizens into armies, and to command armies on campaigns' (Burbank and

Cooper 2010: 28). The Roman Empire was a distinct and organizationally powerful civilization which, like all empires, was guided by the idea of the inherent superiority of its social order and its way of life, conceived by Roman elites as the universal and sole form of dignified existence. For example, for Cicero (2009) there could only be one, universal system of law in the entire world: 'True law is reason, right and natural, commanding people to fulfil their obligations and prohibiting and deterring them from doing wrong. Its validity is universal; it is immutable and eternal.' This view was most clearly articulated in the Roman idea of *humanitas*, which underpinned the imperial proto-ideology. *Humanitas* stood for education, legality, civilized behaviour, cultural advancement and urban living, and was the direct opposite of barbarism, associated with the lifestyle of populations outside the empire. Hence both Julius Caesar in the *Gallic Wars* and Cicero in many of his works used the term in this sense to advocate extending the values of *humanitas* – that is, Romanization – to the entire known world. Strikingly, this view of Roman superiority was often shared by their 'barbarian' neighbours, as illustrated by the words of the Ostrogoth king Theodoric: 'An effective Goth wants to be like a Roman; only a poor Roman would want to be a Goth' (Burbank and Cooper 2010: 40). In addition to a relatively coherent proto-ideology, the Roman Empire was defined by its until then unprecedented social organization, the backbone of which was its military. As many historical sociologists have noted, the legion was the principal organizational source of Roman power. Although its civilian bureaucracy was almost non-existent, the military administration was a well-oiled and pervasive machine able quickly to mobilize, move and utilize hundreds of thousands of soldiers who were well trained and well disciplined, not only to fight, but also to build roads, aqueducts, canals and bridges (Malešević 2010: 100; Mann 1986: 295).

The Chinese Empire was similar in this sense: an all-embracing, powerful, complex and elaborate civilization espousing a strong sense of cultural and organizational superiority. Once the empire was fully unified (under the Qin dynasty in 221 BCE) it controlled huge swaths of territory and a large-scale population, amounting

– just like its Roman equivalent at its peak – to more than 60 million people. The ancient Chinese Empire also operated on the assumption that it ruled the entire (known) world[17] and was able to project a distinct and comprehensive imperial proto-ideology that combined the earlier mythology of the emperor as the 'son of heaven' with the elaborate Confucian teachings that praised the values that confined each individual to his or her designated role in the fixed moral order. In the words of Confucius: 'let the ruler be ruler and the subject a subject; let the father be father and the son a son' (Confucius 2007: 82) With the Chinese Empire embroiled in various conflicts with the nomadic invaders from the North and West, Confucianism also acquired cultural and civilizational overtones as the imperial scholars depicted the inhabitants of the empire as the exact opposite of 'barbarian tribes': 'settled not mobile, eaters of grain not meat; wearers of cloth, not fur' (Burbank and Cooper 2010: 53).

Furthermore, the ancient Chinese dynasties had gradually set up so powerful a bureaucratic organization, with strong meritocratic elements, that no Roman or any other pre-modern polity could match it. The Shang Yang (390–338 BCE) reforms devised efficient systems of land irrigation, reorganized tax collection, standardized weights and measures, created a new imperial currency, introduced the collection of statistical information on the population (with annual reports and forecasts) and created an extensive system of population surveillance. Moreover, the state's allocation of standardized land allotments for each peasant household, which they could sell and buy, fostered stronger links between the military and the households, as the military units were supported, fed and recruited from these households. In fact the rule that each household with more than one adult male had to pay higher taxes 'enforced the nuclear family as the unit of production' (Burbank and Cooper 2010: 35). In other words, unlike most other imperial orders, the Chinese Empire proved successful in weakening the ties of extended kinship networks and enhancing the micro-solidarity of the nuclear family.

The ancient Chinese imperial order went much further than its Roman counterpart not only in creating powerful civilian and military bureaucratic organizations, but in instituting a system of administrative recruitment that had distinct meritocratic elements. The Qin and Han rulers made social status dependent on military performance, introduced new legal codes that linked authority to law, and set up an imperial academy that utilized strict and complicated examination systems which were made compulsory for entering the civil service. Hence education became a principal vehicle for social advancement, and for much of its history, mandarins – that is, centralized officialdom – were the backbone of the imperial order. In contrast to most other empires, in China (Confucian) scholars were simultaneously religious authorities and state bureaucrats and in this sense were seen as more legitimate than generals. Although the empire had a strong and efficient military bureaucracy, the officers, unlike Rome's, lacked political legitimacy: 'Even if a general . . . carried out a successful rebellion . . . to maintain his power the general-turned-emperor had again to establish a close alliance with the Confucian scholars and thus started another civilian government in which generals remained marginal' (Zhao 2006: 15).

Although the Mesoamerican civilizations such as the Aztec/Mexica and Maya appear much later on the historical stage, their geographical isolation from the Eurasian world meant that their social organization, proto-ideologies and technology were at a similar level as those of most ancient Eurasian empires[18] (Mann 1986: 118). The Aztec Empire had a much looser structure of organization than the more centralized and better organized Roman and ancient Chinese polities, but was still a formidable war machine able to conquer large swaths of territory. Nevertheless the Aztec imperial order had a more grounded proto-ideology that was able simultaneously to project the rulers as the representatives of gods on earth and tie this to the popularly shared belief in the Toltec origin of Aztecs: the 'imperial idea was based on the claim that it was the legitimate heir of the near-mythical time of perfection, the Toltec Empire . . . The creator of that empire, the man-god Quetzalcoatl, had sailed away to the east vowing someday to return' (Tsouras 2005: xii). The Toltec lineage was crucial in legitimizing the ruling dynasty, as were the myths of Quetzalcoatl ('Feathered Serpent') and Huitzilopochtli ('Hummingbird of the Left'). Once Huitzilopochtli, the god of war, became a major deity, under the rule of Tlacaelel I (1397–1487), the cornerstone of Aztec proto-ideology centred on human sacrifice. In this view the Hummingbird and other gods required constant supplies of human blood in order to endure in their eternal war to prevent the annihilation of the world. Hence all the subsequent Aztec emperors waged wars of conquest (arrow wars) and wars to capture prisoners for sacrifice (flower wars). Just like the Roman and ancient Chinese, this was a highly militarized empire that rewarded its best warriors by instituting a degree of meritocratic mobility in the military sphere. However, unlike the Chinese and Roman polities, the Aztec imperial order did not incorporate defeated polities into its administrative system but adopted a semi-feudal arrangement, with vassal rulers who were required to provide recruits and tribute on a regular basis (Tsouras 2005: 9). What the Aztec imperial order shared with other empires is the sentiment of cultural superiority vis-à-vis its 'barbarian' neighbours. So the nomadic tribes of the North were depicted as wild people who traditionally ate raw meat, would dress in animal skins and 'did not know how to make houses, but lived in caves' (Soustelle 1995: 217–18).

The fact that these three powerful agrarian empires forged distinct organizational and proto-ideological configurations has led some authors to conclude that they all had important features of nation-states. Hence Gruen (1992) writes about 'the national identity of Rome', Duran (1964) and Soustelle (1995) about the 'Aztec nation' and many scholars insist on the continuity of the Chinese nation over the past 5,000 years. Nevertheless, neither civilization nor empire is a nation-state. While, as we will see shortly, the later empires did have some features of nation-ness, the imperial orders in antiquity lacked all its key attributes. Unlike nation-states, which entail a strong linkage of the units of micro-solidarity with the entire social order, and a shared, egalitarian sense of ideological unity (nationalism), ancient empires not only were hierarchically divided but also developed organizational and proto-ideological mechanisms to block horizontal bonds between groups. These social orders are best described in Hall's (1985) phrase as 'capstone' empires. The essential feature of capstone rule is that the imperial elite centralizes much of its power but, as it is organizationally unable to penetrate deep into the social structure, sits like a capstone on top of different societies. In other words, the rulers control different segments of social order but have neither the institutional means nor the ideological motivation to mould a single society. As Crone (1989: 57) explains: 'capstone government was the response to the problem of organising large numbers of people over large areas with inadequate resources: imperial government was capstone government par excellence ... It made emperors specialists in what has been called extensive power, that is the ability to organise large numbers over large distances for minimal co-operation.' The consequence was that despite nominal commitment to a single, all-embracing proto-ideology such as Confucianism or Roman civilizing ethics, the imperial orders were regularly split between two cultural worlds: the educated and politically dominant elite, which shared one cultural milieu, and the village-based, illiterate peasant masses, who remained culturally different from the elite as well as from other peasantry, as cultural attachments greatly differed from one locality to another. Hence, although some ancient empires such as the Roman, Chinese and Aztec developed much more elaborate and extensive social organizations and proto-ideologies than city-states, early kingdoms or chiefdoms, their internal makeup prevented the emergence of durable and meaningful linkages between pockets of micro-solidarity (village, family, extended kinship) and the broader ideological and organizational structures of the polity. For example, as Hall (1988) shows, ancient China never had enough mandarins to form an efficient ruling stratum able to perform the role modern state administrators have in binding local attachments to the overall state identity. Hence, unlike nation-states, the ancient agrarian empires could not organizationally produce a society-wide, shared normative universe.

The Modernizing Empires

Unlike capstone imperial orders, which were essentially conglomerates of disparate societies that still lacked organizational potency and ideological know-how, and had little need to translate pockets of micro-solidarity into coherent, believable and durable meta-narratives of shared belonging, the empires of the early modern era were in a much better institutional position and, eventually, had greater need of this change. Although this was a very arduous, slow and protracted process, the leading European empires gradually transformed in the direction of polities which had to deal with the increasing politicization of cultural difference. This process is best observed through a brief comparison of the Western European empires, such as the British, French and Dutch, on the one hand and the Central and Eastern European and Middle Eastern empires, such as the Habsburg, Romanov and Ottoman, on the other hand. Whereas in the early periods all these empires exhibited more similarity than difference in their organizational structure, proto-ideological legitimacy, cultural heterogeneity and coercive capacity, the eighteenth and nineteenth centuries saw faster structural transformation of the Western European empires towards nationalizing imperial polities. This particular outcome was a result of different historical and geographical contingencies including increasing population size, the limits of agricultural production and the ever-intensifying conflicts over limited arable land and the prospect of extracting more revenue from such land (Wallerstein 1974: 50–1). In addition, the unique demographic, environmental and geographic conditions of Western Europe (i.e. the abundance of cheap coal, greater population density etc.), coupled with the previously developed multipolar system of competitive states, eventually fostered a breakthrough towards industrialization (Darwin 2007; Diamond 2005; Pomeranz 2000; Hall 1985).

The first significant indicator of social change in the Western European empires was the proliferation of warfare. Although European rulers were at war for much of their history, the technological and organizational changes in the military sphere from the late sixteenth century onwards created the conditions for much deadlier and more protracted wars. As the rulers had constantly to invest in new technological advancements in the production of weaponry, modes of transport and communication, and military training of soldiers, the wars became much more expensive. Hence the rulers had to find new ways to finance such costly adventures. Initially this contributed to the transformation of loose political orders, such as feudalism and the polity of estates (*Ständestaat*), into absolutist monarchies where for the first time the sovereign was a public figure who embodied the entire state: 'the absolute ruler's court was no longer the upper section of his household, a circle of relatives, close associates, and favoured dependants. It was an extensive, artificially constructed and regulated ... exalted stage at the centre of which the ruler stood in a position of unchallengeable superiority' (Poggi 1978: 68).[19] Absolutism was instrumental in the development of state infrastructure, elements of professional bureaucracy, and the codification and implementation of standardized laws over the entire polity of the state. In addition, unlike the previous orders where kings and aristocracy were considered vassals of the emperor, absolutism instituted the proto-ideology of the divine rights of kings as the bedrock of its political legitimacy. In this context the notion of sovereignty was fully attached to the ruler. In other words, if there was a nascent concept of nationhood in early absolutism it could only relate to a single person – sociologically speaking, the king was the nation.[20]

Incessant warfare ultimately stimulated organizational changes as the rulers were forced to centralize power further, reform the administrative structure, and expand taxation and military conscription to include much broader sectors of the population. However, to make sure that the populations under their control paid taxes[21] and fought in the imperial wars, the rulers enhanced the coercive reach of the state but also had gradually to concede some citizenship rights and a degree of state protection for some inhabitants of their polities (Hintze 1975; Tilly 1985; Mann 1988). This incorporation was slow and initially included only small segments of elite strata that were considered, and would consider themselves, members of, say, the English or French nation. For example, unlike the pronouncements of medieval rulers, who made clear that they were above any aristocrats, the speeches of early seventeenth-century rulers were more inclusive and would make reference to lords, bishops and, in some instances, even wealthy merchants as members of the single nation that included the monarch as well. In France the nation consisted of 'the nobility and the clergy'; in Hungary the 1711 Treaty of Szatmár defined the Hungarian nation as 'the barons, prelates and nobility of Hungary'; whereas the German nation 'did not consist of the population that lived in Germany or spoke German, but of a social class of imperial princes who, together with the emperor, constituted the empire' (Schulze 1996: 103–4).

In seventeenth- and early eighteenth-century England 'the nation' was comprised of property-owning groups: in 1740 the House of Commons was elected by approximately 3 per cent of the total population and as Mann (1986: 469) puts it: 'the nation was a class'.[22] Not only was a very small segment of the population considered to be members of the nation, but the concept itself did not have much political meaning until well into the nineteenth century. This was still firmly the world of empires focused on territorial conquest, where cultural similarity and difference were largely a marginal aspect of political discourse.

From the early eighteenth century onwards one of the key differences between the empires was the character of colonial expansion. While the Romanovs, Ottomans and Habsburgs continued the traditional policy of direct territorial incorporation that included entities with different degrees of autonomy and contested/overlapping jurisdiction, the British, French and Dutch empires were in a position to embark on indirect overseas expansion. This particular outcome was in part determined by geography (as the location of the Western European empires largely prevented further expansion in Europe), in part by their highly developed naval power, expanding commodity production, trade and exchange, and in part was also a product of historical contingencies.

As the early European 'voyages of discovery' opened the rest of the world to the Europeans, much of the early colonial expansion by Western European states was haphazard, indirect, and often led and coordinated by privately owned trading companies such as the British East India Company, the Royal Africa Company, the Levant Company, the Hudson's Bay Company or the Dutch East India Company. In this sense, colonial expansion often went hand in hand with the demands of early industrialization and trade at home. The trading companies were interested in acquiring goods and products that were unavailable, in short supply or expensive in Europe, such as spices, sugar, textiles etc., and hence their primary motive was the maximizing of profits. Nevertheless, their actions ultimately contributed not only to the proliferation of capitalism in the world but also to military expansion and the imperial reshaping of the entire globe.

Indirect colonialism meant that the joint stock companies not only established a monopoly on trade in the colonized regions under their control but also had their own militaries and the right to make treaties, wage wars, govern the colonies and even mint money. For example, by the late seventeenth century the Dutch East India Company 'was the richest corporation in the world and an impressive military force in southeast Asia, owning 150 merchant ships and 40 war vessels, employing 50,000 civilians and 10,000 soldiers' (Burbank and Cooper 2010: 161). All these joint stock companies fought numerous wars with local rulers: the British East India Company waged wars in the Indian subcontinent, taking Nepal, Burma and nearly all of India by the 1850s, whereas the Dutch East India Company fought a protracted war in the Malaccas and, 'from its stronghold in Djakarta, acquired territorial control throughout the entire East Indies archipelago' (Opello and Rosow 2004: 185). Hence much of the early colonial expansion was not state-led activity, although the Western imperial powers made the expansion of trade companies easier; it had more to do with the changing nature of entrepreneurship with a global reach. For example, as Darwin (2009; 2007) and Mann (2012: 33) show, in the British and Dutch cases colonial expansion was driven less by the statesmen and much more by 'the freelance adventurers – entrepreneurs, soldiers-for-hire, missionaries, even scientists – raising their own funds, backed by businessmen, churches, and scientific societies'. However, long-distance trade, communication, transport and market expansion generated the new economic and political dynamics and fostered profound social change in the heartlands of Western imperial powers. Once trading companies proved unable, or unwilling, to control the large swaths of territory, and the imperial centres realized that they could utilize colonial expansion for domestic purposes, the colonies became properties of the imperial powers.

The fact that these colonial possessions were not directly incorporated into the mainland territories meant that, unlike their Eastern counterparts, the Western empires were largely spared the painful processes that involved the constant reassembling of the internal imperial structure and the accommodation of various elites. For example, the Habsburg, Ottoman and Romanov empires suffered from pronounced internal tensions between the different aristocratic groupings, which were further fuelled by the uneven spread of industrialization. The large territorial expansion which included the acquisition of Hungary from the Ottomans, large chunks of Poland – after its partition with Prussia and the Romanovs – and the deep penetration into the Apennine peninsula created permanent tensions between the different aristocratic families in the Habsburg Empire. The resolution of this problem was often sought in an asymmetric sovereignty that privileged one set of aristocrats over another. Hence the 1867 dual monarchy compromise saw the Habsburg Empire reconfigured as an entity composed of two separate but integrated kingdoms: Cisleithania (Austria) and Transleithania (Hungary). Nevertheless, such an ad hoc arrangement generated more animosity on the part of other aristocracies, such as the Czech, Croatian or Polish, which were completely excluded from the agreement, thus making the empire less stable in the long term. It is still important to emphasize that this was not an 'ethnic' or national conflict, as it is often presented by the nation-centric discourse of modern historiography, but an elite, status-based struggle. As Lieven (2003: 171) makes clear, the discourse of nationhood did not imply the rights of culturally distinct groups; 'the nation' actually implied 'those groups represented in the estates, and therefore above all the nobility . . . In the eighteenth century many Hungarian nobles were not ethnic Magyars and did not speak the Magyar language.'

In a similar way, the partition of Poland created a situation where the Polish nobility were integrated into the aristocratic system of the Romanovs.[23] The consequence of this change was that by 1795 '66 per cent of the "Russian" hereditary nobility was of Polish origin' (Burbank and Cooper 2010: 275). The Russian Empire was a vast, sparsely populated territory characterized by low levels of urbanization and literacy and an undeveloped civil service. For example, in 1763 the empire's entire administrative apparatus was almost the same size as that of Prussia, which was only 1 per cent of Russia's size (Jones 1973: 182). The resounding defeat in the Crimean War exposed all the internal weakness of the Romanov Empire, including its inability to assimilate fully or accommodate the elites of the lands it conquered or to manage its internal social, political and cultural cleavages successfully.

The Ottoman Empire had a similar problem. As it was created and sustained by military conquest, the backbone of which was the military meritocracy of the devshirme system, once the conquest stopped and the devshirme order degenerated into nepotistic elitism the empire's internal turmoil became more apparent. The religious divide, which for centuries was controlled and moderated by the millet system, together with profound regional unevenness in development, gradually became a central source of political conflict. Since the Balkans were the economic and political centre of the empire, in the early sixteenth century generating revenue for the empire that was four times that from all of Asia Minor, but an overwhelming majority of its population was non-Muslim (Lieven 2003: 130–1), economic and political stagnation galvanized internal elite dissent and instability.

In contrast, the British, French and Dutch empires[24] benefited enormously from the different trajectory of empire-building. Practising colonial expansion abroad, they managed to centralize and expand the administrative apparatuses at home. This was a relatively fast and thorough bureaucratization that soon permeated much of the mainland territory. Furthermore, the expansion of global trade, finance and capital made maritime empires wealthier. The technological and industrial revolutions coupled with incessant war-making ultimately fostered the development of the constitutional state. Such political order meant the development of the organizational and proto-ideological capacity to control one's territory legitimately, the price of which was the (gradual) expansion of citizenship rights on the mainland. Colonial conquest fostered the cumulative expansion of the infrastructural powers of maritime empires. Moreover, as this expansion was successfully justified through proto-ideological narratives such as the British 'white man's burden' and *Pax Britannica*, French *mission civilisatrice* and Dutch *ethische koers* (Foster 2010: 7), it appealed to the broader sections of the British, French and Dutch publics. Although this was still a far cry from the cross-class, egalitarian doctrine that is nationalism, where the pockets of micro-solidarity are fully integrated into the broader ideological narrative, the modernizing maritime empires developed an organizational and proto-ideological potency never seen before.

Hence the different character of the imperial project was crucial in the faster transformation of the Western European empires initially towards statehood and eventually towards nationhood as well. The comparative weakness of the Romanovs, Ottomans and Habsburgs is best illustrated by the size of their revenues. While in 1789 the Ottoman state was able to gather less than 19 per cent of the revenue owing to them and thus collected only £3.75 million, the British and French imperial administrations were able to collect £16.8 and £24 million respectively (İnalcık and Quataert 1994: 714). The uneven development of empires sharpened this divide further as, in order to catch up with Britain and France, the Ottomans, Romanovs and Habsburgs accumulated huge debts to Britain, France and Germany. Nevertheless, the fact that the maritime empires were first to modernize does not mean that they were destined to become nation-states. On the contrary, this was an arduous and still highly contingent process.

There is a near-universal consensus among international relations scholars that the Treaty of Westphalia (1648) represents the beginning of the new era, as the principles of territorial sovereignty, universal recognition of state borders, and religious autonomy[25] were enshrined as the cornerstone of international order. Many argue that this treaty established the nation-state as the principal political actor in the international arena. So Foster (2008: 140) states that 'it was at Westphalia that the nation-state emerged as the defining political unit in Europe and, eventually, of the whole world', and Hoffmann (2007: 75) argues that the 'Peace of Westphalia recorded the birth of an international system based on the plurality of independent nation-states'. Others go as far as seeing the polities represented at the treaty as nation-states: 'the Peace Treaty of Westphalia was negotiated and signed among the European nation-states' (Nanjira 2010: 188). However, not only were there no nation-states in mid-seventeenth-century Europe but the Treaty itself was still a product of imperial geo-politics. As Burbank and Cooper emphasize, the Treaty had nothing to do with the idea of the nation-state; it

> recognised the sovereignty of some three hundred princes on ter-
> ritories under the Holy Roman Empire, but the empire remained an
> overarching political entity, somewhere between a confederation and
> an empire for another 158 years . . . the signatories to the treaty were
> neither very national nor neatly bounded; they pursued and were sub-
> jected to imperial ambitions for the next three centuries. A variety of
> different and nonequivalent forms of state persisted long after 1648:
> strong monarchies like those of France and Spain, a Dutch merchant
> republic, a Polish aristocratic republic, a Swiss confederation, Italian
> merchant republics. Europe kept its popes, emperors, kings, dukes,
> counts, bishops, city administrations, and landholding lords. (Burbank
> and Cooper 2010: 182–3)

Even the notion of sovereignty, as utilized at Westphalia, was a far cry from a centralized, bounded terrain with a single political authority able successfully to claim a monopoly on the legitimate use of force over its territory – a feature that characterizes nation-states. Although Westphalia did eventually have a, rather gradual, impact on the reconfiguration of the existing order, this era remained the world of empires, where 'the layered sovereignty of emperor over king over prince was still a viable European option [even] in the nineteenth century' (Burbank and Cooper 2010:

183). Westphalia did not change the traditional understanding of an empire as a universal polity that aims to cover the entire world and thus ultimately recognizes no rivals. The Treaty only recognized the geo-political status quo where no empire was strong enough to defeat its adversaries. It is much later, in the nineteenth century, that empires started acquiring recognizable features of mutually competing nation-states. The combination of successful and relatively speedy colonial expansion, the proliferation of organizational and proto-ideological power at home, and geo-political rivalry all contributed to the gradual transformation of empires into imperial nation-states. As John A. Hall argues, it is only when it became apparent that 'power can be increased by nationalising one's empire, increasing force through coherence', that 'empires sought to become nation-states' (Hall and Malešević 2013: 17). In other words, the second half of the nineteenth and the early twentieth centuries saw a convergence of imperialism and nationalism where the power of the polity was enhanced on the one hand by the protectionism and economic monopolies which provided safeguarded markets and protected lines of supply, and on the other hand by states' ability to mould a shared, normative (national) universe.

None of this is to say that the modernizing empires were destined to become nation-states or that nationalism was the most important ideological discourse in the nineteenth century. Although the modernizing empires created powerful organizational and proto-ideological structures which are indispensable for the emergence of a large-scale nationalist ideology and practice, as empires they remained profoundly hierarchical orders unable, and often unwilling, to tap fully into the microcosm of interpersonal and inter-group relations and without the ambition to tie this micro-world into a broader nationalist narrative. However, it is important to remember that without empire there would be no nation-state. It is the world of empires that ultimately paved the way for the emergence of the nation-state as we know it.

Conclusion

The advent of the nation-state would be impossible without the organizational, ideological and micro-sociological scaffolding that the pre-modern social and political orders generated. Rather than understanding nation-states and nationalisms as solely the product of modernity, there is a need to acknowledge the structural legacies of empires, kingdoms, city-states and other formations for the emergence of modern nationhood as we know it. However, there is no simple, evolutionary continuity between these orders. The foraging bands had neither the organizational capability nor the ideological know-how to keep large groups of individuals together, and the loose and unstable formation of these bands prevented even the rudimentary development of robust micro-groupings. The complex hunter-gatherer and horticultural tribes were able to forge much stronger forms of micro-solidarity but still lacked recognizable organizational and ideological powers. It is only with the chiefdoms and early kingdoms that one encounters the development of a visible, yet rudimentary, organizational and proto-ideological force capable of fighting protracted wars and instituting stable hierarchical orders. Greater proto-ideological and organizational growth emerges in the city-states and city-leagues, but this often happens at the expense of increased social divisions and dispersal of micro-solidarity. This process dramatically intensifies in the world of empires, which gradually become defined by organizational and proto-ideological might. Nevertheless, such developments are regularly inversely proportional to the degree of cultural homogeneity and social stratification in any given imperial order. In other words, as empires expand their organizational and proto-ideological strength and wider global geo-political reach, they tend to become much more culturally diverse, polarized in terms of status, origin or religion, and their internal worlds of micro-solidarity are further diversified. No empire could mobilize millions of its subjects by linking the imperial doctrine with the microcosm of solidarities in the far-away villages or provincial towns under its control. Although the modernizing empires of the seventeenth, eighteenth and nineteenth centuries differ greatly

53

from their capstone predecessors, it is only with the emergence of the fully fledged nation-states that highly developed organizational and ideological powers become meaningfully intertwined with pouches of micro-solidarity, thus generating the birth of nationalism as the dominant ideology of the modern age.

3

The Birth and Expansion of Nationalisms

Introduction

Unlike empires or composite kingdoms, where political power and cultural identification rarely, if ever, overlap, nation-states are distinct in the sense that their very existence is premised on this overlap. The nation-state is not only a dominant form of political power in the modern era but is also seen by many as the principal locus of one's identity. This is a core idea behind Gellner's (1983: 1) famous definition conceptualizing nationalism as a 'political principle, which holds that the political and the national unit should be congruent'. However, despite its clear merits this definition might give the incorrect impression that the 'political unit' and the 'national unit' are somehow incontrovertible and symmetrical. Nevertheless, while it is fairly clear what a particular 'political unit' might be (i.e. a state, a demarcated autonomous region, a federal unit, a province etc.), the same cannot be said about the 'national unit'. Whereas political units such as a state or a federal region have clear empirical referents, including delineated borders or an administrative structure, it is not certain at all what a nation is, who counts as a member of a particular nation and what are the constitutive ingredients of specific nationhood. Although most nationalist discourses tend to operate with clear-cut understandings of what a nation is and where its boundaries begin and end, there are no unambiguous empirical referents to differentiate cultural differences. Thus, rather than seeing 'national units' as pre-given, it is important to understand that they are the very product of 'political units'. Simply stated, rather than understanding the state as an entity that provides a 'political roof' for the already existing cultural authenticities, it is the process of nation-state formation that creates such 'national units'. Despite the contemporary popularity of the view that every nation should have a state of its own, as the previous chapter indicates, such a belief would have had no resonance for nearly all of our pre-modern predecessors. Hence the central questions of this chapter are: How and why have nation-states come into being? And how and why has nationalism emerged as the dominant (operative) ideology of the modern era?

To answer these questions I firstly engage in a brief debate with the leading approaches in the study of nationalism and nation-states and then articulate an alternative interpretation which focuses on the role played by large-scale organizational and ideological transformations. More specifically, the chapter explores the interplay between the cumulative bureaucratization of coercion, centrifugal ideologization and their gradual interlacing with the grassroots networks of micro-solidarity.

The Dawn of the Nation-State

Despite some dissenting voices that advocate the creation, preservation or resurrection of alternative forms of social organization, the nation-state has no serious rival in the modern era. Not only is the nation-state the dominant form of organized power in modernity but it is also popularly regarded as the only justified form of rule. The principal global political association of polities in the world today, the United Nations, is conceived on this premise that there is no higher power beyond the sovereign nation-state and that no other form of polity could make a legitimate claim for its existence (van den Berghe 1990). For example, the Yanomami of Amazonia, the Ainu of Northern Hokkaido, the Romany Gypsies of Central Europe, Pepsi, Hyundai or the free city of Christiania can never aspire to have a seat in the United Nations or act as a sovereign power in the world. Instead they can only be represented by the independent nation-states in which they are based: Brazil, Japan, Hungary, the USA, Korea or Denmark. Moreover the 'right to nationhood' is defined as one of the key human rights and is as such inscribed in the UN charter. None of this is to say that some non-territorial organizations such as the IMF, the World Bank, NATO, Microsoft, Levi's or 20th Century Fox are not more powerful, wealthier or have greater cultural influence than many nation-states. Nevertheless, even when they have a direct impact on the political, economic or cultural policies of various populations around the globe they inherently lack the popular legitimacy to control the means of destruction, taxation, legislation and education, all of which are seen as the prerogatives of sovereign nation-states. Hence when the IMF takes budgetary control, as was the case in Latvia in 2007 and Greece in 2009, or when NATO leadership decides to undertake military action, as was the case in Kosovo in 1999, this is fiercely resented by large sectors of the population of the countries involved. Similarly when an international court issues a warrant for the head of state, as in Sudan in 2009, or when the Chinese government is condemned for violation of human rights, such actions tend to provoke a great deal of popular resistance, as many interpret these acts as direct attacks on the sovereignty of their nation-state. In other words, regardless of whether a state is considered to be a liberal democracy, theocracy, military junta or state socialist regime, the ideas of autonomy, freedom and self-government are taken as organizing principles that no external authority can tread on.

The idea of national sovereignty is so ingrained and established today that it seems natural and inevitable. However, as shown in the previous chapter there is nothing natural about nation-states, as for an overwhelming majority of their existence on this planet, human beings have lived in other social organizations that have little in common with the nation-state – hunting and gathering bands, tribes, chiefdoms, city-states, city-leagues, composite kingdoms or empires. Even if one discounts hunting and gathering times (which represent more than 200,000 years of our history) and focuses only on the settled social organizations which emerged in the last 12,000 years, the nation-state period counts for less than 2 per cent of human sedentary existence. Thus the key questions are: Where did the nation-states come from? And why have they become such indubitable forms of organized life in modern times?

The doyens of nationalism studies, Gellner (1997; 1983; 1964), Hobsbawm (1990), Anderson (2012; 1998; 1983), Hroch (1985), Breuilly (1993) and Mann (2012; 1995; 1993; 1986), have identified a number of structural, but highly contingent, reasons that gave birth to the nation-state.[1] Although their accounts differently emphasize economic, political or cultural factors as decisive for the emergence of the nation-state, they all share the view that there were no organizational conditions for the development of nation-states before modernity. For Gellner, Hobsbawm, Hroch and Nairn (1981), the nation-state appears on the historical stage as a by-product of broader economic transformations such as industrialization, increasing division of labour, capitalism, uneven regional development, urbanization or secularization, whereas for Breuilly, Mann, Giddens (1985) and Tilly (1992) it is political change that really matters: political movements that seek to control state power or geo-political changes that foster the internal reconfiguration of polities.

Gellner (1997; 1988; 1964) provided a pioneering theory which was built around the contrasting dichotomy of the agrarian and industrial worlds: while the former represented a deeply hierarchical, stratified, stagnant order where avoiding starvation was a principal life ambition for most, the latter was characterized by social and territorial mobility, vibrant economic development, incessant growth, scientific innovation and the exaltation of knowledge. In this context the changing character of the economy shapes social conditions, as industrial production entails a degree of social mobility, linguistic uniformity and specialized knowledge. In contrast to the pre-modern world, where manual labour is the principal mode of production, in the industrial era it is discursive knowledge that becomes the decisive mechanism for the generation of wealth. Thus to work in a factory or an office and to operate successfully in this semantic world, an individual requires a substantial level of literacy, generic and specialized skills, and standardized linguistic proficiency. Hence for Gellner (1983) industrialism fosters the development of large-scale educational systems which, although created to fulfil the needs of industrial growth, ultimately forge cultural homogeneity. In other words, the expansion of (urban-based) industrial production brings huge numbers of culturally diverse peasants to cities where they, and more so their progeny, are gradually moulded through the educational practices into a relatively homogeneous nation. In Gellner's (1983: 57) understanding, nationalism is a direct consequence of industrialism: cultural homogeneity is created through the 'generalised diffusion of a school-mediated, academy-supervised' educational system that is developed to inculcate the values, principles and contents of the standardized 'high (national) culture' into the offspring of former peasants. Simply put, there is no nation-state without standardized vernacular languages, high literacy rates, advanced division of labour, and 'high' culture articulated in institutions such as national academies, theatres, museums, galleries, concert halls, architecture and so on.

Nevertheless, economic growth and institutionally generated cultural capital are not enough for the establishment of nation-states. If this were the case we would live in a world that operates through the medium of a single standardized vernacular and only one high culture (Malešević 2007; O'Leary 1998; Hall 2010). The point is that a nation-state does not emerge in a geo-political vacuum but is always a part of the larger regional and world system that consists of a multiplicity of nation-states and, often, other political entities too.

As Mann, Tilly, Breuilly and Giddens make apparent, wars and revolutions have played a decisive role in the construction of nation-states as we know them. The preparation and mobilization for war and the intensification of European warfare over the past three centuries, together with the insurgent experience of the French and American revolutions, were crucial in the development of centralized power and authority, constitutionalism and the expansion of transport and communication systems. More specifically, as Mann (1986) and Tilly (1985) demonstrate, the rise of the infrastructural powers of the state meant that modernizing polities gradually became capable of monopolizing the use of force on their territory, which allowed them to introduce mass conscription, tax their citizens fully at source, enhance juridical control by using advanced transport and communication networks to link the provinces with the capital, and expand their police forces, censorship and surveillance of the entire population on their territories. Nevertheless, these coercive changes that ultimately expanded the power of the state were often premised on allowing a substantial degree of individual autonomy and citizenship rights. Hence the development of the nation-state involved the simultaneous growth of the state apparatuses and civil society.

As Mann (1995) indicates, from early in the eighteenth century, state development, coupled with the expansion of commercial capitalism, stimulated the spread of discursive literacy among a variety of groups such as officers (reading army manuals), merchants and bankers (using vernacularized contracts), intellectuals (debating political issues in coffee houses, cultural clubs and musical and sport societies), academics and a few other elite groups. He acknowledges that this process was in part initiated by the religious conflicts of the sixteenth and seventeenth centuries when Protestantism and the Catholic Counter-Reformation both encouraged the development of vernacular literacy and helped link family rituals to wider secular practices (Mann 1995). These changes gave birth to a rudimentary sense of civil citizenship and (elite-based) proto-nations.

A much wider sense of nationhood had to wait until the late eighteenth and early nineteenth centuries, when the pressures of fiscal crises forced rulers to become much more politically and socially inclusive. Thus to recruit from the wider base of their populations and to acquire war taxes and war loans, the rulers accepted some of the demands for a greater political voice and representation from the property-owning strata. The nineteenth and early twentieth centuries witnessed a further expansion of both state power and commercial capitalism as they reinforced each other and, in this process, advanced popular identification with nation-states. The intensive development of communications and transport, state-sponsored and state-controlled mass education systems, and mass media have helped nationalize the public sphere and civil society. Most of all, states' direct involvement in welfare provisions and health fostered a strong sense of national homogenization. For example, the militaristic and authoritarian Prussian state initiated the first welfare programmes in the world as early as the 1840s and by the late nineteenth century it operated a welfare system that included old age pensions, accident insurance, medical care and unemployment insurance. Although these were highly paternalistic policies aimed at reducing the influence of the trade unions and left-wing groups, as well as halting emigration to the USA, their chief outcome was a greater popular identification with the state (Beck 1995).[2]

There is no doubt that geo-politics and warfare were crucial factors in the emergence of nation-states. However, as geo-political competition and wars have shaped the history of many different socio-political orders, from chiefdoms and city-states to empires, it is clear that they are important, but not sufficient, reasons for the emergence of the nation-state. If one agrees that nation-states are qualitatively different forms of human organization, then by invoking only warfare and geo-politics one cannot properly differentiate between, for example, the violent processes that created the Roman Empire or the Venetian republic and those that gave birth to modern-day France or Germany.

Modernity differs from previous epochs not only in terms of economics and politics but also in cultural values. As Anderson (2012; 1983: 24–5) emphasized, unlike the pre-modern world where time was generally conceptualized, in either a cyclical or a horizontal sense, as an eternal present, modernity adopts the notion of diagonal, 'homogenous empty time', which is defined by temporal coincidence and is measured by stable and fixed devices such as clocks and calendars. The standardization of time became particularly evident in the everyday life of Europeans and Americans with the proliferation of clocks in public areas (parliament buildings, schools, courthouses, main city squares etc.) and the mass use of pocket-watches, which reached its peak 'in the years leading up to 1914' (Conrad 2006: 51–2). This vertical, calendrical concept of time is perfectly suited to the transformation of multiple and hierarchical communities into large-scale 'sociological entities of such firm and stable reality that their members . . . can even be described as passing each other on the street, without ever becoming acquainted, and still be connected'. The key feature of this new collectivity is a shared, largely teleological understanding of time and space which transforms 'contingency into destiny'. More importantly, the new social understandings are maintained and reinforced by specific cultural products including the institution of the state-wide census, nation-centric cartography with the mass production of national maps, national museums, mass production of books, newspapers and cinematographic portrayals of shared nationhood in its relentless march forward.

All these economic, political and cultural factors identified by the leading theorists of nationalism were highly significant in the transformation of pre-modern polities into modern nation-states. It is impossible to envisage a fully functioning nation-state without effective, state-wide educational systems, relatively high literacy rates, centralized authorities residing in the capital cities, standardized vernaculars, a degree of cultural and even linguistic uniformity, elaborate division of labour, a complex constitutional order, the widespread institutions of 'high' culture, sustainable systems of transport and communication, monopolies on the legitimate use of force, taxation and legislation, the use of calendric time, state-wide mass-media networks and extensive literary production in the native language. It is these unprecedented structural transformations that have taken place over the last three hundred years that made the emergence of the nation-state possible. While these modernist accounts are very persuasive when identifying specific institutional changes that were necessary for the appearance of the nation-state on the historical stage, they have difficulty in explaining the origin of these changes. In other words, in this 'revolutionary' model of modernization (Hutchinson 1994) the pre-modern world resembles an institutional and organizational *tabula rasa*: the structural changes before modernity play little or no part in the development of the nation-state. Gellner's (1996: 366) 'big ditch' thesis, which represents the agrarian and industrial age as polar opposites, is the clearest expression of the modernist position: 'the world was created round about the end of the eighteenth century, and nothing before that makes the slightest difference to the issues we face'.

This inherent weakness of the modernist explanatory models has been challenged by the neo-Durkheimian (ethno-symbolist and perennialist) approaches that insist on a substantial degree of cultural continuity between modern nations and pre-modern ethnic communities. Smith (2009; 2003; 1986), Hutchinson (2005; 1994), Llobera (1994), Hastings (1997) and Armstrong (2004; 1982) among others criticize the idea that nations are a by-product of structural changes such as political, military and industrial revolutions, secularization and state development. Instead, they insist that as nations are first and foremost cultural entities they do not emerge *ex nihilo* but are built on existing cultural repertoires, such as common names, shared foundational myths, collective memories and a sense of homeland, all of which have proved much more durable than modernists imply. For Smith, rather than being a completely novel artefact of the modern age, nations are better seen as a modern articulation of historically sturdy cultural entities – *ethnies*. Whereas for much of history ethnies were a form of (largely non-political) cultural identity, in the modern era they become politicized and 'must begin to move towards nationhood' as they 'take on some of the attributes of *Gesellschaft*, with its features of rational political centralization, mass literacy, and social mobilization' (Smith 1986: 157). Hence, the pre-modern ideas of a chosen people and the myth of a common ethnic descent in modernity are often articulated as the collective memory of the nation and shared 'ethno-history', which combine selective historical truths with political myths that stress 'elements of romance, heroism and the unique' in order to provide 'a stirring and emotionally intimate portrait of a community's history, constructed by, and seen from the standpoint of, successive generations of community members' (Smith 1995: 63).

The neo-Durkheimian critique is right to claim that one cannot properly understand and explain the emergence of nation-states by treating the last two or three hundred years of human history as the beginning and end of everything. It is true that any comprehensive analysis of nation-state formation processes requires a *longue durée* approach which tackles the origins and transformation of human polities *in toto*. However, the neo-Durkheimians miss the point when they focus on the persistence of 'cultural cores' which, allegedly, are destined to undergo a transition in the modern era – from ethnies to nations (Malešević 2006: 109–32).[3] There is a substantial degree of continuity between pre-modern and modern worlds but it is not cultural continuity that is relevant; it is primarily the organizational and, indirectly, ideological continuity that really matters.

Thus to provide an answer to the questions raised above (where the nation-states come from and why they are the dominant form of organized life in modernity), it is crucial to look at the three key processes that have shaped this social change: the cumulative bureaucratization of coercive power, centrifugal ideologization and the transformation of micro-solidarity.

The Nation-State as Social Organization

To understand the origins and development of the nation-state one needs first to define it and differentiate it from other forms of polity. As convincingly argued by Brubaker (2004; 1996) and Collins (1999), 'nation' is a popular, folk concept that has no clear empirical referents. In contrast, the nation-state is a social organization with clearly distinguishable features. Firstly, unlike empires and composite kingdoms, whose territorial domains are internally contested and externally undefined, nation-states have fixed, stable and, for the most part, internationally recognized territories that are run, directed and organized from the capital city. Simply put, empires and kingdoms have frontiers while nation-states have borders (Colas 2007: 19). Whereas an emperor can, in principle, legitimately claim ownership of the entire planet, no government of a nation-state would ever attempt to make such a claim. The pre-modern European polities were built around personalized ties between rulers and ruled with complex and often contradictory systems of legal obligations: 'a vassal was free to accept fiefs from a number of feudal overlords . . . Even kings might be vassals: the English king, John Lackland (1199–1216), was a vassal of the French crown.' More importantly, territory was conceptualized in different terms: 'medieval Europe was unfamiliar with the idea of states on a purely territorial basis, it acknowledged only personal bonds based on an oath of allegiance . . . the medieval personal bond . . . was limited in duration' (Schulze 1996: 7).

Secondly, in contrast to nearly all other sedentary social orders the nation-state is built on principles that delegitimize inherent social hierarchies and innate status-based rights. In other words, unlike empires, kingdoms and chiefdoms, where one does not question hierarchies of status descent and the inborn superiority of emperors, kings, lords and chiefs, nation-states are built on principles that espouse the moral equality of all human beings. This obviously does not mean that citizens of nation-states necessarily enjoy economic or actual political equality, but simply that no full member of a nation-state is legitimately regarded as having less or more moral worth than others.

Thirdly, unlike empires and composite kingdoms, which embrace universalist creeds such as a civilizing mission or world-wide religious doctrine, and unlike sedentary tribes, chiefdoms and city-states, which derive their legitimacy from kinship structure and local attachments, nation-states are ideologically particularist polities where citizens largely celebrate themselves. In other words, nation-states justify their very existence in terms of being unique, special and different from other nation-states. As Weber (1968 [1921]: 925) was already aware, despite its empirical ambiguity the idea of the nation is 'anchored in the superiority or at least the irreplaceability of the culture values that are to be preserved and developed only through the cultivation of the peculiarity of the group'.

Fourthly, and linked to the previous point, nation-states, unlike any other sedentary polity, entail a substantial degree of cultural homogeneity. Whereas the populations of complex tribes, chiefdoms and some city-states often exhibited linguistic and religious unity and shared ritualistic practices and beliefs, it is only in the nation-state that cultural uniformity becomes an ideological and organizational prerogative. In the pre-modern world, collective cultural capital beyond one's social stratum, such as language or religious practice, generally does not have political meaning; thus there is no institutional impulse to mould cultural homogeneity. In contrast, as nation-states are defined by politicized culture, both rulers and the general public strive to forge greater linguistic and other cultural similarity.

Finally, in contrast to all its historical predecessors the nation-state is an institution largely built through and around secular principles. In the early kingdoms and empires, rulers justified their right to rule by invoking the idea of the divine origins of monarchs and emperors. The oligarchs of city-states tried to replicate the religious blueprints of the heavenly city in their communes. The chiefs of sedentary tribes and chiefdoms utilized kinship mythologies, whereas the simple hunter-gatherers relied on totemistic myths of non-human descent. The nation-state is the only form of polity that justifies its very existence in secular terms. This is not to say that religious discourses have disappeared from the political rhetoric or that some nation-states, such as Iran, Afghanistan, Sudan or Mauritania, do not combine the ideas of popular sovereignty with theocratic principles. The point is that even in these instances the organization of the state rests on an Enlightenment-based secular legacy that insists on the moral equality of all human beings, the rational organization of one's rule, the popular sovereignty of distinct nations, and autonomous decision making on the national level. As Roeder (2007: 9) indicates, the concept of popular sovereignty has become so widespread that 72 per cent of 143 state constitutions open with a line stating that the people, 'such as "the Burundian Nation" or "the Chadian people", have a right to govern themselves and to choose the form of their government'.

Thus, to sum up, a nation-state can be defined as a secularized social organization with a fixed and stable territory and a centralized political authority underpinned by intensive ideological particularism and the promotion of moral egalitarianism, social solidarity and cultural homogeneity among its populace. More specifically, the nation-state rests on the principle, rooted in the popular beliefs of its population and the recognition of other nation-states, that it has the legitimate right to monopolize the use of violence, taxation, education and legislation in its territory.

Although the nation-state is a quintessentially modern institution, it did not appear out of thin air. Its organizational capacity, its ideological potency, and its ability to tie the two together successfully through the projection of micro-solidarity on the society-wide level are all consequences of long-term historical change. The key feature of this historical continuity is the fact that the nation-state is first and foremost a social organization. As such, despite its ability to invoke strong sentiments with the projection of kinship, through metaphors such as 'our French brothers who sacrifice themselves on the front line', 'dear mother Russia' or 'the need to protect our American sisters and wives', a nation-state is far from being a spontaneous and natural hub of group solidarity. Just like all social organizations, such as hospitals, schools, business corporations or military regiments, the nation-state is a created and externally imposed entity. All social organizations have similar features: the division of labour, a hierarchy of responsibility, the disciplining of subordinates, the fulfilment of specific tasks and the general presumption of organizational loyalty. As Mann (1986), Tilly (1985), Ertman (1997), Downing (1992), Service (1978) and others have convincingly argued, the emergence of, first, potent social organizations such as chiefdoms, early city-states and pristine empires was a highly contingent process that involved a gradual transfer of the individual liberty and self-control of large numbers of individuals to social institutions. In Mann's (1986) view this process, whereby human autonomy and power are slowly but surely 'exchanged' for a sense of security, protection and material well-being, is a form of social caging. Hence the development of the first known large-scale organizations had a strong coercive dimension: rather than being a natural form of social life, a social organization is an externally imposed entity that directs and controls the actions of numerous human beings. Once the process of social caging was fully set in motion, around 12,000 years ago, there was no escape from the organizational power. One chiefdom could destroy or enslave another chiefdom or a small city-state; one capstone empire could defeat and conquer another empire; but once pristine forms of large-scale social organizations had taken root it was almost impossible to live outside their reach.

Furthermore, as polity development often went hand in hand with the proliferation of warfare, the demand for military protection and security has often translated into the strengthening of the coercive powers of subsequent polities. Thus the rise and expansion of social organizations were followed by their greater penetration into civil society, neighbourhoods, family, and kinship and peer networks. In the context of European warfare between 1500 and 1850, as Tilly (1992) shows, social caging was reinforced by 'political racketeering', with state rulers offering protection from the 'external enemy' as much as from themselves in exchange for a greater economic contribution (taxes and war loans) and popular participation in protracted wars. The key point here is that over the last 12,000 years the power of social organizations vis-à-vis societal groupings has constantly been on the increase, as has their coercive potential. Throughout history the dominant form of social organization has been a polity that is often referred to as a 'state'. This is clearly a misnomer as it makes no distinction between such diverse entities as chiefdoms, composite kingdoms, city-states or city-leagues, which lacked most attributes of 'statehood', and the more statist but very different entities that are empires and nation-states. However, there is an important element of continuity between all of these polities. This is their organizational power. Even though there is no simple evolutionary transition between hunter-gatherers, chiefdoms, city-states, kingdoms, empires and nation-states, as they often exist in parallel and there is a great deal of historical reversibility, including the presence of mixed models of polity, it is possible to notice that the organizational capacity and reach of large-scale social organizations have, for the most part, been cumulative. Not only are most contemporary social organizations, such as police, business enterprises, educational systems, state administrations or prisons, vast, complex and powerful when compared with those of the last two centuries, but there is a clear, identifiable pattern in the cumulative increase of organizational power over the last 12,000 years (Malešević 2011b; 2010).

This cumulative bureaucratization of coercion has played a crucial role in the transformation of imperial orders, absolutist kingdoms, city-states and city-leagues into nation-states. The conflict and competition between diverse forms of polity have stimulated further the growth of organizational competence, and it is only when this competence has reached sophisticated levels that technological discoveries can be utilized to foster the further organizational and technological development of the polity. For example, the early nineteenth-century boom in technological invention (steamships, railways, telegraphs, machine guns etc.) rested firmly on the earlier organizational changes which created conditions for the application and mass use of these inventions (Giddens 1985). In this sense, large-scale destructive events such as wars, revolutions and even natural disasters have in some instances proved catalysts of organizational change as they opened the space for innovation, creativity, adaptability and new knowledge. Although military competition can lead to mutually assured destruction, as both Sombart (1913) and Hall (1985) show, when there is a common normative roof but the lack of a single omnipotent coercive power, protracted small-scale warfare can ultimately create unintended consequences of social action, thus generating unprecedented social change, as was the case in the birth of modernity in Europe. The key point is that there is no political development, economic growth or cultural transformation without organizational change. Organizations are the primary locus of power. What matters in wars, revolutions, party politics, economic contests and cultural rivalries is the organizations which are the backbone of social action. As Collins (1989: 366) argues: 'Armies fight, not in order to kill soldiers, incapacitate weapons, and take the ground, but to destroy the ability to resist. Organization is both the weapon and the target of war.' Similarly, business enterprises embark on 'hostile takeovers' and revolutionaries invade parliaments and government buildings, whereas political parties work on undermining opponents' capabilities to fight back. In all of these instances the focus is on containing or expanding one's organizational power at the expense of the opponent. In this sense Pareto's (1963 [1902]) claim that history is the graveyard of aristocracies should be reformulated to read: history is the graveyard of social organizations, as more powerful ones tend to replace their weaker and less complex predecessors.

The rulers of pristine social organizations such as capstone empires, city-states and composite kingdoms were already aware that organizational capacity was decisive in the takeover, maintenance and expansion of one's power, and as such generally fostered the proliferation of the organizational capabilities of their polities. If this had not been the case there would have been no transition from chiefdoms and city-states to capstone empires and from empires to nation-states. Nevertheless, the intensive organizational development of these polities was often severely constrained by the structural obstacles they had to face, including infrastructural underdevelopment, widespread illiteracy, localism, the entrenchment of kinship and nepotistic networks, a highly stratified social order, the lack of shared value systems etc. Hence it is only in the last three hundred years or so that the process of cumulative bureaucratization has dramatically accelerated. Without going into the origins and causes of this acceleration,[4] it is important to distinguish briefly between pre-modern and modern social organizations. Weber's (1968 [1921]) distinction between the patrimonial and the bureaucratic organization is important here as unlike capstone empires, chiefdoms or composite kingdoms, which are regularly grounded in a highly personalized and nepotistic (that is, patrimonial) order, the nation-state is a prime example of a bureaucratic social organization. Even when nation-states do not live up to the ideal of rational bureaucratic order, the combination of what Weber called instrumental and value rationality remains an ultimate goal and a principal vehicle of legitimacy in the modern era.

The French and American revolutions were symbolic watersheds in this regard as they inaugurated the idea of the nation-state. Deeply rooted in the ideals of the Enlightenment, which glorified human reason, individual autonomy, social solidarity, peace, the moral equality of human beings and popular sovereignty, the two revolutions initiated the gargantuan social change that would eventually see the traditional imperial monarchies being replaced by nation-states. The transition from the patrimonial order that characterized early kingdoms and empires to the bureaucratic order associated with nation-states is often seen through the sanguine prism of gradual evolutionary advancement driven by noble Enlightenment principles and liberal visions (Pinker 2011). However, the ideas of the Enlightenment, including all its organizational trappings, were not disseminated through reasoned debates and discussions but, paradoxically, were coercively imposed from above. Not only were the two revolutions brought about through excessive violence that included the decapitation of monarchs and the killing of hundreds of thousands who opposed the new social order, but once established the new regimes embarked on decades of ruthless warfare, aiming to 'convert' the rest of the world to their noble cause. Hence the aftermath of the French Revolution involved the virtual annihilation of the reactionary peasantry in the Vendée and Brittany. Opposing the ideas of *fraternité*, *égalité* and *liberté* for the sovereign French people meant instant imprisonment and most probable death. As revolutionaries were confronted with the large number of the counter-revolutionary population they invented new techniques to kill their opponents – from the guillotine to packing hundreds of Vendée peasants into barges and sinking them below the water, and then replacing the corpses with a new group of prisoners (Bell 2007; Opie 2006). The revolutionaries were not just opposed to the nobility, the clergy and the conservative peasantry but were particularly hostile to any pronounced signs of cultural difference. In this respect the leading revolutionary Abbé Grégoire developed the new linguistic policy of the Republic with the principal aim of destroying what he termed 'highly degenerate' dialects such as Breton, Basque, Corsican and others. The direction of the new policy was bluntly stated in the title of Grégoire's document: *Report on the Necessity and Means to Annihilate the Patois [minority tongues] and to Universalise the Use of the French Language* (Nimni 1991: 20). From the outset, opposition to the Revolution was defined in cultural terms: 'Federalism and superstition speak Breton; emigration and the hatred of the Republic speak German; counter-revolution speaks Italian; and fanaticism speaks Basque' (Brubaker 1996: 7).

Both French and American revolutions represented seminal events in organizational development. Their novel form of popular legitimacy allowed for relatively swift state penetration into the realms of civil society, locality, kinship and family. Combining explicit coercive pressure with moral blackmail, the French revolutionary state was able to mobilize nearly a million recruits who were sent to export revolutionary nationalist ideals violently throughout Europe (Keegan 1994). Building on the organizational legacy of the revolutionary social order, the Napoleonic state further expanded its infrastructural powers, as it was capable of policing, monitoring and forcing the entire population of France to produce for, or fight in, the protracted wars of 1803–15, with more than six million casualties. The new Napoleonic order was coercive and bureaucratic to the core, as the whole of French society was now modelled on its military, with a clearly defined and developed division of labour and responsibility, a centralized command structure, meritocratic recruitment, fixed salaries, professionalism and a transparent system of promotion.

In a similar vein the American revolutionaries combined Enlightenment-inspired liberal ideals with an organizational transformation that saw a handful of small colonies turning relatively swiftly into an omnipotent imperial nation-state. Despite later nationalist historiography which paints the rise of the USA in reference to the founding fathers' fondness for liberty, tolerance and progress, much of its sudden development is rooted in warfare and ethnic cleansing of the native population. As Anderson and Cayton (2005) have convincingly argued and empirically demonstrated, from the early wars such as the Indian conflicts, the war of 1812, the Mexican–American war and the US Civil War to the Spanish–American war and the two world wars, the unprecedented organizational power of the US polity was created and shaped by organized violence. Whereas the early wars of conquest secured huge 'empty' territory, taken away from native inhabitants and from Mexico, the first industrial war – that is, the American Civil War (1861–5) – represented a decisive moment in state development as it dramatically enhanced the organizational and coercive powers of the federal state: the military victory of the North created the conditions for the monopolization of organized violence (the unified federal military and federal police), centralization of state power (strong federal government), fiscal reorganization and economic control (the formation of a national banking system and a national currency), and substantial state influence in the schooling of the young (the allocation of federal resources for public education).

In both of these cases, the USA and France, just as in other nation-states that emerged and developed in this period, organizational power was crucial. In many respects the new polities were the epitome of social orders undergoing a transition from patrimonialism to bureaucratic rationality. However, what is often neglected is the fact that greater efficiency and rational conduct are not synonyms for freedom and lack of restrictions. On the contrary, organizational effectiveness rests on coercion: the hierarchical division of labour and responsibility, discipline and self-control, organizational loyalty and obedience to (legitimate) authority. As the French commander during the Napoleonic Wars appealed to volunteers, without a hint of irony: 'have but a single sentiment: love of liberty and of equality; but a single principle; obedience to the law' (Hippler 2008: 66). Hence the nation-state is principally a bureaucratic entity, and since all bureaucracies rest on control, discipline, hierarchy and obedience, the nation-state is inherently a coercive organization. Once this polity had established a monopoly on violence, taxation, education and legislation over firmly delineated territory its cumulative coercive power only increased.

Nevertheless, unlike a hospital, a school or a business enterprise, all of which have a specific purpose – healing individuals, educating pupils or generating profit – the nation-state has no ultimate purpose. Although its constitutive units all have particular purposes (i.e. defence, policing, law-making, educating, etc.), the nation-state as such has no definitive rationale. The nation-state can generate security for individuals, create an environment for comfortable living or provide resources for one's survival, but no nation-state is purposely created for any of these specific goals, and other polities, such as empires or city-leagues, could accomplish these tasks just as well. Thus to understand better how the nation-state came into being and why, and how it became the only legitimate form of rule, it is also important to analyse its ideological foundations.

The Magic of Nationalism

The fact that the nation-state is a coercive social organization which does not have a specific, instrumentally defined, purpose means that its very existence remains dependent on its ability to secure and maintain popular justification. Although all historical polities entailed a degree of legitimacy, which usually rested on the proto-ideological power of mythology, religious creeds or imperial doctrines, the nation-state is the only polity that derives its legitimacy from the idea of popular sovereignty. This means that no group or individual other than the nation itself is considered to have supreme authority over a specific geographic area that constitutes a particular nation-state. The Declaration of the Rights of Man and the Citizen (1793), the fundamental document of the French Revolution, states this idea clearly and bluntly: 'The principle of sovereignty resides essentially in the Nation; no body of men, no individual, can exercise authority that does not emanate expressly from it' (Kedourie 1993 [1960]: 12). Hence the rulers of the nation-state are considered legitimate as long as they express the 'will' of the nation. In this sense, unlike other historical formations, nation-states are profoundly ideological creations, as their very existence is tied to a specific ideological doctrine and to practices shared by the majority of its population – nationalism.

Some political theorists, such as Freeden (1998; 1996) and Sutherland (2012), argue that unlike liberalism, socialism or conservatism, which are fully fledged ideologies that provide a complete set of principles covering nearly all aspects of social and political life, nationalism is a thin ideology that lacks complex and comprehensive ideas and principles that stretch 'from the general to the practical, from the core to the periphery' (Freeden 1998: 750). Nevertheless, if one conceptualizes nationalism not only as a political doctrine but as a particular way of thinking and acting that is integral to the organization of everyday life in modernity, then nationalism has to be understood as a thick ideology in the sociological sense of the word.

Nationalism can be defined as an ideology that rests on the popularly shared perceptions and corresponding practices that posit the nation as a principal unit of human solidarity and political legitimacy. In this view nations are understood to be self-evident and natural forms of social organization, with each nation exhibiting a unique character. In nationalist discourse one's devotion and commitment to the nation should supersede all other allegiances, and fully fledged nations are envisaged as free, sovereign and independent. Moreover, nationalist ideology espouses the view that every human being belongs to a nation, and estrangement from one's nation is often seen as a form of moral failing (cf. Malešević 2013b; Breuilly 1993: 2; Smith 1971: 21; Kedourie 1993 [1960]: 1). What this implies is that compared with liberalism or socialism, which are built on a sophisticated corpus of knowledge but generally do not permeate everyday interaction for most individuals, nationalism might be conceptually less developed but is much more present in the routine, habitual encounters of everyday life. While only a small number of highly committed activists and adherents understand the world through the prism of 'the invisible hand of the market' or 'the dictatorship of the proletariat', an overwhelming majority of individuals on this planet are fully aware of their nationhood and tend to see the world through nation-centric lenses. A randomly selected average 14-year-old schoolboy from Paraguay, a 90 year old pensioner from Russia or a 36-year-old nurse from Ghana probably would not be able to spell out the key differences between conservatism and liberalism but would, with relative ease, give a thorough account of what a nation means to them.

In this sense, as I have argued in my previous work (2006; 2002), nationalism is a dominant operative ideology of the modern era without which the nation-state would hardly be able to exist. Nationalism is the social glue that holds members and institutions of the nation-state together. While modern social and political orders usually exhibit a great variation in their normative ideological commitments, ranging from liberal poliarchy, state socialism, theocracy and military dictatorship to the monarchist nation-state, on the operative level all these societies supplement these official doctrines with a hefty dose of everyday nationalism. For example, the comparison of official ideological doctrines as codified in state constitutions and other legislative documents, or of the manifestos of leading political parties, or of influential books written by mainstream intellectuals and ideologues, in such diverse political orders as Islamic Iran, communist Yugoslavia and the liberal democratic UK, shows that these three social orders exhibit huge ideological differences. However, a careful, in-depth analysis of everyday discourses as formulated in school textbooks, tabloid newspapers, the speeches of political leaders, bestselling novels, adverts or mainstream news and entertainment programmes clearly demonstrates much more similarity than difference between them, as in all three cases nationalism emerges as the dominant operative ideology (Malešević 2006: 83–108; 2002).

To understand the palpable strength of nationalism, it is of paramount importance to explore the origins and structure of this ideology. One of the first theorists that tackled these issues, Kedourie (1993 [1960]), found Immanuel Kant and other German Enlightenment and Romantic thinkers responsible for the origin of nationalism. Others have identified Herder, Mazzini, Fichte, Rousseau or Garibaldi as the originators of nationalist ideas. There is no question that, as with all ideologies, nationalism requires intellectual articulation and persistent agitation. However, without a successful organization and a highly receptive audience, nationalist ideas and practices would have had little impact. Hence for nationalism to become a dominant operative ideology of modernity it was essential that its 'recipients' as well as its organizational basis were in place. In other words, without relatively high literacy rates, compulsory education systems, mass publishing, affordable and accessible mass media, enforced military conscription and a developed public sphere no early nationalist programme could

possibly have succeeded. These organizational means were necessary for the successful dissemination of nationalist ideology but
were not sufficient in themselves to generate the truly seismic ideological transformation that has taken place in the last 250 years or
so. What is just as important is the changing values and practices
of the population. It was only when a large number of individuals
started believing in the moral equality of all inhabitants of their
polity and acting on that belief that nationalism could take hold
and gradually become a dominant ideological narrative. This was
a complex and historically contingent process which was initiated
by the revolutionary upheavals and by the profound delegitimization of the ancient regime. Rather than most individuals 'maturing'
and suddenly deciding to abandon their 'self-incurred tutelage',
reflected in one's 'incapacity to use one's own understanding
without the guidance of another', as Kant (1990 [1784]) saw it,
the dramatic ideological transformation came mostly as an unintended consequence of regime collapse (in France) and colonial
downfall (the USA). Rather than being a fully developed ideology
that motivated revolutionary overthrow or rebellion against the
colonial usurpers, as later nationalist narratives would portray
the French and American revolutions, nationalism was largely a
by-product of these events. Although in both instances, the French
and American, the revolutionaries were guided by the ideas and
principles of the Enlightenment, their ultimate creations, the sovereign republics, were historical novelties that combined elements of
Roman republicanism, Athenian democracy and the warrior class
proto-parliamentarism of pre-modern Europe (O'Leary 2000;
Hintze 1975; Marx 2003; Mann 1993; Downing 1992). Neither
nationalism nor the nation-state emerged from clearly formulated
blueprints. What transpired in the aftermath of the two revolutions was an organizational hotchpotch that would eventually and
only slowly transform into a nation-state one would recognize as
such today. The inherent fragility of early republics was quickly
tested in Napoleon's declaration of the French Empire as well
as in the American Civil War. This experience was repeated on
numerous occasions throughout the nineteenth century as many
leaders, such as Iturbide and Maximilian I of Mexico, Pedro I of

Brazil, and Louverture and Dessalines of Haiti, imitated Napoleon by embracing titles such as 'emperor', 'first consul' or 'governor-general for life'.[5] For much of the nineteenth century the imperial and the national were not seen as mutually exclusive concepts and many leading polities were amalgamations of the two. For example, until well into the twentieth century the major European powers, such as Britain, France and Germany, were simultaneously nation-states and empires; that is, imperial nation-states. As empire was the only known form of durable social order, the early nineteenth-century nation-states were often experimental polities that shared many imperial features. In this context, nationalist ideologies were the direct product of state formation. This is not to say that nationalism, as an elite-formulated doctrine, did not exist before the two revolutions; as Leerssen (2006), Smith (2009; 1986) and Hutchinson (1987) convincingly demonstrate, cultural nationalism dominated many intellectual discourses well before the French and American revolutions. One could also identify specific political associations and movements that advocated the destruction of the empires and the creation of some form of republican polity modelled on the ancient Greek ideal. Nevertheless, it is only in the aftermath of the two revolutions that nationalist ideology developed its recognizable shape, as the revolutionary polities provided a new organizational vehicle for nationalism's societal and institutional proliferation. In other words, most of these pre-revolutionary nationalist visions combined fiction and reality, as nobody could imagine what the destruction of monarchical power would bring about.

Hence it is the demolition of the ancient regime that called for new interpretative horizons that would fill the void of legitimacy based on the divine origins of monarchs. Furthermore, the political and economic pressures of the radically changing social order fostered a popular sense of possibility and insecurity, as peasantry and urban poor, just like the property-owning strata, were trying to make sense of the new world. It is in this post-revolutionary environment that ideologies such as republicanism, socialism, liberalism and conservatism took hold among much larger sections of the population. These new doctrines were able to provide competing interpretations of a new social reality as well as to offer grand vistas of a better future.

The traditional lifestyle in which an individual would derive security and emotional comfort from the small-scale networks of one's family, clan, village and commune[6] was suddenly being replaced by a new life in a complex, centralized and increasingly bureaucratized polity. In this new environment the local world was overpowered by the omnipotent nation-state, which gradually supplanted the family, neighbourhood, clan and village as it took responsibility for the economic sustenance, education, physical protection, juridical support and even emotional needs of millions of anonymous individuals. Once the new post-revolutionary polities embarked on intensive industrialization, this process contributed further to uprooting hundreds of thousands of former peasants, who moved, or in the American case migrated, to and settled in the large urban congregations. As both Gellner (1983) and Weber (1978) emphasized, this generational transition was particularly painful, as making Frenchmen out of peasants involved coercive assimilation and the crude obliteration of any form of local attachments. Instead, the post-revolutionary world was a world of grand abstractions – liberty, fraternity, equality – with the nation as a pinnacle of organizational identity. In this new historical context individuals became much more political, as attaining a sense of equality, justice, freedom and fraternity often implied very different understandings of these concepts. While socialism, liberalism or conservatism provided persuasive and sophisticated, but mutually exclusive, interpretations of these grand abstractions, it is nationalism that has proved to be the most potent operative ideological discourse, able to capture the hearts and minds of huge sectors of the population (Malešević 2006; 2002).

There is no doubt that nationalism was a novel ideological discourse, as its central message of national sovereignty and the moral equality of citizens could not have had popular resonance before modernity. However, the relatively swift development and expansion of this ideology among the ordinary population indicate that there is a substantial degree of continuity at play here as well. Nevertheless, this is not a question of the cultural continuity of ethnies simply transforming into nations, as suggested by Smith, Hutchinson and other neo-Durkheimians; it is the organizational continuity articulated in the cumulative bureaucratization of coercive power of social organizations which created the conditions for the rise and social embedment of nationalism. Despite later, nationalist reinterpretations of American and French history, cultural difference had a negligible role, if any, in the revolutionary upheavals, and even the idea of nation lacked a cultural dimension. Moreover, as there was no consensus on who could be considered a legitimate citizen of the new republic, the notion of nationhood remained vague and undefined. While the middle-class leadership and most participants in the American Revolution were culturally indistinguishable from their British counterparts against whom they were fighting, the educated leaders of the French Revolution, including the Jacobins, could not have been more culturally dissimilar from the peasantry and urban poor whose interests they officially represented (Chavez 2009; O'Leary 2000; Spillman 1997; Mann 1986). As Chavez (2009: 107) points out, the American rebels 'were basically English' and 'they initially demanded their rights as Englishmen'. Similarly Spillman (1997: 22) argues that 'revolutionary claims were not framed in nationalist terms . . . colonists rebelled in order to claim rights they understood as British'. What is important to emphasize here is the highly counterintuitive point that nationalism, in its original form, did not emerge as a demand for the preservation of one's cultural authenticity. On the contrary, both American and French revolutionaries couched their claims in strictly universalist, Enlightenment-inspired terms. There was no room for ethnies in the brave new republics; they were seen as an obstacle to the universalist march of Reason.

It is only later, when the republican power found itself under threat internally and externally, that it opted to rely on the politicization of cultural difference to secure a broader legitimacy. In other words, as the universalist and highly abstract messages of Reason, Liberty and Equality lacked popular appeal, the new social organizations had to embrace the idioms of national particularism: instead of *citoyens du monde* and the land of the free it was the French and American people that really mattered. Hence the survival of the nation-state became increasingly tied to nationalist ideology. Although the nation-states had much better organizational prerequisites to justify their existence in nationalist terms than did empires or city-states, this was not a smooth and simple process. Instead nationalism only slowly and gradually became a dominant ideology of the masses. Mosse (1975) explained how this 'nationalization of the masses' took nearly a century to materialize and to transform something that was initially the prerogative of a small, elite minority into a mass phenomenon. These changes were an integral part of the process I have termed 'centrifugal ideologization': an organizational effort, often shared by the civil society groupings, to forge a sense of collective unity for large-scale social organizations such as the nation-state by successfully projecting images and actions associated with kinship and local, community-based, micro-solidary groups (Malešević 2010). To understand how this process works, let us briefly analyse the micro-universe of nationhood.

The Micro-Universe of Nationhood

Traditional historiography, which one can still encounter in history textbooks all over the world, identifies the unification of Germany and that of Italy as the pinnacle of the 'age of nationalism', when the popular urge to live together under a single political roof was finally realized in the belated national unification of each of the two countries. Nevertheless, this latter-day, and profoundly nationalist, reinterpretation of events that took place at the end of the nineteenth century is deeply misleading, as nationalism was not a driving force behind these two events. Neither the political elites, who accomplished this feat, nor the majority of the population, who were the subject of this 'unification', had much sense or appreciation of nationalist ideals. Instead the territorial fusion was a direct result of imperial projects led by the ambitious monarchs of Prussia and Piedmont. The general ignorance of nationalist aims was clearly visible in Bismarck's lack of any interest in extending the process of unification to the German-speaking populations in Austria, Luxembourg or Switzerland, and in Piedmont's monarch's ambivalence towards the Italian language and culture. Even more importantly, for large sections of the population of the 'unified' and 'liberated' territories these actions were seen as hostile and unwelcome events. For example, the majority of the population in Württemberg were firmly opposed to any attempts to forge new, shared, all-German symbols, many of which were locally perceived as a Prussian imposition. Hence the endeavour to institute Sedan Day as the all-German unification day was firmly resisted and 'the celebrants of Sedan Day were derided as "our Prussians at any price", and "those who beg to become Prussians"' (Confino 1997: 78). Similarly, at the meeting of the first Italian assembly in Turin in 1860, the delegates spoke French and an overwhelming majority of 'Italians' had no sense of what the Italian nation was (Schulze 1996: 161).[7]

Hence, rather than Germany and Italy emerging as the natural realization of any thousand-year-long dream of unification, these two nation-states came about through the same highly contingent, coercive and bureaucratic geo-political processes that characterized the emergence of other nation-states. Furthermore, just as in the case of French and US nationalisms, the popular ideology that binds state sovereignty and cultural authenticity became significant only once the bureaucratic apparatus of the state was able to penetrate deeply into the various pores of each society. Here too, just as in many other cases, ideological unification had to be built on top of a sturdy organizational scaffolding, and this took a lot of time. Furthermore, the rulers themselves were often ambivalent and even ill-disposed towards nationalist projects. Hence Bismarck resolutely opposed the introduction of the key national symbols as 'they implied a transference of legitimacy from the dynasties to the people'. So unified Germany 'lacked a national flag until 1892, a national hymn until after Wold War I, and a national holiday' (Confino 1997: 31).

Despite strong and vibrant nationalist cultural and political associations, often led by the leading intellectuals in Germany and to a lesser extent in Italy, in each case the overwhelming majority of the population did not see themselves as Germans or Italians at the time of the country's unification. The often-quoted statement, wrongly attributed to the prime minister of the Kingdom of Sardinia, Massimo d'Azeglio,[8] that 'we made Italy, now we have to make Italians' was right on the spot in its realization that most inhabitants of the new state did not see themselves in national terms,[9] but the statement was completely wrong in assuming that a simple proclamation of a novel polity would automatically result in a new state. Not just Italians but Italy too had to be made, in both an organizational and an ideological sense.

The new German polity could rely on a much more robust organizational base that included better transport, communication, military, police, and educational and juridical systems, and which was also able to generate a more muscular high culture and much higher literacy rates. Nonetheless, the legacies of various regional wars, religious divides and the nascent institutionalization of diverse polities, including city-states, city-leagues, small kingdoms and mini-empires, meant that until well into the early twentieth century local and regional attachments overpowered national ones. In both instances it was the state and state-sympathetic civil society networks that were decisive for the gradual 'nationalization of the masses'. Breuilly (1993) has argued convincingly that nationalism developed out of the tension between the public (the state apparatuses) and the private (civil society, family), a tension triggered by the rise of the modern, rational state organization. Moreover, the success of nationalist ideology was often rooted in its commitment to rectify this rupture and re-establish the unity of state and society. However, for Breuilly (1993: 390), this is a paradoxical process, as to abolish this distinction would also mean the end of nationalism: 'Only if there is a distinct notion of the sovereign and bounded public sphere does the idea of political self-determination make sense. Only if there is a distinct notion of a private civil society which is regarded as the source of sovereignty can one claim that power ultimately rests with the nation defined in "private", that is cultural, terms.' Hence, in his view, once national sovereignty is established and the new state is fully formed, nationalism is likely to evaporate as a principal ideological discourse.

Although Breuilly is right that nationalism derives much of its ideological power from the public vs. private/state vs. society tension, he is wrong in the view that nationalist ideologues can, or even seek to, abolish this dichotomy. On the contrary, nationalism thrives on this state/society ambiguity and it is at the heart of the legitimacy of all nation-states. Rather than trying to abolish this distinction, as Gellner (1997: 74) nicely put it, nationalists speak in the idiom of *Gemeinschaft* but are in fact bent on building yet another *Gesellschaft*: 'a mobile anonymous society, simulating a closed cosy community'. This is not to say that nationalist discourses are necessarily manipulative or cynical; many such claims are fully genuine and sincere. The point is that, like all large-scale social organizations, the nation-state is a contrived, external entity that can only secure and boost its legitimacy claims by projecting the image of a closed, familiar micro-world associated with kinship, family, friendship or locality. In this sense the nation-state is not unique: business enterprises foster symbols of loyalty and rewards linked to family and friendship, and the leaders of political parties and social movements address their members in terms of kinship metaphors such as 'our proletarian brothers' and 'the universal sisterhood of women'. Hence the nation-states are also portrayed as super-families of equally cherished siblings where the nation is depicted as the mother of all. For example, in the aftermath of the French Revolution, the mayor of the small provincial town of Cesson appealed to future recruits in the following words: 'consider yourselves as citizens of France as a whole, as children of the common mother country, and as actual brothers of all those of your kind whom she carries in her womb' (Hippler 2008: 51). Thus all large-scale social organizations require the social glue that will hold them together. However, since the nation-state lacks a clearly defined instrumental role it requires much more of this (and much stronger) glue than other organizations. In other words it requires the superglue that is nationalism.

Nevertheless, nationalism's historical success was not preordained. It was highly contingent and uncertain. It entailed long-term processes of centrifugal ideologization of different sectors of the population, which were regularly embedded in the stable and protracted cumulative bureaucratization of coercive powers. However, the key issue was always the capability of organized ideology to penetrate the micro-world. This was often achieved slowly, gradually and, in many instances, with a lot of resistance. The centralized, unitary symbols of nationhood were often linked to and reinterpreted on the micro-level so as to integrate local traditions and practice into the broad national narratives. For example, for the Sedan Day ceremony to succeed in the largely anti-Prussian environment of late nineteenth-century Reutlingen, the organizers had to draw on local experience and local heroes: 'The Reutlingen war memorial successfully captured this spirit by symbolically placing the fallen sons of the locality within a larger national context . . . the names of the local soldiers were engraved on the north and south sides of the memorial; Württemberg soldiers who died in Reutlingen's hospital were engraved on the west side; and fallen North Germans on the east side.' This attempt to merge the local and the national experience symbolically was also reinforced by the various actions of war veterans, including an event where a Dorzbach veteran, 'accompanied by the members of the newly formed Veterans Association, got married on 2 September 1873, thus linking the personal and the national'. Similarly, in school celebrations 'children related to the abstract concept of nation through the immediate local world in which they lived' (Confino 1997: 43–6). As with all ideological discourses, nationalism too rests on highly abstract ideas and concepts that require 'translation' into popular, familiar, beliefs and practices to make its central message much more comprehensible and meaningful. As Kedourie (1993 [1960]: 40) puts it: 'the rulers have [regularly] tried to persuade the ruled that the relations between citizens are the same as those between lovers, husbands and wives, or parents and children'. While there is no doubt that the state apparatuses, such as the educational systems, mass media or military institutions, put a lot of effort into making nationalist imagery and rituals part of compulsory activity, nationalist ideology could not have had such a spectacular success if it had not been for the actions of the non-state agents such as the civil society networks, esteemed cultural and sport enthusiasts, small-town poets, leaders of the local communities, valued family members, trusted neighbours, activist spouses, respected local clergymen or committed lovers. Simply put, it is the micro-universe, the grass-roots, where the nationalist narrative becomes a matter of habit, a second nature. Individuals are often loyal, proud and comfortable in their 'national skins' precisely because their friends, family members, neighbours and other local significant others espouse the same feelings. Once the nation becomes indistinguishable from one's close family, any sign of an attempt at national humiliation is likely to be interpreted as an attack on one's close family members. In some instances this can go even further, when nation comes before the family. For example, when in 1821 poet Leopardi's sister got married he composed a poem in which this marriage is understood solely through nationalist eyes: 'O my sister, in these times of dejection, in these times of mourning, you will add one more unhappy family to unhappy Italy. Your sons will be either unhappy or cowards. Wish that they be unhappy!' (Kedourie 1993 [1960]: 79).

As both Barthes (1993) and Bourdieu (1990) emphasized strongly, ideological power is best measured by its ability to make particular, historically specific social relations seem normal, natural and universal. Thus, in early nineteenth-century Europe it was taken as given that women were intellectually inferior to men, that the 'white race' was much more competent than other 'races' and that homosexual love was a form of perversion. These beliefs were not only espoused at the macro-level of large-scale social organizations or in the writings of the leading cultural, political and economic elites but, more significantly, were deeply ingrained in the everyday practices of ordinary Europeans. Hence male chauvinism, racism and homophobia were part and parcel of everyday life: such attitudes and practices were widely shared and rarely questioned in the micro-world of one's family, neighbourhoods, local communities or close friendships (Mann 2012; Darwin 2009; Banton 1997).

In contrast to these three ideological discourses, nationalism is a doctrine that generally does not polarize the citizens of one state in terms of gender, sexuality or physiognomy. Furthermore, its discursive repertoire is much more attuned to the intimate metaphors of family, friendship and community. Most importantly, this doctrine serves as the key legitimizing foundation of the nation-state. All of this makes nationalism much more amenable for deeper ideological penetration at the grassroots level. Hence, whereas late twentieth-century Europe witnessed a decline in the popular belief that one's gender, sexuality or physiognomy is superior to those of others, the conviction that one's nation is above others has only increased. For the large majority of Europeans the normality and naturalness of nationhood largely remain intact.

Conclusion

The organizational and ideological apparatuses of all nation-states tend to depict such entities as the primary and self-evident hubs of one's identity and group solidarity. Furthermore, such views are equally promulgated by the plethora of civil society groups and are just as present and visible in highly localized spaces, from neighbourhoods to friendships, peer groups and family settings. In this context it comes as no surprise that an overwhelming majority of individuals on this planet tend to see the nation-state as the natural and authentic form of organized social life. Moreover, it is this form of polity that is presently regarded as being the only legitimate political entity able to represent and express the will of its population. No other large-scale political structure is currently entitled legitimately to claim it is the political incarnation of popular sovereignty, and from the United Nations onwards no international institution recognizes such claims if and when made by other political entities. However, rather than being the innate and self-evident source of group solidarity and identity, the nation-state is an organizational and ideological product of many historical contingencies. There is nothing natural or predetermined in how nation-states came to be the pivot of organized social and political life in modernity.

This is not to say that the institution of the nation-state or the ideology of nationalism has emerged out of thin air or that they exist against the will of the majority. On the contrary, nationalism is not a false consciousness; it is a real and powerful ideological discourse that permeates modern institutions and underpins the thoughts and practices of billions of human beings. This particular state of affairs did not arise overnight; the development of nation-states and nationalisms is rooted in long-term organizational and ideological transformations. There is a great deal of historical continuity in the formation of nation-states, and even nationalist ideology is, in part, grounded in the dispositions of previous creeds and doctrines. Nevertheless, and in contrast to neo-Durkheimian views, it is not cultural but organizational and, indirectly, ideological continuity that was crucial in transforming empires, city-states and composite kingdoms into nation-states, and religious doctrines, imperial creeds and various mythological beliefs into nationalism. There is no one-directional change from ethnies to nations, as envisaged by Smith (1986) or Hastings (1997).[10] This was never a simple evolutionary process but involved, and still involves, historical ups and downs, reversibility, hybridity, blind alleys and the parallel co-existence of different polity forms. Even today not all nominal nation-states are actual nation-states. They differ in terms of the strength of their state-ness and how widespread their nation-ness is. Obviously, the Democratic Republic of Congo is a much weaker state than Sweden and the nation-ness of Belgium can hardly compare to that of Poland. Nevertheless, it is only under modern conditions that the organizational and ideological powers have increased so much that they have reached the point of being capable of fully penetrating the micro-sociological universes and of stimulating peculiar synergic relationships between the powerful social organizations that comprise the nation-state, the dominant ideologies that legitimize such nation-states, and the grassroots solidarities of citizens that inhabit those nation-states.

4

Nationalist Ideologies and Violence

Introduction

Many famous artistic representations of nationalism, such as Delacroix's *Liberty Leading the People* (1830), Goya's *The Third of May, 1808, The Shootings at Mount Principio Outside Madrid* (1814) or Sandor Wagner's *The Self-Sacrifice of Titusz Dugovics* (1859), depict national glory through the prism of excessive violence. In these and many similar works of art, nationalist ideals are born, bred and perish amid pools of blood. It seems as if the deep intensity of nationalist sentiments and aspirations cannot be fully expressed without being accompanied by an imagery of armed soldiers, the sacrifice of innocents, fervently waved national flags, bloody battlefields, and scores of wounded and dead people. Such paintings reflect the view, which has been prevalent since the revolutionary upheavals of 1848, that nationalism and violence are conceptual twins. This assessment has often been shared equally by opponents and supporters of nationalism. Hence Ernest Renan (1990 [1882]: 11) argued that national unity 'is always effected by means of brutality' while many German nationalists, from Arndt, Jahn, Schleiermacher and Fichte to Treitschke, saw violence as the principal means for achieving national unification. In the words of an 1848 German revolutionary: 'Mere existence does not entitle a people to political independence; only the force to assert itself as a state among the others' (Kedourie 1993 [1960]: 109). Similarly Treitschke argued that 'over and over again it has been proved

that it is only in war that a people becomes in very deed a people'
(Davis 1915: 150). However, despite the pervasiveness of such
views there is nothing intrinsically violent in nationalist ideology.

This chapter explores the complex relationships between nationalism and violence. It aims to show that rather than operating
on the principle of simple causality, in most instances, the link
between nationalist ideology and violent action is indirect and
inadvertent. In other words, nationalism is rarely a single and
direct source of violence. Instead, to understand how some nationalist ideas might ultimately lead to brutal outcomes it is necessary
to shift our gaze towards broader, long-term historical processes,
which make the transformation of nationalism into violence possible. Thus this chapter analyses the role that the bureaucratization
of coercion, centrifugal ideologization and micro-solidarity play in
making wars, revolutions, insurgencies, terrorism, ethnic cleansing
and genocide into nationalist phenomena. I argue that to understand the multifaceted and contradictory relationships between
violence and nationalism it is crucial to demystify the workings of
both. Hence the chapter challenges views that locate the origins
of nationalism and violence in human agency or biology and
emphasizes the decisive role of social organizations and structured
historical contingencies in this process.

Is Nationalism Inevitably Violent?

The popular mass media, as well as critics of nationalist doctrines
and many scholars, tend to see nationalism as being intrinsically
linked with violence. Such views emphasize the variety of historical and contemporary cases in which nationalism is the alleged
driving force of violent action. Hence both French and American
revolutions are often interpreted as being provoked by the 'nationalist aspirations' of revolutionaries who wanted to 'bestow a
homeland upon themselves' (Gerstle 2002: 148; Taylor 1993: 40).
The enormous casualties of the Napoleonic and Franco-Prussian
wars and the upheavals in the nineteenth-century Balkans are also
regularly viewed as having origins in the rising and competing

nationalisms of European nation-states: 'Nationalist yearnings set off thirty wars of independence in Europe and led to autonomy for Belgium, Greece, Bulgaria, Albania and Serbia' (Pinker 2011: 238). Furthermore, much conventional historiography tends to identify nationalism as the principal cause for the outbreak of two world wars. As Snyder (1968: 71) makes explicit: 'European nationalism was a major force in the origins of both world wars of the twentieth century. The peoples of Europe went to war in 1914 in an outburst of nationalistic fervour – the French "*à Berlin*", and the Germans "*nach Paris*".'

Nationalism is not only linked to revolutions and wars but also to violent insurgency, terrorism, ethnic cleansing and genocide. Hence the actions of clandestine militant movements such as the Basque separatist movement Euzkadi Ta Askatasuna (ETA), the Provisional Irish Republican Army (PIRA), the Irish National Liberation Army (INLA), the Kosovo Liberation Army (KLA), the Liberation Tigers of Tamil Eelam (LTTE) or the 1970s Palestine Liberation Organization (PLO) are all attributed to strong and uncompromising nationalist ideologies (Burleigh 2009: 268–345). Most twentieth-century genocides and ethnic cleansings, such as the Armenian, the Rwandan or the Bosnian, as with the Holocaust, are directly linked to nationalist projects pursued by extremist organizations in charge of the state apparatuses, such as the Committee of Union and Progress (CUP) in Turkey, the Hutu-dominated Coalition for the Defence of the Republic (CDR) in Rwanda, the Serbian Democratic Party (SDS) in Bosnia and Herzegovina, and the National Socialist movement in Germany (Midlarsky 2011; Kiernan 2007). Nevertheless, the relationship between violence and nationalism is more complex, more contradictory and much more indirect than is usually assumed.

Firstly, some of these popular views are built on the premise that cultural difference in itself, or in a milder version as a claim for the existence of such a difference, ultimately or inevitably leads to hostility. For example, much cognitive and developmental evolutionary psychology insists on an innate proclivity for kin selection. These socio-biological accounts see aggression as the principal means through which an organism attains scarce resources and mating partners to secure self-reproduction. In circumstances where direct reproduction is not possible, the genetic tendency is to favour one's kin over non-kin and close kin over distant kin. In this context, nationalism is understood to be a recent articulation of an innate and universal ethno-centric tendency to privilege members of one's own group over others. In this way violence is seen as the optimal tactic for an organism in securing successful reproduction of its gene pool (Gat 2006; Pinker 2011).

The softer, non-biological incarnation of this argument sees in-group favouritism as a product of irreconcilable cultural differences. Hence for foremost military historian John Keegan (1994: 12), war is not the product of political disputes and rational calculations but is 'an expression of culture'. More specifically, warfare is 'the perpetuation of a culture by its own means' whereby violent conflicts from the ancient Greek world to the Yugoslav wars of the 1990s are seen by Keegan (1994: 58, 192) as being 'fed by passions and rancours' and 'nationalist hatreds', which are deemed to be 'apolitical, to a degree for which Clausewitz made little allowance'. Similarly, mainstream interpretations of recent suicide bombings by Islamist groups have focused on the centrality of religious, and also, in the cases of Hamas and Chechen insurgency, nationalist, doctrine in motivating social and political action (Burleigh 2009). Nevertheless, neither one's biology nor one's culture predetermines violent action. If this relationship between culture/biology and violence were based on a simple causality one would expect to see violent conflicts whenever there is a cultural/ biological difference, but this is obviously not the case. Nearly every patch of territory on this planet is populated by culturally diverse collectivities, most of which never engage in violence. As Laitin (2007: 4–5) shows, even in the regions that are colloquially known as hotbeds of incessant ethnic conflicts and nationalist uprisings, such as much of Africa, violent confrontation is an exception rather than a rule: 'the percentage of neighbouring ethnic groups that experienced violent communal incidents was infinitesimal – for any randomly chosen but neighbouring pair of ethnic groups, on average only 5 in 10,000 had a recorded violent conflict in any year'.

These socio-biological and culturalist assumptions also tend to converge on viewing groups as inherently homogeneous and bounded units whose actions are somehow determined by group membership. Hence when discussing nationalism and violence there is a tendency not only to write about 'Frenchmen' fighting 'Germans', 'Serbs' killing 'Croats' or 'Hutus' attacking 'Tutsis' but also to assume that all individuals who are categorized as 'French', 'Hutu' or 'Serb' will automatically act on the basis of shared cultural/biological attributes. Nevertheless, since human beings are not ants or buffalos, mere cultural/biological similarity cannot serve as a trustworthy forecast for collective action. In cases of nationalism and violence, both of which are multifaceted phenomena, this is even more so, as neither comes naturally to human beings. Nationalism entails long-term political mobilization over specific, often arbitrarily selected, cultural markers, and such political mobilization can only succeed in very specific historical circumstances. For every successful nationalist movement there are hundreds which fail (Gellner 1983: 42–6). With violent action this is even more the case as most individuals will avoid the use of violence whenever there is the possibility of doing so (Malešević 2013b; 2010; Collins 2008; Bourke 1999). Hence rather than being the 'natural' expression of group belonging, nationalist-based violence is extremely difficult to achieve. As Brubaker (2004) rightly points out, 'nation' is not a social actor; it is a category of practice used by social actors themselves. As such there are always competing understandings of what the nation is, where it is headed and what it stands for, and these interpretations are often articulated by competing social organizations and 'political entrepreneurs' who claim the right to speak and act in the name of a specific nation. Nations are not clearly defined billiard balls with singular wills and predictable courses of action. Instead nation-ness is a messy, contingent, multifaceted process which depends on the workings of particular social organizations, civil society groupings, family networks, social movements and many other organized entities (Malešević 2006: 24–30). Hence the transformation of nationalist doctrine into an effective, organized, violent action is a mammoth task that rarely succeeds.

Secondly, the view that nationalism is one of the principal causes of large-scale violent action cannot explain the many instances of organized violence before modernity. In other words, as wars, revolutions and violent uprisings have a much longer historical presence than nationalism, most forms of protracted collective violence could not possibly be caused by nationalist aspirations. For example, even if nationalism were a key cause of warfare, as it is less than 300 years old and the institution of warfare is at least 10,000 years old, this would mean that nationalism could only account for less than 3 per cent of wars fought through history (Malešević 2013a; 2010). The same argument applies equally to violent uprisings, riots, rebellions, pogroms and other forms of organized violence that were widespread before modernity.

Nevertheless, even if the argument is confined to the last 300 years or so, there is little empirical evidence that nationalist ideology by itself is the root cause of revolutions, insurgency, terrorism, war or even genocide. Much recent scholarship on these indicates that nationalist ideologies have generally played a more marginal role than is usually assumed. The popular perception of revolutions, reinforced by the traditional Marxist and nationalist accounts, is that such events result from popular dissatisfaction arising from class- or nation-based exploitation or a combination of both. The view is that this popular discontent creates conditions for the rise of ideologically committed revolutionaries bent on the radical transformation of the existing order. In this view, nationalist and class-based ideologies serve as a motivating force for revolutionary action. The revolutionaries are often seen as individuals who become resentful towards the existing order in part because their social mobility has been blocked (Smith 1998; Gellner 1983).

However, as Goldstone (1991), Skocpol (1979), Tilly (1978) and Collins (1999: 21) have demonstrated convincingly, revolutionaries and repressed masses do not cause revolutions. Instead revolutions occur when there is a 'breakdown from above, not because of insurgency from below'. Regardless of how profound and severe popular discontent is, no revolution has been successful where there was unity among the state elites, military and police apparatus (Calvert 1970). According to Goldstone (1991), for popular revolts to succeed it is crucial that there is a prolonged conflict between state elites, which ultimately paralyses any decisive action, and the state experiences such severe financial difficulties that it becomes unable to pay its civil servants, soldiers and police. For Skocpol (1979) such financial strain is often the product of changing geo-political conditions. Her analysis shows how the huge debts accumulated during unsuccessful American wars impoverished the French monarchy and weakened the state's ability to control its population. Hence the French and American revolutions did not occur in the manner of carefully prepared and well-planned events, executed by nationally conscious or class-conscious revolutionaries. Neither class nor nationhood had anything to do with these events, as in both cases the revolutionaries and their opponents were members of the same class and 'nation'.

In a similar fashion, terrorist actions are often linked to the fierce and uncompromising ideological commitments of fanatical individuals. Hence terrorists are commonly understood to be extremely religious and motivated by specific religious tenets (e.g. Al-Qaida, Hezbollah or Aum Shinrikyo) or extremely nationalist (e.g. Tamil Tigers, Chechen insurgents, IRA, KLA or ETA). However, much of the recent empirical research indicates that rather than being a product of individual fanaticism most terrorist activity is collectively planned, collectively executed, strongly rooted in specific political and strategic goals, and often motivated by specific micro-level concerns (Gambetta 2006; Kalyvas 2006; Hopgood 2006; Ricolfi 2006; Pape 2005). The volunteers chosen for terrorist actions often come from the pool of those less prone to nationalist excesses and violent outbursts.

For example, the elite units of Tamil Tigers, the Black Tigers, who were involved in assassinations and suicide bombings were not selected on the basis of their strong nationalist commitments or propensity for violence. On the contrary, only highly self-disciplined, almost ascetic individuals with a strong sense of loyalty to their regiment and of personal responsibility and a strategic understanding of each mission were chosen: 'while a heightened sense of personal responsibility may be essential for volunteering, its consolidation and testing under training conditions may increase the sense of being "chosen", of being one of the elect with others, and therefore of having a special obligation to one's own comrades to uphold the honour of the unit' (Hopgood 2006: 76).

Although most modern wars are understood to be caused by nationalism, this too is a highly questionable proposition. As recent studies demonstrate, even the conflicts which were traditionally regarded as being initiated by 'nationalist fever', such as World War I, the Franco-Prussian War of 1870, the Crimean War or the Balkan wars of independence, in fact had little to do with nationalism. Whereas World War I, the Crimean War and the Franco-Prussian War were imperial conflicts waged along similar lines to most eighteenth- and nineteenth-century imperial wars, the Balkan uprisings of the nineteenth century were a combination of socio-economic frustrations and imperial geo-politics (Mann 2013; Burbank and Cooper 2010; Figes 2011; Malešević 2013a; 2012a). The Balkan case is particularly interesting as it is regularly used to undermine the classic modernist theories of nationalism, such as those of Gellner (1983) or Nairn (1981). Hence Mouzelis (2007), Minogue (2003) and Orridge (1981) insist that the early nineteenth-century Balkan 'wars of independence' falsify Gellner's and Nairn's approaches, since nationalism in this part of the world had allegedly arrived long before industrialization. However, such criticisms are victims of latter-day nationalist historiography which cannot be taken at face value. There was very little if any nationalism in the early nineteenth-century Balkans. Rather than being motivated by the ideals of popular sovereignty, national authenticity and territorial autonomy, the Balkan uprisings were the by-product of a changing historical context that brought together the interests of local elites and the geo-political aspirations of the Great Powers. These shared interests were expressed in successful attempts to foster, and later utilize, the traditional peasant jacqueries in the direction of political autonomy (Malešević 2012a; 2012b).

The continuous decline of the Ottoman Empire fostered direct intervention on the part of the British, French and Russian imperial governments, which openly supported and in some instances, such as the Greek war of independence, directly fought for the creation of new Balkan polities. Whereas the representatives of the Great Powers were driven by imperial ambitions, local notables such as Đorđe Petrović Karađorđe, Miloš Obrenović, Alexander Ypsilantis or Tudor Vladimirescu, who would later become canonized in nationalist historiography, were principally interested in establishing personal fiefdoms. Hence Karađorđe and Obrenović, the leaders of two Serbian uprisings, were large pig dealers interested in monopolizing the pork trade with the Habsburg Empire, and once this was achieved they offered quickly to 'restore order on behalf of the Sultan' (Stokes 1976: 84; Meriage 1977). Similarly the paramilitary units involved in these violent events, *hajduks*, *khlepts* and *armatoloi*, who too were later rebranded as national heroes, were for the most part completely oblivious to any nationalist ideology, were prone to defection to the Ottomans, and were inclined to rob Muslims and Christians alike (Malešević 2012a; Pavlowitch 1999). The rest of the essentially peasant and illiterate population had little or no understanding of what nationhood is, and would most probably have identified with their locality, clan, kinship networks and specific religious denomination rather than with 'ethnicity' (Kitromilides 2010).

The link between nationalism and violence is not clear cut even in the case of genocides. While there is no doubt that nationalism has played an important part in projects that eventually resulted in ethnic cleansings and genocides, the link between the two is often more indirect than one would ordinarily assume. The conventional assumption is that most if not all genocides were carefully planned and premeditated events with clear origins in the ideological discourses of extremist movements (Goldhagen 1996; Neurberger 2006; Dadrian 1995). Thus conventional historiographical interpretations trace the Final Solution directly to specific passages from *Mein Kampf*, the ethnic cleansing of Bosnian Muslims to the pre-war speeches of Milošević and Karadžić, and the Armenian genocide to correspondence between Mehmed Talaat, Ismail Enver, Ahmed Djemal and other members of the CUP (Scheff 1994). However, as several recent studies demonstrate (Mann 2005; 2004; Snyder 2000; Bauman 1989), rather

than being the outcome of well-planned scenarios, most genocides came about through gradual radicalization in the context
of changing geo-political conditions. As Mann (2005: 7) argues,
genocides typically emerge in the later stages,

> as a kind of Plan C, developed only after the first two responses to
> a perceived ethnic threat fail. Plan A typically envisages a carefully
> planned solution in terms of either compromise or straightforward
> repression. Plan B is a more radically repressive adaptation to the
> failure of Plan A, more hastily conceived amid rising violence and
> some political destabilization.

It is only when these strategies fail that 'some of the planners
radicalise further'. In other words, systematic mass murder often
emerges as a series of unintended consequences resulting from
complex interactions. This is not to say that genocides are the
result of historical accident. It is obvious that the presence of
extremist ideologies and policies is crucial in mobilizing and later
justifying the mass murder of human beings. The point is that
there is no direct, causal link between radical nationalism and
mass slaughter. This is apparent in the fact that the last 200 years
have spawned thousands and thousands of extreme nationalist
movements, hundreds of which have attained significant political
power, but only a handful of cases involving systematic ethnic
cleansing and genocide (Midlarsky 2011). As Mann (2006b;
2005) shows, with the exception of the Nazis, most movements
involved in genocide started off from generally democratic ideals,
but the changing geo-political situation, and in particular the escalation of war conditions, led to an extremist reconceptualization
of 'demos' as 'ethnos'.

The Armenian case is illustrative in this regard, as genocide came
about in a haphazard and contingent way following the escalation
of warfare in 1915. After unsuccessful attempts to forge alliances
with the Armenian political parties, the purpose of which was to
oppose the Russian and British offensives jointly, the Young Turk
government perceived its Armenian population as a potential
threat. By late 1914 it embarked on forced deportations to prevent

the fraternization of Ottoman Armenians with the Armenian volunteer units from the Caucasus fighting for the Russian Empire (Tehcir Law). With ongoing war operations preventing quick deportations to planned destinations in Syria and Mesopotamia, and feeling besieged by the onslaught of the Russian forces by May 1915, the Young Turk leadership decided to replace the forced deportations with mass murder (Kiernan 2007; Mann 2005). As Mann (2005: 178) concludes: 'This was committed by a state possessing overwhelming military superiority, recently destabilised, factionalised, and radicalised, mostly by unexpected geopolitical crises. It would not have happened without such contingent pressures, and it was not long premeditated.'

Therefore nationalism and violence are not conceptual twins. An overwhelming majority of nationalist movements and much nationalist action is distinctly non-violent. It commonly involves peaceful practices such as setting up specific associations, cultural clubs and political parties, organizing cultural events, writing nationalist literature and programmatic documents, educating children in a nationalist tradition, policing the use of one's 'native' language, or simply agitating for the nationalist cause. The tendency to see nationalism as a primary cause of such violent events as wars, terrorism, insurgency, revolutions or genocides is often the result of the fact that in modernity most political action is articulated and justified in nationalist terms. This omnipresence of nationalism in everyday political discourse can easily cloud one's analytical judgement so as to attribute too much explanatory power to nationalist ideology. The central argument of this chapter is that the link between nationalism and violence is rarely direct, and that to understand how and when nationalist ideas acquire violent consequences one has to focus on broader historical processes, such as the cumulative bureaucratization of coercion, centrifugal ideologization, and in particular how these two processes operate in the micro-contexts of everyday life.

What Makes Nationalisms Violent?

Much of the scholarship on nationalism and violence is focused on the role that individual or collective agents play in the initiation and organization of violent actions. Hence one strand in the literature identifies specific and powerful leaders such as Robespierre, Napoleon, Hitler, Mussolini, Prabhakaran or Milošević as individuals who are deemed responsible for the escalation of nationalism into mass murder. Hence these authors argue that without Hitler there would have been no Holocaust, without Robespierre no Age of Terror, and without Prabhakaran no Tamil suicide bombing missions (Pinker 2011; Eatwell 2003; Griffin 2007). For example, a substantial number of historians and political scientists are of the view that key to 'the causes of the Second World War were the personality and the aims of Adolf Hitler' (Muller 2007: 54, quoting Hinsley 1967; Stoakes 1986) or that without Hitler there would have been no mass extermination of Jewish and other populations (Eatwell 2003; Bartov 1992; Himmelfarb 1984). In a similar vein many scholars have identified Milošević and Prabhakaran as being the principal initiators of nationalist violence in the former Yugoslavia and Sri Lanka respectively (Cigar 1995; Cushman and Meštrović 1996; Ramet 2004; De Votta 2004).

Some authors attempt to explain the actions of these leaders by tracing the traumas of their childhood and youth, with an emphasis on feelings of shame, guilt, resentment and anger which allegedly created violent, fanatical nationalist personalities bent on the mass destruction of groups held responsible for their psychological state. So Bromberg and Small (1983), Miller (1983) and Davidson (1977) explain the emergence of National Socialism and its path to genocide through the prism of Hitler's psychological problems: isolation as a child, the presence of an abusive father and a weak, complicit, mother. Thomas Scheff (1994: 118) argues that the extreme nationalism and violence that characterized the Nazi movement were caused by Hitler's feelings of shame and rage, which were shared by his audience: 'Hitler and his public were united by their individual and joint states of emotion, a triple spiral of shame-rage. They were ashamed, angry that they were ashamed, ashamed that they were angry, and so on, without limit.' Hence for Scheff (1994: 140) both radical nationalism and excessive violence are the direct product of psychopathology of shame: 'I attribute the fanaticism of Hitler's policies to this cause: A continuing shame-rage spiral means madness, whether for an individual or a group.' A similar model of 'psychological autopsy'[1] is also used on the traumatic childhood of Milošević, with both of his parents committing suicide, thereby accounting for his transformation from a communist apparatchik into a violent nationalist (Sell 2002; Djukic 1994).

The other strand of this literature gives more explanatory weight to collective relationships between the groups involved in various ethno-nationalist conflicts. Thus the appearance of violent nationalist movements such as the IRA, ETA, KLA or LTTE is interpreted through the historical analysis of group relationships between Irish and English/British, Basque and Spanish/Castilian, Albanian and Serbian or Tamil and Sinhala peoples. Although there are several different perspectives in this strand, ranging from socio-biological, interactionist, functionalist and rational choice to neo-Marxist analyses,[2] they all explain specific ethno-nationalist conflicts with reference to changing group relations (Connor 2005; 1994; Horowitz 2001; 1985; Kaufman 2001; Gurr 2000; 1993). Hence the rise of Irish or Basque nationalisms and their trajectory towards violence, represented by the actions of the IRA and ETA respectively, is viewed through the history of unequal relationships, or in some accounts of a direct exploitation by English of Irish and by Spanish of Basque peoples (Midlarsky 2011; Cordell and Wolff 2010).

Most of these authors see ethnic groups and nations as acting and behaving in a stable and coherent mode, thus exhibiting distinct psychological characteristics. Thus Horowitz (2001), Gurr (1993) and Connor (2005) see ethno-national relations through the prism of strong psychological bonds. For Horowitz (2001: 45–7) 'the foundations of ethnic loyalty reside in the need of individuals to belong to groups', where ethnicity is rooted in a 'strong sense of similarity, with roots in perceived genetic affinity, or early socialization, or both'. In Gurr's view ethnic groups are 'psychological communities' able to 'pursue their interests' and 'maintain their identities' (Gurr 1993: 3; Gurr and Harff 1994: 14–17).

For Connor (1994: 102) ethno-nationalism stems from the psychological bonds of kinship and ancestral relatedness, which can be real or mythical. In this context nations and ethnic groups are understood to be the major social agents that, in pursuit of their material or symbolic interests, engage in conflict. The focus is not on social organizations but on groups. As explicitly stated by Connor (1994: 90),

> an intuitive bond felt toward an informal and unstructured subdivision of human kind is far more profound and potent than are the ties that bind them to the formal and legalistic state structure in which they find themselves. Present and recent large-scale violence within such Third World states as Burma, Burundi, Chad, Ethiopia . . . amply testify to the widespread failure of governments to induce a substantial segment of their citizenry to transfer their primary loyalty from a human grouping to the state.

Despite the pronounced differences between these perspectives, the psychological autopsy model and psycho-collectivism share the view that the roots of violent expressions of nationalism are to be found in specific (individual or collective) actors. Such a view suffers from several pronounced explanatory weaknesses.

For one thing these approaches wrongly assume that both nationalism and violence are simply given, mental states of individuals or groups. In other words, regardless of whether nationalism is understood to be a cause or a product of violence, in all instances both are seen as an asset of individuals or groups. However, as Collins (2008) convincingly shows, to understand how violence is produced it is of paramount importance to shift one's focus from individuals and groups to the social contexts that generate violent outcomes. Rather than being an innate quality of an individual or group, violence is a form of contingent social relation that can potentially engulf any group and individual. Hence the research focus has to shift from 'brutal individuals' and 'violent groups' to 'violent situations': 'We seek the contour of situations, which shape the emotions and acts of the individuals who step inside them. It is a false lead to look for types of violent individuals, constant across situations' (Collins 2008: 1).

This is even more the case with such a historically recent and particular phenomenon as nationalism. There is no question that powerful leaders such as Hitler, Robespierre, Napoleon or Prabhakaran played a decisive role in the concrete historical events that saw the transformation of nationalism into excessively violent phenomena. However, there were many historical instances when nationalist doctrines have mutated into violence without the presence of a single omnipotent individual (e.g. 1970s and 1980s Basque and Irish nationalism) and when powerful nationalist leaders have avoided the use of violence (e.g. Gandhi, Rugova, Parizeau or Pujol). The view that history is made by powerful individuals has been a staple food of traditional historiography since Thomas Carlyle (1963 [1857]: 17), who made this explicit with the formulation that the history of the world is nothing more than 'the biography of great men'. Nevertheless, this 'heroic determinism' has proved very weak in accounting for the structural contexts and specific social circumstances that create particular conditions for the transformation of nationalism into violence (Sztompka 1994).[3] For example, this approach cannot explain why the late 1920s and 1930s saw large parts of the European continent witness a dramatic and sudden rise of radical nationalist, fascist and paramilitary movements led by 'strong men', while such movements largely did not exist before this period (Midlarsky 2011; Mann 2012; 2006b; Griffin 2007). By focusing on Hitler's traumatic childhood one cannot possibly explain the proliferation of hundreds of violent paramilitary nationalist formations in 1920s and 1930s Germany, Italy, Austria, Hungary, Spain, Romania or Yugoslavia. This is even more the case in the context of 1990s Bosnia and Rwanda or 1915 Turkey. As Mann (2006b: 296) puts it: 'if Milošević or any other single leader from these cases had been removed from the scene, ethnic cleansing would probably have occurred anyway'. While the character of individual leadership matters, it is not in itself sufficient to explain either the emergence of nationalism or its mutation into violence.

Psycho-collectivism is equally problematic, as its starting position rests on the reification of group membership and an essentialist treatment of social action. Hence in this perspective groups resemble individuals and are seen as being able to 'pursue their interests', 'maintain their identities' and engage in violent conflicts.[4] Moreover, they are seen as clearly differentiated and bounded entities that have an 'intuitive bond' and shared psychological foundations. This rigid groupist[5] view operates with a strong intentionalist understanding of collective action. On the one hand this approach attributes too much power to social agents, who are seen as overly coherent, determined and fully self-aware of their group membership. On the other hand this approach tends to take the pronouncements of nationalist actors and movements at face value. So when an individual or group of individuals makes a claim to being Hutus who fight Tutsi supremacy, the inclination of psycho-collectivism is to define the situation in terms of 'a violent conflict between Hutus and Tutsis'. However, to understand fully the complexity of each violent and nationalist episode it is crucial to identify the following:

1. Who are the agents making the specific claim that they represent millions of individuals who regard themselves as 'Hutu'? (Obviously there is never a single interpretation of what constitutes 'Hutu-ness'.)
2. When and how is this claim articulated? (For example, whereas in the pre-colonial period wealthy Hutu could be redefined as Tutsi, in the twentieth century being a Hutu implied not being a Tutsi.)
3. How and when do such sweeping claims acquire popular resonance? (Before modernity, no large-scale mobilizations of clan- and tribe-based collectivities were possible around quintessentially modernist categories such as 'Rwandan', 'Hutu' or 'Tutsi'.)
4. When and how are the opponents categorized as 'Tutsi'? (Before the escalation of macro-level violence many Rwandan

citizens were not aware of who was a Tutsi and who was a Hutu.)
5. Who on the 'Hutu' side defines the conflict in such ethno-national, violent or exploitative terms? (Is it radical groups such as the ideologues of 'Hutu Power', the CDR and *Interahamwe*, or the moderate political parties and civil society organizations?)[6]

In other words, every violent and nationalist episode has a specific historical and social trajectory which allows individuals and representatives of different social movements and organizations to make a specific claim about groups' existence, motives, ambitions, needs, feelings and so on. As human beings are complex and often contradictory creatures, no claim made in the name of millions of individuals can be taken as given. As Brubaker (2004: 12) rightly emphasizes, the psycho-collectivist and other groupist approaches often confuse groups with categories, since unlike categories, which are mere collections of entities, a group is a 'mutually interacting, mutually recognizing, mutually oriented, effectively communicating, bounded collectivity with a sense of solidarity, corporate identity, and capacity for concentrated action'. The overwhelming focus on agency and the lack of differentiation between the micro-individual and macro-structural levels prevent this approach from realizing what are the historical and organizational trajectories that create both nationalist and violent situations and that link nationalism with violence.

To explain adequately how and when nationalist ideologies and movements embrace violent action, it is necessary to take a historical bird's-eye view and look at the relationship between the cumulative bureaucratization of coercion and the emergence of popular mass ideologies. Instead of looking at nationalism and violence as properties of individuals and groups the attention will shift to social organizations, for it is organizations that are the generators of large-scale violence and mass-level nationalism.

The dominant view, reinforced by blockbuster films, crime thrillers and pop science books, is that both violence and national attachments come naturally to human beings and that if they are not constrained most individuals are likely to revert back to their original state as in-group favouring predators. Although this is obviously a caricature, the more sophisticated version of this argument has been advanced by much social and political theory, historiography and social science from the times of Hobbes and Machiavelli all the way to contemporary evolutionary psychology, realist international relations theories and Eliasian sociology, to name a few. However, this is an upside-down view of historical reality. Rather than seeing human beings as innately violent and ethnocentric, while social institutions and organizations are portrayed as the guardians of peace and civility, it is the social organizations that foster both the proliferation of organized violence and mass nationalism (Malešević 2011b; 2010).

Human beings have no natural propensity either for violence or for nationalism. As decades of painstaking research on the behaviour of soldiers on the battlefield, the history of homicide and the dynamics of gang cultures demonstrate, ordinary humans as individuals are neither good at nor comfortable with the use of violence (Bourke 1999; Collins 2008; Grossman and Christensen 2008; Grossman 1996; Holmes 1985). These studies clearly show that most are reluctant to injure seriously or kill another human being. Consequently nearly all of the killings in wars, genocides, revolutions and terrorist actions have been committed by a relatively small number of highly determined and well-organized individuals, whereas most ordinary humans, if not coerced or emotionally blackmailed, avoid or show deep aversion to these practices. US Colonel Marshall's (1947) early studies revealed that during World War II less than 25 per cent of soldiers would shoot at the enemy, with an overwhelming majority opting to misfire purposely or not shoot at all. Later studies have only confirmed the intensity of this universal human tendency (Griffith 1989; Miller 2000; Grossman and Christensen 2008). In close, interpersonal, face-to-face encounters, violence generates intensive tension and fear, with most individuals opting for flight over fight. On this face-to-face level most violent action is chaotic, messy and difficult to initiate (Collins 2008). Killing or severely injuring others goes very much against the moral grain of one's primary socialization in most societies. In contrast to popular, Hobbesian views of the pre-modern world as a universe of incessant violence, anthropological and archaeological studies have demonstrated that for 99 per cent of human existence on this planet the institution of warfare did not exist. As before the Mesolithic era human beings lived in very small, non-sedentary bands of gatherers and scavengers who roamed vast, depopulated savannahs and forests, they had no means, motivation or organization to engage in protracted violent conflicts (Malešević 2010; Fry 2007; 2005; Kelly 2000).

It is only with the development of a permanent sedentary lifestyle, the invention of agriculture, rudimentary technology, fortifications, mass production of weaponry, writing and intensified networks of trade and exchange that organized violence becomes the cornerstone of social life. It is no coincidence that the birth of civilization and of protracted warfare happens at the same time in the early Bronze Age (Kelly 2000; Eckhardt 1992). What is crucial in this transformation is the gradual and cumulative expansion of organizational power: as the organizational potency and reach of polities such as chiefdoms, capstone empires and early city-states were expanding so was their destructive capability. Although this was a slow, *longue durée* process that took off in the last 10,000 years, with pronounced expansion in the last 3,000 years, its cumulative coercive and organizational capacity has dramatically escalated in the last 250 years (Malešević 2010). In other words, rather than being an inborn human quality, the gradual and cumulative expansion of violence was fostered by the proliferation of social organizations which have proved capable of coercing (and later ideologically mobilizing) hundreds of thousands of men to fight, kill and die. Once the process of social caging was in place there was no turning back: the cumulative bureaucratization of coercion proved highly successful in converting the individual capacities of human beings into organized violence. Hence the direct consequence of the ever-increasing power of social organizations was the monopolization of violence within one's internal realm, resulting in the coercive pacification of societies and the simultaneous expansion of external violence, most visible in the proliferation of destructive inter-state warfare. The dramatic expansion of warfare, revolutionary uprisings, insurgencies, terrorism and genocide in the modern era stems directly from the ability of sophisticated modern social organizations to direct the actions of millions of individuals and create specific conditions where most of the killings and destruction are committed at a safe psychological and spatial distance. Instead of engaging in gruesome and psychologically gruelling, but numerically inefficient, face-to-face killing, millions are slaughtered by aerial bombardment, heavy artillery, long-range ballistic missiles, closed gas chambers and atomic bombs. As a result more people were killed in the twentieth century alone than in the previous 5,000 years of human history (Eckhardt 1992). Thus the proliferation of organized violence is rooted in the development and expansion of social organizations: simple hunter-gatherers cannot fight wars or organize genocides, for this is a prerogative of the highly complex state organization. Similarly, revolutions, insurgency and terrorism entail superior organizational capacity, division of labour, professionalism, specialized knowledge and a discursively articulated vision of the better future rarely found in the pre-modern world.

If violence does not come naturally to humans, this is even more the case with nationalism. There is no obvious biological, psychological or any other reason for 1.3 billion individuals to feel so attached to each other that they would express their willingness to kill or die in the name of protecting 'the Chinese nation'. While the previous chapters show why there were no material, ideological or organizational conditions for popular nationalism before modernity, and why most pre-modern individuals could not articulate their sense of attachment in national terms, it is important to explore briefly the link between the emergence of nationalism as the dominant operative ideology of modernity and the cumulative bureaucratization of coercion.

The gradual historical transformation from the disorganized social life of mobile, non-sedentary and non-hierarchical bands into settled, hierarchical agrarian orders entailed not only the concentration of coercive power but also a substantial degree of proto-ideological justification. Before modernity, much of this legitimizing power was derived from mythological traditions, comprehensive religious canons or imperial doctrines. Nevertheless, as the overwhelming majority of the population were not part of political life, coercion always remained a more central tool to secure mass obedience. It is only in modern socio-political orders which ground their legitimacy in the sovereignty of the people that ideology, and nationalism in particular, becomes a key ingredient of political discourse.

Obviously this could not happen without major structural changes, such as an unprecedented increase in literacy rates, the proliferation of standardized national languages, the introduction of compulsory primary education and conscription, urbanization, industrialization and all the other modernizing processes. These material changes coincided with, and helped reinforce, the value transformations that posited a human being at the centre of the moral universe. Underpinned by the ideas of the Enlightenment and Romanticism but also of Classicism, Rationalism and other novel discourses, nearly all new ideologies insisted on the equal moral worth of all human beings. While there were pronounced differences between such normative ideologies as liberalism, socialism and republicanism, with some privileging social equality over individual liberty and vice versa, no popular ideology rejected the values of liberty, equality or popular sovereignty. However, as the nation-state replaced empire, city-state or city-league as the key organizing principle of rule,[7] despite their inherent universality, these central principles were popularly conceptualized and organizationally implemented only at the level of the nation-state. Hence what on the normative level was formulated as the moral equality of all human beings, on the operative level was largely understood as the equality of all Frenchmen in France, all Britons in the UK or all Dutchmen in the Netherlands and so on. Not only were colonial subjects excluded but so were all those who were not full members of the nation: no *liberté* and *égalité*, without *fraternité*. Although most post-Enlightenment-era individuals were fully committed to the belief that these ideals should become a universal norm for all, there was a sense of understanding that this could only be achieved within the framework of one's nation-state. Even such radical intellectuals as Marx and Engels could not envisage the next stages of social development without the contours of existing nation-states. So when they advocated the assimilation of Czechs, Serbs or Ukrainians and other 'ethnographic monuments' and 'residual fragments of peoples' (Marx and Engels 1977) into the larger political entities, this was seen as being fully congruent with proletarian egalitarianism and individual freedom. In other words, the territorial and organizational form of the nation-state has from the very beginning shaped the form and the content of dominant ideological discourses. The borders of the nation-state set the outer limits of one's ideological universalism. Hence to mobilize or legitimize mass-level political action, one had to operate within the existing organizational structure (nationhood) and embrace the widest possible discourse within this social organization (nationalism).

Therefore it is social organization itself that sets the parameters of ideological disputes: socialism, liberalism, conservatism and other isms could only succeed in mobilizing mass support by having their messages rearticulated in nationalist terms (see chapter 3). However, the link between nationalism and the dominant social organization of the modern era, the nation-state, goes further than this. It is no coincidence that the principal values of modernity, inaugurated by the Enlightenment, such as peace, merit, reason, autonomy, efficiency, division of labour, legitimate hierarchy, transparency, achievement and so on, are also the fundamental principles of all modern bureaucratic organizations. There is a non-accidental compatibility between the structure of modern bureaucratic organization, its organizational ethos and nationalism. As with all modern social organizations, the nation-state is built on principles that extol instrumentality and value rationality over traditionalist and patrimonial conduct. As Figes (2011: 468–84) shows, although the Crimean War was still an imperial conflict, its direct legacy was the delegitimization of aristocratic patrimonialism and the simultaneous affirmation of the meritocratic and nationalist models of social organization. Since the incompetence of the traditional, aristocratic order was held directly responsible for the huge human casualties among ordinary British soldiers, the new national commemorations celebrated ordinary soldiers: 'If the British military hero had previously been a gentleman all "plumed and laced", now he was a trooper, the "Private Smith" or "Tommy" . . . of folklore' (Figes 2011: 468). This was a pivotal moment in redefining war from an aristocratic enterprise towards 'the idea of the soldier defending the national honour, right and liberty'. Nevertheless, this radical shift came about through long-term historical change which 'triggered a new assertiveness in the middle classes, which rallied round the principles of professional competence, industry, meritocracy and self-reliance in opposition to the privilege of birth'. It is no accident that the Crimean War triggered the mass creation of memorials, monuments and commemorative plaques and the institution of a new medal devised, for the first time in British history, to reward bravery regardless of one's rank or class.

Furthermore, the nation-states could not operate without a clearly defined division of labour underpinned by specialized professionalisms, established systems of promotion based on skill and experience, reliance on a coherent system of abstract rules (such as the constitution) and legitimate obedience to an impersonal order where authority stems from one's position in the hierarchy. Most importantly, as with other social organizations, the nation-state cannot tolerate the presence of violent conflicts within its domain. Instead all conflicts are externalized as similar social organizations (i.e. neighbouring nation-states) are portrayed as potentially hostile competitors. With the intensification of conflicts between different social organizations any sign of disloyalty becomes interpreted as immoral if not treasonous. In this context organizational principles become moral principles, with nationalism acting as a widespread organizational glue that holds individuals together. Hence the nation-state as a bureaucratic organization requires internal pacification, which is brought about and maintained through the combination of coercion and ideological legitimization. Whereas the cumulative bureaucratization of coercion provided the structural contours of modern-day nation-states, nationalism supplied the principal ideological adhesive.

Nevertheless, it is important to emphasize that despite its rhetoric of kinship solidarity, nationalism has nothing to do with biology and very little with shared culture. Obviously 150 million Russians could not possibly have a common ancestor, nor could they all share the same cultural practices and values. What really matters in nationalism is a shared sense of loyalty to a specific social organization which is popularly defined as a 'nation', but in reality is either a bureaucratic unit (a nation-state) or a social organization that aspires to set up such a unit (a nationalist movement or a political party). Hence nationalist ideology espouses the view that the nation is a natural and principal form of human solidarity and stipulates that obedience to the nation should surpass all other attachments. However, rather than being a sentiment of adherence to a 'nation', as is portrayed by nationalists, nationalism is an ideology that in fact demands loyalty to a specific social organization (either the nation-state or the nationalist movement). In this sense nationalism is not an extension of kinship or feeling of attachment to a shared culture, but rather a legitimizing ideology of a very specific social organization – the nation-state.

Although nationalism is usually associated with explosive and strong emotions, which particularly come to life in times of extraordinary events such as wars, terrorist attacks or revolutions, most nationalist experience is distinctively non-sentimental and ordinary. As Billig (1995) has convincingly demonstrated (and I elaborate this more extensively in the next chapter), it is the habitual, everyday, almost unconscious activities that are much more important for the reproduction and maintenance of nationalism than violent emotional outbursts. If nationalism were just an emotional state rather than an institutionalized and organized ideological doctrine it would evaporate quickly. No single emotion, and particularly such intensive emotions as anger, arousal, ecstasy or rage, can last for decades or centuries. Hence everyday nationalism is generally muted, routine and uncharacteristic. In Billig's (1995: 8) well-known example 'the metonymic image of banal nationalism is not a flag which is being consciously waved with fervent passion: it is the flag hanging unnoticed on the public building'. Nevertheless, despite its 'invisibility', once established as the principal source of popular legitimacy (and the dominant operative ideology) of the modern era, nationalism is unlikely to vanish. On the contrary, as long as the institutions of the modern nation-state reproduce nationalist ideology in routine form, such as the educational systems, mass media, governmental departments, military, police, courts, public sphere etc., so too will nationalism continue to thrive. Moreover, rather than being a sign of its impotence, the routine, habitual quality of banal nationalism is in fact a marker of its deep institutional entrenchment and its ideological strength. As Barthes (1993) demonstrated, ideological penetration is best measured through its invisibility and naturalization: once specific social relations are taken as normal and natural they are rarely questioned. Gellner's (1983: 6) quip that in the modern era 'a man must have a nationality as he must have a nose and two ears' is a good illustration of how successful centrifugal ideologization has been over the last 300 years or so. In the nation-centric world that we inhabit, not having a national affiliation is generally seen as an unusual if not also a bizarre choice. In this sense banal nationalism has become second nature to most individuals. Nevertheless, this has nothing to do with the 'profound' spontaneous bonding indicated by Connor, Gurr or Horowitz but is a product of long-term historical processes: the cumulative bureaucratization of coercion and centrifugal ideologization. Hence, contrary to Connor's (1994: 90) claim, nationalism is not a potent 'intuitive bond felt toward an informal and unstructured subdivision of human kind' but exactly the opposite: it is an institutionally generated sense of loyalty towards a specific social organization (the nation-state or the social movement). The fact that most people see it as a normal, 'intuitive bond' is in itself a potent indicator of how institutionally widespread and successful the process of centrifugal ideologization has been.

Therefore the link between violence and nationalism is neither direct nor natural. Since both are products of organizational development, in order to understand when and how nationalism becomes violent the focus has to shift to the workings of specific social organizations that generate, maintain and reinforce both violence and nationalist ideology. It is social organizations that initiate and wage wars, commit genocides, start revolutions, organize, or fight against, terrorist actions. In a similar vein, there is no nationalism without organizational power. It is the cumulative bureaucratization of coercion and centrifugal ideologization that foster historical conditions which transform organizational loyalty into national identification. Despite the popular, and some academic, perceptions that see wars as struggles between individual leaders and their peoples, all warfare is, in fact, a violent conflict between two or more social organizations. Similarly, rather than being the expression of a natural bond with culturally, or biologically, similar individuals, nationalism is first and foremost an expression of loyalty to a concrete social organization – the nation-state, the social movement, or a political party. Since banal, ordinary nationalism is the dominant form of nationalist experience in modernity, its shift towards violence always remains dependent on the workings of these social organizations. In this context triviality is not a synonym for harmlessness. On the contrary, it is organizational entrenchment and routine that sustain nationalism in the public domain and make its transition to violence in times of crisis possible (see chapter 5).

This is also the case with the violent actions present in revolutions, genocides and terrorism. Revolutions are not events initiated by the subjugated masses but, in most instances, the result of organizational breakdown exploited by other small and large social organizations, from insurgency cells to neighbouring states. Genocides are not the result of blind, irrational hatred instigated by pathological individuals and groups, but a consequence of macro-organizational blind alleys and can only happen in the presence of highly sophisticated micro-organizational coordination. Finally, instead of being a product of individual fanaticism, terrorism, both nationalist and religious inspired, is rooted in the supremacy of well-organized political networks.

Hence wars, terrorism, revolutions, insurgencies and genocides are not the direct cause of, and are not directly caused by, nationalism. They are all products of long-term organizational and ideological development. Wars and revolutions cannot provoke nationalist outbursts among populations that have no such sentiments in the first place. Terrorism and genocides are highly unlikely to happen without the presence of certain ideological vistas. The onset of wars, insurgency, terrorist activity, genocides and revolutions can only serve as catalysts for the eruption of already existing outlooks, affects and experiences; they cannot instantly create such attitudes and behaviour *ex nihilo*. Before modernity, any call for national unity in the wake of an external threat could not possibly resonate with a majority of an essentially peasant population. Moreover, no pre-modern commoner would be willing to die or kill for an abstract notion such as political sovereignty or national liberty. It is only through the long-term historical processes such as the cumulative bureaucratization of coercion and centrifugal ideologization that populations of distinct nation-states become organizationally and ideologically prepared for both nationalism and violence.

However, even after the long-term impact of these two processes, there is still no guarantee that in times of war, revolutions or other violent macro-events, citizens of modern states will answer the patriotic/nationalist call to engage in violence. For this to happen it is crucial to tap into the micro-cosmos of interpersonal relationships. The studies on the behaviour of soldiers, revolutionaries, terrorists and genocide perpetuators demonstrate that despite an abundance of nationalist and aggressive rhetoric, once they find themselves in violent situations most individuals are more motivated by micro-level concerns. That is, when people are making a decision to kill or die, grand ideological narratives, such as the 'national cause', 'socialism', 'race purity' or 'Islamic *umma*', mostly give way to feelings of responsibility, obligation and emotional attachment to one's micro-group (Hassan 2011; Pape 2005; Sageman 2004; Kalyvas 2006; Collins 2008; Bourke 1999). All the key decisions, from joining a national military, terrorist organization or revolutionary cell to volunteering for a suicidal mission or genocidal operation, are largely motivated by feelings of micro-solidarity towards one's friends, peers and family. Soldiers go to the front lines with a sense of obligation to their mothers, sisters, brothers, wives, girlfriends and fathers and because their friends do the same. Revolutionaries persist with their struggle even when the cause is lost because they feel responsible to their comrades and the experience of shared solidarity.[8] Terrorists engage in violent missions out of a sense of moral obligation to their friends, peers and family. Even taking part in genocide has often more to do with conformity and group attachment than with grand ideological vistas (Browning 1993; Mann 2012; 2005; 2003; Kalyvas 2006; Shils and Janowitz 1948).

In all of these cases both nationalism and violence play an indirect role. While soldiers, revolutionaries, genocide perpetuators and terrorists absorb both violent and nationalist messages and understand the wider world in nationalist and violent terms, it is only when social organizations manage to 'translate' these macro-narratives into a micro-reality that nationalist violence is likely to occur. It is no accident that despite their commitment to bureaucratic – in contrast to patrimonial – rationality and detached formal structure, most modern social organizations heavily utilize the rhetoric of kinship ties and local attachments. Instead of fighting, killing and dying for a particular bureaucratic unit (a nation-state), soldiers and ethnic cleansers are called on to sacrifice and slaughter in order to protect their brothers, sisters, wives, girlfriends, children, mothers and fathers. Despite centuries of bureaucratization and ideologization, human beings remain active and reflexive creatures who crave the emotional attachment and solidarity of micro-, face-to-face groups. Although, in the modern era, all human beings are born, live and die in the world of large-scale social organizations, there is a universal inclination to find comfort, love, friendship and security in much smaller units: nuclear family, peers, neighbourhood, networks of friends and similar groupings. It is only in such small groups that one can develop meaningful long-term relationships built on unconditional trust, love, care and attachment. Such deep emotional ties require a genuine and sincere long-term commitment and emotional investment that is further reinforced in times of profound crises when one's sense of solidarity is fully tested. It is a parent's love for their sick child that would galvanize them to make any sacrifice imaginable to heal that child. It is a willingness to replace a lover in Death Row that tests the strength and intensity of one's personal commitment to that relationship. In a similar way soldiers, revolutionaries and even terrorists and genocide perpetuators are motivated by the principles of micro-solidarity: someone is willing to die and kill to conform with the wishes of significant others, to please or impress those she or he admires or fears, to avoid the humiliation and shame which could result from not acting, out of a sense of micro-group attachment, a feeling of responsibility to those one loves and so on. In all of these instances, even when it is loudly proclaimed to be so, nationalism is rarely a primary source of violent action. Instead the specific organizational and ideological context integrates the genuine hubs of micro-solidarity into broader, all-encompassing, organizationally produced, maintained and reinforced macro-nationalist narratives. Thus what is an instance of deeply personal voluntary sacrifice for one's platoon, family, revolutionary or terrorist cell of close friends becomes reinterpreted as martyrdom for a national cause. For example, World War II Japanese kamikaze pilots were regularly seen as being motivated by extreme nationalism and loyalty to the central symbol of Japanese nationalism – the emperor. However, as Shimazu's (2009) analysis of soldiers' diaries and Hill's (2006: 24–6) interviews with surviving kamikaze pilots show, the soldiers' motivations were highly complex and diverse, ranging from personal vanity, pride and feelings of humiliation to a more pronounced sense of loyalty and duty towards family and friends. For example: 'I am not going out for the Emperor of the Japanese Empire. I am going for my beloved wife . . . I am dying to protect her' or 'I didn't see myself throwing my life away for him [the emperor], nor for the government either, nor for the nation. I saw myself dying to defend my parents, my brothers and sisters. For them I must die.' Similarly, the soldiers of the Bosnian Serb army are often depicted as inherently violent nationalists but, as my interviews with a number of these former soldiers indicate, their motivations for joining the military and taking part in extreme forms of violence were also complex and had much more to do with loyalty and feelings of attachment to micro-groups than to the grand nationalist vistas (Malešević, in preparation).

The success of bureaucratization and ideologization is rooted in the organizational ability to envelop, integrate and 'translate' these hubs of micro-solidarity into a wider nationalist vista where most citizens will be able to recognize themselves and their personal life stories. Hence neither violence nor nationalism came easily or naturally to human beings. Nor is the link between the two inevitable. Without large-scale social organizations, nationalism and protracted violent conflicts would not be possible. It is only through particular, historically contingent developments, such as the cumulative bureaucratization of coercion, centrifugal ideologization and their successful incorporation of the pockets of micro-solidarity, that nationalisms can acquire violent manifestations.

Conclusion

In a number of recent, empirically meticulous studies, Andreas Wimmer and his collaborators (Wimmer and Heirs 2013; Wimmer 2012; Wimmer and Feinstein 2010; Wimmer and Min 2006) have emphasized the role war and other forms of organized violence have played in the transformation of empires into nation-states. In this view, rather than nation-states emerging as an unintended consequence of imperial breakdown, the argument is that the collapse of empires was largely caused by violent nationalist movements: 'the rise and global proliferation of nationalist movements has been a crucial factor in re-shaping the structure of the state system over the past two hundred years' (Wimmer and Heirs 2013: 212–13).

Without disputing the fact that some nationalist movements deliberately utilize violent means, in this chapter I have tried to demonstrate that the relationship between violence and nationalism is much more complex, unpredictable and accidental than usually envisaged.[9] There is no doubt that in some instances, such as Algeria or Vietnam, the emergence of the nation-state was a profoundly violent affair and nationalism has been intertwined with violence for long periods of time. However, most expressions of nationalism are not violent and there is no unambiguous relationship between the two. Nationalist ideologies are often present long before any signs of violent activities, and nationalism burgeons just as well, if not better, after the guns have been silenced. Both Vietnam and Algeria demonstrate this amply (Sutherland 2010; McDougal 2006).

Although nationalisms often accompany modern wars, revolutions, insurgencies and genocides, such phenomena are not dependent on nationalist discourses and can occur without coherent nationalist ideologies. More importantly, the fact that both nationalism and organized violence dramatically expand in the modern era does not necessarily mean that one is a cause or consequence of the other. Instead it is the gradual and cumulative expansion of organizational and ideological powers, together with the ever-increasing capability of modern social organizations to penetrate the micro-sociological universe, that has indirectly stimulated the proliferation of both – violence and nationalism. Since neither violence nor nationalism comes naturally to human beings, their institutional and societal escalation entails the continuous expansion of bureaucratic and ideological might.

5

The Omnipotence of Triviality

Introduction

In *Swann's Way* Marcel Proust (2004 [1913]: 8) makes much of the idea that ordinary, everyday, habitual action provides a sense of comfort and security for most human beings. As he puts it, habit is 'that skilful slow-moving arranger' without which our minds 'would be powerless to make any room seem habitable'. Indeed, one of the defining characteristics of everyday social life is its ordinariness, its triviality. Since Durkheim (1995 [1915]) it has become apparent that moments of collective effervescence and shared emotional intensity are quite rare and that much of our everyday social life is not particularly eventful. For most of our lives we are engaged in cosy but mundane activities and more or less pleasant but repetitive tasks. Although our primary-school history textbooks are filled with dramatic narratives, colourful events and heroic actors, most of human life has always been defined by triviality and more or less comfortable insipidness.

Since nationalism is colloquially associated with highly momentous events such as wars, revolutions, insurgencies, terrorism or genocides, there is a tendency to overemphasize the emotional at the expense of habitual acts in the nationalist experience. Far more attention is given to the proclamations of revolutionaries, the voluntary sacrifices of soldiers and the inflammatory speeches of radical politicians than to the everyday manifestations of nationalism as expressed in sports, cinematic productions, tourism, beauty pageants or cuisine. It is only recently that everyday, banal forms of nationalism have become an object of serious scholarship. This chapter explores the significance of habitual nationalism in modernity. More specifically, it engages in an ongoing debate with recent approaches that make sharp distinctions between the 'hot' and 'banal', or 'official' and 'vernacular', nationalisms and that emphasize the inherent weakness of the everyday expressions of nationalist practice. In contrast to these approaches that see banal nationalism as an institutionally weak force, a bottom-up phenomenon that characterizes the late modern condition in the post-World War II Western world, I argue that triviality is the defining feature of nearly all nationalisms. Furthermore, by focusing on the historical transformations of organizational and ideological power and their ability to break gradually into the intimacies of the micro-social world, the chapter underscores the institutional strength of banal manifestations of nationalism. Instead of being a mere synonym for frailty, it is the trivial and habitual acts that both reflect and reinforce the organizational and ideological powers of modern nation-states. In this sense nationalism is much more powerful when it appears in an invisible, routine and habitual, rather than in a hostile, guise.

Hot vs. Banal Nationalisms?

The aftermath of World War II has changed the character of nationalism in two distinct ways. Firstly, the massive wartime mobilization of local populations in Asia and Africa, together with the worldwide delegitimization of the imperial projects and the supremacist doctrines that have traditionally justified such projects, made the maintenance of colonial power a virtual impossibility. Like the experience of World War I, when mass conscription of the urban poor and peasantry forced the rulers to extend citizenship provisions to the 'great unwashed', so the mass participation of 'colonial subjects' in World War II meant that their rights could not be overlooked either. Moreover, once large sections of a population were armed and trained how to fight and expel Japanese,

German or Italian enemies, these same skills could be used just as well to put pressure on the 'colonial masters' to leave. Hence the 1950s, 1960s and 1970s saw a dramatic proliferation of nationalist and separatist movements all over the world. In some instances, as was the case with most British 'overseas territorial possessions', the process of decolonization was relatively smooth[1] (Mann 2012; Darwin 2009; Boyce 1999). In other instances, as with the French and Portuguese authorities, reluctance to relinquish imperial possessions led to new waves of war. Hence in Algeria, Vietnam, Angola and Mozambique, to name a few, full state sovereignty was achieved through the protracted, violent conflicts of 'national liberation'. In most of these cases nationalist movements were led by individuals and groups inspired by the rhetoric and practice of nineteenth-century European nationalist ideologues.

Secondly, the new, bipolar world of cold war, bloc-based politics brought a substantial degree of geo-political stability which, combined with intensified economic growth, better employment prospects and the expansion of welfare provisions, created more prosperous conditions for most ordinary citizens in Europe and America.[2] Furthermore, the shared anti-fascist legacy helped delegitimize most forms of virulent racism and national chauvinism in both Soviet- and US-dominated spheres of influence. The political stability of the post-World War II settlement largely enshrined the existing borders, with little or no possibility for violent clashes over territory in Europe, America and even further afield. In addition the direct legacy of two brutal total wars, genocides and ethnic cleansings – which took place in war as well as immediately after the war – was an unprecedented degree of ethno-national homogeneity throughout the European continent (Mazower 2000). All these changes had a significant impact on the transformation of nation-states and nationalisms. Hence instead of a violent pursuit of claims for territorial expansion, expulsion of ethnic minorities and wars of unification, most European and American nationalisms acquired an informal, ordinary shape. The aggressive jingoism, virulent flag waving and militarist mobilization of the public for war gave way to milder expressions of national attachment and international competition. These included such diverse practices as sporting competitions (Olympics, football world cups, six nations rugby tournaments, World University Games, Islamic Solidarity Games or Commonwealth Games), national cuisine (e.g. the globally recognizable characteristics of Italian, Chinese, French, Japanese or Mexican food), international beauty pageants (Miss and Mister Universe, Miss Earth, Miss International or Miss Bikini Universe), popular song contests (from Eurovision to the national versions of *The X Factor*), public consumption of 'national' labels (Irish Guinness beer, German BMWs, Japanese Toyota cars, Italian fashion brands etc.), thematic Hollywood productions that glorify a particular nation (e.g. *Braveheart*, *Patriot*, *Michael Collins* or *Independence Day*), specific museum and gallery exhibitions (from the Terracotta Army to Caravaggio), idealized tourist destinations (from the Taj Mahal to Connemara) or widely advertised public festivals (from Songkran to Oktoberfest).

This change in the character of nationalist experience has led a number of influential scholars (Billig 1995; Cohen 1996; Edensor 2002; Eriksen 1993) to argue that what one could witness happening in the late twentieth and early twenty-first centuries is something distinctly new. Thus Billig (1995), Hutchinson (2006; 2005) and Sutherland (2012: 57–72) differentiate between the 'hot nationalism' of those aspiring to create a nation-state of their own and the 'banal nationalism' of 'established nations', which are those states, as Billig (1995: 8) put it, 'that have confidence in their own continuity, and that, particularly, are part of what is conventionally described as "the West"'. In other words, while violent nationalism is to be associated with independence movements, wars of national liberation or insurgency, banal nationalism, the daily 'flagging' of nationhood, is, for the most part, a feature of the modern Western world.

In a similar way Edensor (2002) sees everyday nationalism as a late twentieth-century phenomenon characterized by the distinctive spatial framing, performance and consumption of well-established national identities. Other scholars, such as Eriksen (1993), Wilk (1993), Cohen (1996), Whitmeyer (2002) and Jenkins (2010; 2008), differentiate between the official, elite or formal nationalisms articulated by the state authorities and the popular, informal, personal, vernacular or 'visceral' nationalisms of civil society groups and autonomous individuals. Despite their obvious differences, all of these approaches insist that everyday nationalism is a highly distinct and novel type of nationalist experience which differs significantly from the virulent expressions of nationalism in previous periods. Furthermore, some argue (e.g. Miller-Idriss 2009; Hearn 2007; Fox and Miller-Idriss 2008; Thompson 2001; Thompson and Day 1999; Wodak et al. 1999; Skey 2009) that unlike its traditional nineteenth- and early twentieth-century counterpart, which was essentially a top-down affair, the new everyday nationalism is defined by bottom-up activities and as such is 'creatively and self-consciously deployed and manipulated by ordinary people' (Fox and Miller-Idriss 2008: 59). Thus the two principal features of nationalist experience in the post-World War II context come together: mild, banal, nationalism is understood to be the dominant form whereas violent expressions of nationalist ideology are either confined to past eras or seen to be a property of the periphery (the former colonies and the political or geographical margins of the 'established states').

Although it is clear that since the early 1950s most nationalist rhetoric in Western Europe, North America or Australia has become softer and more placid, it is less certain that this is a completely novel or permanent transformation. More importantly, by rigidly separating 'banal' from 'hot' nationalisms one cannot properly explain their social origins or how they periodically metamorphose into one another. Hence in this chapter I will argue that any firm distinction between hot and everyday nationalism is conceptually vapid and empirically unsustainable. Banal expressions of nationalist ideology are not the sole preserve of the late modern West but were just as present at the inception of mass nationalism in late eighteenth- and nineteenth-century Europe, and also continue to be integral to all nationalisms worldwide. Secondly, I contend that everyday nationalism cannot be firmly distinguished from 'official' nationalism. In most contemporary, as well as historical, contexts, such banal manifestations of nationalism cannot be interpreted as the simple product of a spontaneous, bottom-up reflection of individual resistance or creativity. Instead they remain decisively tied to their organizational shells, which firmly set the parameters of their development. Thirdly, and perhaps most importantly, I argue that the proliferation of everyday forms of nationalism is not a sign that nationalism is becoming a weak or benign political force but, in fact, is an indicator of its ever-growing strength. Let us elaborate on each of these three points in turn.

Firstly, the strong distinction between banal and hot nationalism presupposes the existence of two different phenomena: the violent nationalism associated with the aspirations to establish a sovereign and independent nation-state or unite different political entities under a single national roof, and the non-violent, habitual sense of national attachment present in stable nation-states. In Billig's (1995: 41) own terms, 'as a nation-state becomes established in its sovereignty ... then the symbols of nationhood, which might once have been consciously displayed, ... become absorbed into the environment of the established homeland. There is, then, a movement from symbolic mindfulness to mindlessness.' Nevertheless, such a rigid polarity is built on the incorrect assumptions that virulent nationalism has been the historically dominant form of nationalist experience and that there was no mundane nationalism before the second half of the twentieth century. As discussed in the previous chapter, rather than being the norm, violence rarely accompanies nationalism. Despite the memorable revolutions, wars and insurgencies, there is little direct link between nationalism and violence, and when nationalist ideology acquires violent features these tend to emerge in short, explosive episodes which are then followed by long periods of non-violent habituality (Collins 2012; Malešević 2013a; 2011b; 2010). In other words, the nationalisms of state formation or unification are not defined by the omnipresence of violence: here, too, violence appears sporadically and unevenly and tends to be interwoven with the everyday routine.

The key point is that the nationalist experience has always been defined by routine and everyday habit. From the way French revolutionaries would address each other, the clothes they wore and the mannerisms they espoused, through the Englishness depicted in the novels of the early nineteenth century, to the World's Fairs of the late nineteenth century (including the Great Exhibition of the Works of Industry of all Nations) or the reinvention of the Olympics in 1896, mundane forms of nationalism have been around for much longer than is usually thought. Furthermore, the constant overlaps between banal and hot nationalisms were well documented in history. For example, Raento and Brunn (2005) have explored the popular use of Russian postage stamps in Finnish nationalist experience in the late nineteenth century. In this context the use of stamps was often both a reflection of banal, official (Russian), state nationalism and a form of political resist-ance, as many nationalist Finns attempted to sabotage official, banal nationalism by placing the disliked stamps upside down on the envelope. In a similar fashion Jones and Merriman (2009) and Azaryahu and Kook (2002) have demonstrated the inherent frailty of the hot/banal distinction in their respective analyses of Welsh and Palestinian everyday nationalism. Azaryahu and Kook (2002: 208–10) provide a historical analysis of nationally con-tested street-naming practices in Haifa in the 1930s, Jerusalem in the 1920s–40s and the Palestinian-dominated district of Haifa, Umm al-Fahm, in the 1990s. In all of these cases the renaming of streets was simultaneously a form of habitual action and a political statement that would provoke hostility from the authori-ties. For example, the decision to name a street in Umm al-Fahm after Muhammad Izz ad-Din al-Qassam, who led militant actions against British, French and Zionist associations in the Levant in the 1920s and 1930s and whose name was appropriated by several jihadist organizations, was deemed scandalous by the Israeli public. In a similar vein Jones and Merriman (2009) analyse the dynamics of popular campaigns for the establishment of bilingual road signs in Wales in the 1960s and 1970s and emphasize the impossibility of differentiating between hot and banal national-ism in this particular context, as the road signs were understood differently by different actors. In their own words:

> Welsh nationalist organizations, as well as individuals and organiza-tions involved in the governing of Wales, were adept at understanding these road signs in a multiplicity of ways: as symbols of (in)justice and

as conveyors of information; as linguistic eyesores and as symbols of Britishness. . . . the effectiveness of road signs as conveyors of information also influenced their status as markers of identity politics in Wales, whether through the use of particular fonts or through the ordering of Welsh and English versions of place names. (Jones and Merriman 2009: 172)

Thus rather than existing in two different and mutually incompatible forms, both, habit and hostility, are integral and often interdependent segments of nationalist experience. Furthermore, rather than being a novel, Western exception, banal nationalism has been and remains a dominant expression of nationalist practice from the time of the French and American revolutions. And it is as such that nationalist ideology has managed to capture the hearts and the minds of individuals all over the world.

The fact that the late twentieth and early twenty-first centuries are witness to a greater proliferation of mundane expressions of nationalism is not a reliable indicator of novelty but a direct consequence of broader organizational and ideological changes. Just like other forms of nationalism, its banal manifestations entail a substantial degree of technological advancement in communication, transport, printing, increased literacy rates, mass educational systems and other macro-structural transformations. There is no possibility of envisaging one's nation through topographic maps and weather reports without having a mass media that will transmit such reports and a public able to recognize and understand such maps.[3] There can be no identification with the images displayed on national notes and coins without the mass production and circulation of a single and standardized national currency. There can be no thousands of unnoticed national flags hanging on public buildings and private homes without the mass manufacturing and mass distribution of such flags.[4]

Hence in this sense the experiences of both hot and cold expressions of nationalism are similar, as in the early modern era there was neither the organizational nor the ideological know-how to transmit either of the two. To reach a wide audience, both nationalist militants and sports enthusiasts require developed systems of

127

communication, transport and a (nationalized) public responsive to their messages. Therefore the key organizational vessels for the development of 'hot' and 'cold' nationalisms are essentially the same: the large-scale social organizations – military, educational system, mass media, political parties, social movements, civil society groupings and so on. The historical record shows that banal and virulent symbols of nationalism have developed together. As O'Leary (2000), Spillman (1997), Hobsbawm (1983), Cannadine (1983) and Anderson (1983) document, nationalist mobilization for World War I was preceded by the mass production of national monuments, the invention of public ceremonies, the popular canonization of national martyrs and symbols, the mass printing of historical stamps and world maps, the mass creation of national associations and the institutional proliferation of sports on a mass scale.

For example, within a year of Bismarck's death in 1898 no fewer than 470 municipalities had erected 'Bismarck columns', and by 1902, 372 monuments of William I had been built throughout Germany. By the 1890s the national tricolour became an obligatory symbol at every civil marriage and other prominent ceremonies in France. Statues of Marianne, the image of the French Republic, were mass produced in a variety of sizes to cater for the expanding market, which included state officials just as much as ordinary citizens. It is only from the 1890s that US flags were placed in most American schools and that Uncle Sam became a national symbol sought after by the larger audiences. The second half of the nineteenth century witnessed huge interest in souvenirs of George Washington, with his image appearing 'on everything from clocks, ceramics, and glassware to yardage, homemade quilts, handkerchiefs, and banners' (O'Leary 2000: 17). Even quintessential international days such as 1 May had a distinctly national flavour, with workers from different parts of Europe wearing different 'national' flowers: carnations in Austria, red roses in Germany, sweetbriar and poppies in France. This was also a period when sports enthusiasts were instrumental in animating mass participation and articulating different sporting traditions, from cycling in France, football in England

and gymnastics in Germany to rifle shooting in Switzerland and the codification of Gaelic games in Ireland (Hobsbawm 1983: 263–307; Spillman 1997: 25; Mosse 1975: 167–82). Hence from the early days mundane nationalism was the dominant form of nationalist experience. In contrast to Giddens's (1985: 215) view that nationalism is a phenomenon that interrupts a daily routine, something that is 'not so much a part of regular day-to-day social life', nationalism is, and has always been, first and foremost a routine activity.

Secondly, the firm distinction between official/formal and informal, personal nationalism is also difficult to sustain empirically. There is no question that nationalist ideology nearly always appears in a variety of forms, some of which may be mutually exclusive, and that the state authorities are regularly interested in establishing a particular version of a nationalist doctrine as the dominant, society-wide, national narrative. There is also no dispute with the view that official nationalist messages can have very different local resonances or that such messages can be subverted, distorted or rearticulated to suit local situations or personal interests (Fox and Miller-Idriss 2008). Precisely because nationalism is not a rigid, uniform, inflexible ideology but something prone to continuous contextual metamorphoses, it can appeal to very diverse groups of individuals.

Nevertheless, saying that nationalism is a flexible ideology does not mean to suggest that its plasticity has no bounds. While the classic accounts of nationalism, such as those of Gellner (1983), Breuilly (1993) or Deutsch (1966), were certainly too much focused on top-down analysis and made little room for the role of human agents, some contemporary approaches went to the other extreme by completely privileging agency over structure. For example, Thompson (2001: 21) draws on Schutz's phenomenology not to find out why individuals employ the concepts of national identity or why nationalism has become a powerful popular ideology; he is only interested in how agents comprehend their world in national terms. In this view what really matters is 'how individuals actively employ their "common stock of knowledge" about nations and national identities'. In a similar way Brubaker et al. (2006: 15,

358) focus on everyday nationalism in the Romanian city of Cluj with the view of interpreting the daily encounters between Romanians and Hungarians from the agents' own point of view. Thus in this perspective ethnicity and nationhood are understood to be 'an interpretative prism, a way of making sense of the social world', 'a frame of vision, a cultural idiom, and a political claim'. This emphasis on the view of an agent is equally visible among those scholars who make a strong distinction between popular and elite nationalism (Whitmeyer 2002), formal vs. informal nationalism (Eriksen 1993), official vs. visceral nationalism (Wilk 1993) or political vs. personal nationalism (Cohen 1996). In all of these cases, popular nationalism is identified with the action, creativity and manipulation of ordinary individuals in contrast to the rigidity of the formal nationalism of states and elites.

Although this approach rightly acknowledges the importance of human agency in the variety of articulation and consumption of nationalism, its epistemological idealism makes it insensitive to the complexities of the organizational and ideological embedment of nationalist experience. While it is obvious that individual and social agents differ in how they perform, consume or frame their nationhood, there are objective structural limits to what or how widely one can choose. For one thing it is very difficult, if not almost impossible, to articulate a believable popular nationalist narrative which would operate completely outside of the main organizational and ideological channels for the creation and dissemination of nationalist ideas. One does not have to be a structuralist or historical determinist to recognize that social action is regularly shaped or constrained by the existing institutions: we are all born, live and die in the world of states and a myriad of other bureaucratic entities without which it would be very difficult, if not impossible, to function. And so are our parents, siblings, peers, neighbours and close friends. Hence even the most radical civil society groups have to work in the world that already exists; they can contest, subvert, reinterpret existing nationalist frames but they cannot create completely new interpretative frames. To initiate any large-scale change one still needs to interact with the bureaucratic institutions – from the publishing houses, universities, schools, courts, mass media and various outlets of the public sphere to internet providers.

The young Romanians and Hungarians in Cluj may be completely ignorant of the broader nationalist frames articulated by the political entrepreneurs, such as Cluj's mayor Funar (Brubaker et al. 2006), but they simply cannot escape the structural, organizational and ideological processes that are embedded in the institutions of the modern nation-states under which we all now live. Nationalism is not an omnipotent leviathan that cannot be resisted or transformed. However, as long as one lives in a world that is both physically and ideologically nation-centric, the choices an individual and groups are able to make will generally remain more or less nationalist. As Baert (1998: 74) observes: 'even if certain choices are thought as theoretically possible, the internalized generalized other is constraining in that it links particular imaginary choices with particular effects'. The cumulative bureaucratization of coercion and centrifugal ideologization have set the organizational and ideological foundations for a world where individuals and groups can subvert, ignore, reject, make fun of or even openly hate nationalist discourses, but as long as the nation-state is the dominant organizing mechanism of living on this planet, none of these practices could substantially undermine the potency of nationalist principles in everyday life.

In this sense, rather than being a profoundly different, creative or independent force, banal nationalism is largely a popular symbiote of 'official' nationalism. The habitual reproduction of nationhood through newspaper discourses, landscapes, shared currency, unnoticed flags or weather reports always remains dependent on the broader organizational and ideological scaffolding of the existing state structure (Malešević 2007; 2006). There could be no mundane, everyday nationalism without the institutions and elaborate doctrines of 'official nationalism'. For example, the popularly shared belief that the nation is a normal and natural unity of collective solidarity is reproduced daily through such banal practices as the pledge of allegiance to the flag and the Thanksgiving turkey dinners in the USA or wearing a red poppy on Remembrance Day in the UK. Nevertheless, such a specific nationalist *Weltanschauung* is not a product of local spontaneity but has a distinct ideological and organizational origin: it is a product of a deliberate action on the part of the nationalizing state elite, and its persistence and society-wide proliferation remain dependent on the institutions of the modern nation-state (Siskind 1992; Hobsbawm 1983; Spillman 1997: 25). As O'Leary (2000) and Löfgren (1993) demonstrate, the popularization and mass use of national symbols in the USA and Sweden were a direct consequence of the prolonged nationalizing policies of the two states which acquired popular support during periods of economic growth and a general rise in living standards. Most American national symbols and rituals which are popularly articulated as timeless representations of American-ness are novel creations: 'The first national observation of Memorial Day took place in 1868, but it was not uniformly observed on the last Monday of May until 1971; Francis Bellamy's Pledge of Allegiance was not written until 1891; "The Star-Spangled Banner" was finally approved as the official national anthem in 1931; and Congress did not enact a national law against "flag desecration" until 1968' (O'Leary 2000: 3). Hence rather than interpreting everyday nationalism as 'the practical accomplishment of ordinary people'[5] (Fox and Miller-Idriss 2008: 539), it is better to focus on its intrinsic parasitic quality. Rather than having an autonomous existence, the habitual is only one form of the complex set of processes that encompass nationalism.

Finally, there is a general tendency to assume that banal nationalism is a largely harmless and weak phenomenon. To be fair, Billig (1995: 6–7) is adamant that for him banality is not a synonym for benign acts: 'banal nationalism can hardly be innocent: it is reproducing institutions which possess vast armaments[6] . . . The armaments are primed ready to use in battle. And the national populations appear to be primed, ready to support use of those armaments.' However, others (Gellner 1983: 42–6; Collins 2012) emphasize the alleged feebleness of everyday nationalism as opposed to the intensity and strength of hot nationalism. Thus Collins (2012: 384–5) argues that 'most of the time, nationalism is low-strength: latent, perhaps, but far from the thoughts and feelings of most people', or that 'even in societies where nationalism is institutionalized, it is not necessarily very strong or constant'. This point is illustrated by the general popular ignorance of national monuments ('the statue of the victorious general in the park splattered with pigeon droppings'), or national holidays which ordinarily end up as hedonistic occasions for eating and drinking and 'invoke little sense of national solidarity'.

Collins is absolutely right that national symbols by themselves do not create meanings. For symbols can only become the markers of group solidarity through intensive social action. In this sense neither monuments nor national days per se would guarantee nationalist mobilization. As Robert Musil (1986 [1936]) noticed a long time ago, 'there is nothing as invisible as the monument'. Similarly, many official national days such as 3 October in Germany (National Unity Day) or 6 June in Sweden (National Day) are largely ignored by the majority of the population, while some states, such as the UK or Denmark, do not even have a national day (McCrone and McPherson 2009). Nevertheless, and regardless of their relative invisibility, such national symbols can relatively quickly acquire a potent mobilizing, even totemic, quality at specific historical moments. The point is that meaning can be bestowed on such 'unstable signifiers' (Geisler 2009).

For example, the statue of the *ban* (duke) Josip Jelačić in Zagreb is highly indicative of the way changing historical contexts can infuse a dormant monument with different symbolisms. The statue was originally installed in 1866 by the Habsburg rulers to commemorate Jelačić's support in crushing the 1848 revolution in Hungary. The statue was oriented towards the north with Jelačić's sword deliberately pointing towards Hungary. The building of the monument was initially fiercely opposed by the Zagreb councillors, and the majority of the population were not particularly enthusiastic about its building. After all, it was only a memorial for a loyal Habsburg aristocrat. However, with the intensification of the Budapest policies of cultural assimilation by the 1880s, the statue became a symbol of Croatian national resistance against Hungarian hegemony. With Hungary out of the picture after World War I the monument remained popularly invisible, just as did most such statues all over Europe. This all changed after World War II. Seeing Jelačić as a traitor to the South Slav cause and an aristocratic stooge, the communist authorities removed the statue in 1947. This move was resented by many nationally conscious individuals and groups in Croatia but this issue did not feature prominently until the late 1980s, when the political situation changed, with the new national symbolism gaining in visibility. In this new context Jelačić was reinterpreted as the protector of Croatian sovereignty and an opponent of Serbian hegemony. By 1990 the nationalist opposition was highly successful in mobilizing mass support for the reinstalment of the statue, with a petition signed by 70,000 Croatian citizens. In this period the leading nationalist movement, the Croatian Democratic Community (HDZ) – which was soon to assume power – issued a declaration stating that 'the fate of the unhappy *ban*'s statue has become a symbol of how Croatian national feelings were trampled on in socialist Yugoslavia, a symbol of a policy of heartless hatred for one's own nation, its history, culture and heritage'. The monument was soon reinstated but this time Jelačić's sword was set to point in the opposite direction – towards Serbia (Goldstein 1999: 206; Magaš 2007). What one can see in this example is that although symbols such as monuments can and often do remain invisible, empty markers, they can relatively quickly be infused with intense and very different nationalist imaginings.

It is so too with other nationalist symbols, from the commemorations of national days to public festivals, sports competitions, beauty pageants, tourist destinations, national cuisine, triumphal arches or war memorials. In everyday life all of these and many other symbols can became powerful mobilizers of nationalist action, and just as readily can remain completely outside of any nationalist discourse. It is the specific historical context and one's organizational ability to articulate a monument's significance ideologically that will determine which symbols will become the object of nationalist mobilization and which will remain empty shells. The key point is that one should not confuse invisibility with irrelevance. Although such symbols can remain unnoticed for very long periods of time, it does not mean that they are insignificant. Examples of monument desecration in the UK in 2011 demonstrate well that despite the ordinary inconspicuousness of memorials, any attempt to desecrate them is likely to provoke a public outcry. Thus the damaging of the Tidworth war memorial in Wiltshire was described by the tabloids as the act of 'sick yobs' who 'flog statues for scrap'. Their behaviour was deemed scandalous since they 'left communities across the UK outraged at the appalling insult to the heroes of two world wars' (*Sun*, 31 October 2011: 1).

Similarly the organized burning of red poppies on Remembrance Day in 2010 by a group called Muslims against Crusaders was equally seen as shocking by local residents, the media and magistrates. The case was brought quickly to court, where witnesses described this action as 'sickening': 'I felt sick inside. It is something that means so much to me. So to see what I believed was a wreath of poppies fall to the ground, it was despicable.' Even the prosecutor deemed such actions to be going 'far beyond the boundaries of political protest and freedom of expression' (*Mirror*, 24 February 2011: 5). In both cases similar feelings were voiced by the online readers:

> Absolutely disgusting! How can these ungrateful people do this? The war memorials are a tribute to all those people who have given their lives to provide the society these horrid people cherish. Desecrating these sites is unforgivable! The plan to disrupt the Remembrance Day ceremonies by the Muslim Extremists just baffles me! The only reason they are in a society that allows them to behave in that way is because these service men and women have given their lives in so many conflicts across the world. They should be thanking them and honouring their memory not denigrating it. (*Mirror*, 24 February 2011: 5)

Since hot and banal nationalism share the same symbolism, what at one point might be seen as an indiscernible and irrelevant symbol can on other occasions provoke an intense and hostile emotional reaction. Most individuals will not pay much, or any, daily attention to the flag hanging on the government building, the framing of a particular weather report or the images displayed on the national currency. However, any attempt to burn that previously unnoticed flag, to desecrate the image of the national hero on the banknote or deliberately to omit part of the country from the weather report is likely to incite a mass public outcry in any contemporary nation-state.[7]

All of this suggests that rather than being a weak, sporadic, thin and largely insignificant phenomenon, banal nationalism is in fact an extremely powerful force. Nonetheless, its potency does not come from periodic emotional outbursts but from its structural embeddedness. It is its routinized, normalized, taken-for-granted, indiscernible quality that signals its omnipotence.

Collins (2012: 385) argues that nationalism is characterized by time bubbles, 'capsules of collectively experienced time, on the whole rather sudden in onset, lasting for a while, then declining back to banal normality'. He illustrates this with the metaphor of a rocket which zooms into the sky, 'exploding in an eye-catching blast, then dispersing into fallout fading slowly from vivid to drab'. Collins is completely right that nationalism is a dynamic phenomenon that waxes and wanes and that violent outbursts of high intensity cannot last for long periods of time. An intense feeling of solidarity, the Durkheimian collective effervescence, is by definition a temporary state.

However, what is neglected in this account is that such momentary periods of concentrated nationalist frenzy cannot emerge without an already existing organizational and ideological scaffolding. To experience the eye-catching blast in the sky one needs to build a rocket first. There can be no hot nationalist bubbles and no effervescence without long-term organizational and ideological 'preparatory' work. Not only can there be no nationalism without modernity but there is no nationalism without social organizations and ideologization. No matter how heightened their collective emotional encounters might have been, no medieval European peasantry could possibly have experienced nationalist fervour. Collins is well aware that the existence of nationalism presupposes a high degree of state penetration, but he makes no attempt to explore the relationship between the two. For the very prevalence of mundane, habitual nationalism is deeply rooted in the cumulative bureaucratization of coercion and centrifugal ideologization and in the capacity of modern social organizations to absorb these bubbles of micro-solidarity dexterously into a synchronized and lasting, society-wide, shared nationalist experience. Let us explore these links in greater detail.

The Organization and Ideologization of the Mundane

Nationalism is a doctrine that thrives on ambiguity and paradoxes. Gellner (1983: 124) captures some of this paradox in his well-known statement that nationalism 'claims to defend folk culture while in fact it is forging a high culture; it claims to protect an old folk society while in fact helping to build up an anonymous mass society . . . It preaches and defends cultural diversity, when in fact it imposes homogeneity both inside and, to a lesser extent, between political units.' Gellner is of course right in this account, but there is an even greater paradox at work in the development and expansion of nationalism over the last several centuries. This paradox is discernible in the inversely proportional relationship between the visibility and strength of nationalist ideology. The common-sense view is that virulent and loud nationalist outbursts indicate its pervasiveness and its force. When one thinks of nationalism the general tendency is to pinpoint radical movements on either the right or the left of the political spectrum – from the Front National in France and the National Democratic Party in Germany to the Basque Herri Batasuna and Eusko Alkartasuna or Golden Dawn in Greece. While it is clear that such movements and political parties have a significant support base, they are generally shunned by the majority of citizens in their respective nation-states. In other words, whereas these movements are highly visible and well known to the electorate they do not command such large-scale popular support as the mainstream political parties. This is not to say that such nationalist movements are unlikely to gain a wider support base in the future or that the mainstream political parties are not nationalist. As discussed in chapter 4, in the modern era no political party can succeed in electoral contests if its patriotic credentials are seen to be suspect. In this context the radicalism of far right or some far left parties is not a novel ideological discourse; it is just a radicalized extension of the mainstream nationalist discourse.

However, the much more important point is that radicalism or high discernibility should not be viewed as synonymous with political strength. For one thing, the heightened state of emotional tension or stimulation cannot last for a long time and quickly amplified feelings are bound just as quickly to deflate. Hence in the long term the habitual reproduction of national attachments is much more effective than highly intense but sporadic nationalist frenzies. For another thing, aggressive defensiveness and intolerant posturing are more often than not signs of insecurity and weakness rather than strength. As Pareto (1963 [1902]: 79) was already aware, one should not confuse violent rage with power: 'The strong man strikes only when it is absolutely necessary, and then nothing stops him. Trajan was strong, not violent: Caligula was violent, not strong.' It is the sense of insecurity that breeds fear and violence (Bauman 2006). When one feels comfortable in her or his ideological skin there is little necessity for Freudian defence mechanisms or aggressive self-righteousness. When being Swedish or Brazilian is simply taken for granted and perpetuated through the daily routine there is no need to hurl one's Brazilian-ness or Swedish-ness in somebody's face. Thus greater power stems from familiarity and predictability. If one defines strength mechanically as a capability to produce or withstand applied stress without failure, then this is a quality that entails long-term institutional work rather than an instant spark. So the vitality of nationalism presupposes a long-term organizational and ideological build-up. As decades of sociological research demonstrate, both organizational and ideological penetration require prolonged periods of time and this penetration develops unevenly in time, in space and among different social strata.

Many analysts agree that nationalism is likely to proliferate further and faster in the presence of strong social organizations, be they state institutions or well-organized social movements (Breuilly 1993; Lachmann 2010; Hearn 2011). However, as

Mann (2012; 1993; 1986) shows, there are different forms of organizational power. The despotic power of elites – which can make and implement decisions at will, with little or no negotiation with other elites and civil society groupings – differs profoundly from the infrastructural power whereby state organizations have the capacity to permeate civil society deeply. It is the infrastructural power that really attests to the ever-increasing ability of organizational power. One of the key features of the cumulative bureaucratization of coercion is this ever-increasing infrastructural potency of modern social organizations. This includes the ability of state institutions to tax income and wealth at source; to collect and use a huge volume of personal data; to enforce the use of identity documents including birth certificates, passports or driving licences; to recruit their citizens to fight in wars; to nationalize privately owned property if deemed necessary; and so on. As Mann (2012; 1993; 1986), Tilly (1992) and Lachmann (2010) show, these powers have dramatically increased in the past 150 years, as before the second half of the nineteenth century states did not have the organizational or ideological know-how to tax, mobilize and control their populations fully without their consent. Even the defining characteristic of the state – its ability to monopolize the use of violence over its territory – could only be implemented in the modern era when states acquired relatively sophisticated transport, communications and technology that would allow the policing of the entire territory.

However, this process has affected not only states but also non-state social organizations from private corporations and international associations to social movements. All these entities have experienced a dramatic increase in their organizational powers and infrastructural reach. Thus there is a much greater compartmentalization of responsibilities, stricter divisions of labour, increased disciplinary control, a hierarchical ordering of tasks and cultivated hostility towards competing organizations (Meyer et al. 1997). These organizational changes have stimulated the expansion of compatible values that on the one hand praise obedience and respect for the rules of the organization and on the other hand commend one's dedication and loyalty to that organization. As

Merton (1952: 365) noticed a long time ago, the increase in social disciplining presupposes a shared belief in the validity of such organizational practices: 'discipline can be effective only if the ideal patterns are buttressed by strong sentiments which entail devotion to one's duties, a keen sense of the limitation of one's authority and competence, and methodical performance of routine activities'. All of these structural changes had a profound impact on values that underpin one's attachment to a specific organization. Since the nation-state and social movements that seek the establishment of a particular nation-state are social organizations par excellence, they too have been affected by these changes. Whereas the pre-modern, patrimonial organizations utilized kinship, age, religion and clientelistic networks to foster a fairly narrow sense of attachment to one's social unit, the modern bureaucratic institutions stimulate the detached, meritocratic and instrumentalist ethics of belonging. Hence instead of public proclamations of unquestioned allegiance to the ruler, head of the household or religious authority, loyalty is now expressed through routine compliance with the rules. And it is this detached, routinized setting of the bureaucratic unit that gives rise to banal nationalism. The modern social organizations, including the nation-state, cultivate an ideal institutional context for the proliferation of a mundane, habitual sense of attachment. The bureaucratic machine of the nation-state supplies the coercive organizational frame that helps create and reproduce habitual actions, while banal nationalism operates as the ideological glue that binds the members of a specific nation-state together. Banal nationalism is nothing else but a habitual expression of loyalty and attachment to a specific social organization. Like any modern bureaucratic unit, the nation-state and the movements aspiring to set up a nation-state encourage timid compliance with what they consider to be a legitimate authority. The ever-increasing organizational power of these entities means that they are able to structure the modern world in such a way that it becomes almost unthinkable to envisage this world without the presence of social organizations, and most of all without nation-states.

While the long-term historical process of the cumulative bureaucratization of coercion has provided the organizational frame for the development and expansion of everyday nationalism, it in itself could not create and disseminate nationalist ideology. Hence this structural process was regularly accompanied by the gradual ideologization of the different social strata. As George Mosse (1991; 1975) and Eugen Weber (1978) have demonstrated, this 'nationalization of the masses' combined top-down indoctrination by the state institutions (education, military, mass media, courts, public administration) and the cultural, political and economic elites with the initiatives of civil society groups and local communities. What started off as a doctrine of a small, elite, minority had by the early twentieth century become a dominant ideology of the majority of the population. Nevertheless, it is important to emphasize that this centrifugal ideologization could not have emerged through the rigid imposition of a nationalism that was red in tooth and claw. Instead it was the gradual and relatively slow but constant and continuous exposure to mundane images, practices, ideas and actions that transformed 'peasants into Frenchmen'. In other words, rather than aggressively foisting 'hot' nationalist doctrine onto the unsuspecting peasants, manual labourers or their children, much of the centrifugal ideologization was accomplished through trivial acts.

For example, from the second half of the nineteenth century, nationalist imagery became widespread in board games, jigsaw puzzles, picture postcards, children's toys, school plays, circuses, photographs, subsidized pilgrimages and the early forms of tourism. Mosse (1991: 127–56) shows how mass production of illustrated postcards, themed board games and children's toys was crucial in making one's nationhood palpable, familiar and habitual. What in the earlier periods was a privilege of elites, who would spend their leisure time playing war-themed board games or solving jigsaw puzzles, by the early twentieth century became a mass pastime phenomenon involving nearly all strata of the population. Hence the popular jigsaw puzzles and board games depicted 'anything from the sinking of the *Lusitania* to the shooting of a small French boy by the Germans . . . to the chasing of Marianne by a German soldier' (Mosse 1991: 128). In a similar fashion this period witnessed the mass production of picture postcards – which by 1910 had a print run of 125 million in France alone – that contained highly nationalized and romanticized images of national landscapes, ordinary soldiers and domestic life, and humorous representations of other nations (Jones and Howell 1972: 11). The mass manufacturing and distribution of toys such as tin soldiers, playing cards, toy cannons and competitive sports toys, which were initially used by adults as much as by children, further contributed to the reproduction of mundane forms of nationalism. Tin soldiers in particular were generally seen not as simple playing devices but as educational tools: 'in 1902 tin soldiers in France were actually called the educators for tomorrow's war. They were also said to encourage loyalty to the flag' (Mosse 1991: 141). What is important to emphasize here is that these trivial nationalizing devices were produced, distributed and consumed by social organizations, groups and individuals working outside of the state administration. Differently put, the process of centrifugal ideologization involved civil society, the family, one's peers, neighbours and private businesses just as much as the state bureaucracy.

The distinctive feature of successful centrifugal ideologization is the ability to portray social action through the prism of normality. Since the early works of Bourdieu (1990), Foucault (1975) and Barthes (1993) it has become apparent that the potency of any ideology is best gauged by its popular inconspicuousness. That is, when a particular belief system or a specific course of action is deemed to be normal and natural this in itself is a reliable indicator of its effective ideological penetration. When historically specific and contingent social relations such as patriarchy, racial segregation, the use of child labour or criminalization of homosexuality are normalized and naturalized so that they are taken for granted and rarely, if ever, questioned, then one can identify hegemonic ideological processes at work. For example, as already mentioned in chapter 3, for much of the late nineteenth and early twentieth centuries public opinion in Europe and America subscribed to the view that women are instinctive care-givers who should stay at home and mind children while men go to work. The gendered division of labour was seen by most citizens as normal and natural (Mann 2012: 6–8, 75–6). Moreover, such a belief system was enshrined in the constitutional documents of many states.[8] For example, the Irish Constitution still has a clause that states: 'the State recognises that by her life within the home, woman gives to the State a support without which the common good cannot be achieved. The State shall, therefore, endeavour to ensure that mothers shall not be obliged by economic necessity to engage in labour to the neglect of their duties in the home' (Article 41.2). Today such beliefs, together with those supporting racial segregation, homophobia or the exploitation of child labour, are perceived as anachronistic and are confined to the margins of popular opinion. However, this has not happened with nationalism.

On the contrary, the view that human beings are naturally divided into specific nations and can only fully express their individual freedom through membership in a nation-state has become so dominant that it has been enshrined in the UN Charter, which states that 'Everyone has the right to a nationality. No one shall be arbitrarily deprived of his nationality nor denied the right to change his nationality' (Universal Declaration of Human Rights, 1945: article 15). It is interesting that there is no universally guaranteed right to have no nationality or to opt out from nationhood altogether. Since nationalist ideology is articulated as a project capable of traversing nearly all internal divisions in terms of class, gender, religion, region and in many cases ethnicity, its normalization and naturalization are often even more pervasive. While it is acceptable to feel alienated or even hostile to one's nation-state, to change a nationality or have two or more national allegiances, to have no nation at all is not seen as a serious option (see chapter 6). The fact that in the early twenty-first century declaring that one has no nation is almost tantamount to saying that one is from another planet is a poignant indicator of how dominant and undisputed this belief system is.

The long-term historical processes of cumulative bureaucratization and centrifugal ideologization have fostered the emergence of distinct and mutually exclusive national habituses which are largely resistant to changes in political or economic systems. This is best illustrated when comparing two contemporary nation-states that could not be more different in terms of their economics, politics and culture: Denmark and North Korea. One is a liberal democratic state with a vibrant, globalized, capitalist economy, an extensive, locally based welfare system and a decentralized power structure; the other is a highly centralized communist partocracy with a centrally planned economy that officially proclaims its military as the privileged stratum (Kim Jong Il's military first policy). While the former has a highly developed and vivacious civil society and a lively public sphere, with free mass media and a variety of educational outlets, the latter rigorously punishes any attempt at criticism, has no legitimate non-state channels for the articulation of public debate and has no identifiable civil society networks. Yet despite all of these enormous differences both nation-states rely on nationalism as the principal ideological glue for their political legitimation.

Despite the official Marxist commitment to the internationalism of the world proletariat, much of the everyday rhetoric in North Korea is saturated with intense nationalist imagery. This is not only visible in the official declarations, documents issued by the government and military, the fiercely nationalist state mass media and the education system, but also in the various outlets of everyday life from children's games, jokes and family relationships to parenting techniques (Seth 2010; Kang 2012). In all of these instances one can encounter highly belligerent nationalist expressions that portray the Korean people as a racially distinct, ethnically homogeneous, primordial and superior nation while depicting its alleged enemies, such as Americans, Japanese and the South Korean regime, in extremely negative terms (Shin 2006). For example, the primary school mathematics textbook describes an action from the Korean War (1950–3) in the following terms: 'In the last war for national liberation, our soldiers killed and dismembered a total of 278 bastards, a sum of American imperialist bastards, wolves and South Korean puppet soldier bastards' (Kang 2012: 10). The children's magazines publish poetry which glorifies equally voluntary self-sacrifices for the nation and the killings of 'unscrupulous' enemies. Thus the poem 'My Mother's Military Cap', written by a primary school student, Yumi Li, tells the story of her brave mother who 'grabbed a rifle with the mind of revenge

[and] how many enemies did she shoot in every decisive combat'
(Kang 2012: 10–14).

While it is clear that these state-sponsored publications reflect
official doctrine, such pugnacious discourse is just as present
in everyday interpersonal communication and among family
members and friends. Jin Woong Kang (2012) interviewed sixty-
two North Korean refugees and defectors living in South Korea,
many of whom testify that belligerent nationalism was and
remains widespread among ordinary citizens in everyday life.[9]
Rather than being solely a top-down phenomenon, North Korea's
militant nationalism 'was also productive and diffusive from
below'. An integral part of this nationalist rhetoric is rampant
anti-Americanism, often combined with an intense dislike of
South Korean and Japanese societies. Kang (2012: 14–15) documents how one interviewee recalled the common practice of North
Korean mothers telling their children to stop quarrelling in the
following words: 'Why are you guys fighting? You should rather
fight against American bastards.' Calling a person 'an American
imperialist bastard' or 'a South Korean puppet' was the worst
insult in the Democratic People's Republic of Korea (DPRK),
while 'beating American scarecrows with a stick' was one of the
most popular children's games. The combined traumatic legacies
of the Japanese occupation and the Korean War stimulated a proliferation of nationalist ideas throughout North Korean society.
In the aftermath of the Korean War the regime relied extensively
on nationalism to secure its legitimacy. By the 1970s, nationalism
trumped socialism as the primary source of ideological justification of rule, with the doctrine of *Juche* (national independence
and self-reliance) becoming a constitutionally enshrined official
ideology (Seth 2010; Shin 2006).[10]

Notwithstanding its much greater popular support – grounded
in political pluralism, democratic institutions, a liberal civic
culture and an open public sphere – the Danish state still
derives most of its legitimacy from nationalist principles. Here
too national symbolism permeates equally state institutions and
popular discourse and practices. The *Dannebrog*, the Danish
flag, accompanies all public events and is just as much present

in the private sphere – from town councils, *kommunes*, schools and kindergartens, streets and military barracks to weddings and birthday celebrations (including the standard flag-sporting cakes), funerals, the *Dannebrog*-decorated family Christmas trees or even hot-dog vans. School children learn that this is the oldest flag in the world, which fell 'from Heaven in June 1219 during the battle of Lyndanisse' to save King Valdermar II and his brave knights. This event is commemorated in numerous paintings, folklore, novels and songs, some of which are part of the school curriculum. One such popular poem glorifies the flag in the following terms: 'There is nothing that means as much as the flag being raised, while it draws our hearts and minds towards Heaven' (Jenkins 2010: 131). The national songs are widely performed and sung by official state representatives and by the ordinary public. Denmark has two national anthems – the royal, 'King Christian', and the secular, 'There is a Lovely Land' – both of which exalt the special and unique national virtues of Danes (Østergaard 2006: 96).

Moreover, the Danish state consciously promotes a particular set of educational values that emphasize the cultivation of character formation – *dannelse*. As Korsgaard (2008) explains, from the nineteenth century onwards this concept acquired a less elitist meaning,[11] as it became integral to Grundtvigian-inspired 'enlightenment of the people' movements which were highly instrumental in establishing the system of private primary folk schools and 'people's colleges'. Nevertheless, in both public and folk schools the values and principles of *dannelse* helped reinforce many tenets of Danish nationalism. Even though Grundtvig's guiding principles clashed with those of the official state elite nationalism, they were just as nationalist. The popular enlightenment was conceived as 'emanating from the people itself', unlike the foreign-influenced academic enlightenment which 'never reaches the people as living words, nor does any good for the fatherland, but leaves the people dumb and spiritually defenceless to be ridiculed by foreigners' (Korsgaard 2008: 61, quoting Grundtvig).

Furthermore, the Danish royal family (the House of Glücksburg) is another potent national symbol revered equally in official and popular discourse. Just like the *Dannebrog*, the royal house is publicly and popularly deemed to have the oldest royal lineage in Europe. The genealogy of the current queen regnant, Margrethe II, is traced all the way back to Gorm the Old (936–58 CE), and as Jenkins (2010: 127) points out, this long lineage is a powerful source of state legitimacy and national pride: 'it offers a plausible narrative, and despite the usual multi-national European royal family tree, allows the family to claim timeless and authentic Danishness'.

Therefore, regardless of profoundly different political, economic and social systems, Denmark and North Korea, just as all modern nation-states do, derive most of their legitimacy from nationalist ideas and practices. In both cases nationalism permeates not only state institutions such as the educational systems, mass media, military, courts or town councils but also the realms of civil society, family, neighbourhoods and even children's playtime. Despite the enormous political differences, the two nation-states, as nation-states, share a similar organizational structure, and it is this structure that sets up the specific ideological and organizational scaffolding that supports and maintains nationalist understandings of social reality. The direct legacy of the long-term historical processes that are the cumulative bureaucratization of coercion and centrifugal ideologization is a nation-centric world.

However, this is not to say that the nationalisms at work in North Korea and Denmark are the same. Even a superficial observation of the two cases would show that while most occurrences of Danish nationalism tend to be subdued or trivial, the displays of nationalism in the DPRK are often characterized by intense hostility. This difference is most stark in such symbolic representations as the imagery of the Danish flag on the wedding cake or in the shopping mall, in contrast to the melodramatic and often vicious performances of the North Korean TV and radio newsreaders who shout nationalist slogans and curse 'the American bastards' and 'the South Korean puppets'. Whereas much of the North Korean nationalist rhetoric is full of passionate and aggressive language and metaphors, a great deal of the Danish nationalism is rather trivial. This obvious difference in the intensity and character of nationalist expression in the two societies has led a number of scholars to see Denmark as less nationalist than many of its West European neighbours (Korsgaard 2008; Østergaard 2006), while North Korea is regularly seen as epitomizing an extreme nationalist order (Lim 2009; Kang 2012).[12] In other words, while North Korean nationalism is understood to be strong and well entrenched, Danish nationalism is viewed as a weak and ineffective force.

Nevertheless, in line with the general argument of this chapter I would argue that the opposite is the case. The fact that the North Korean state has to engage in the nearly permanent mobilization of its population is in itself a reliable indicator that, despite its widespread appeal, North Korean nationalism is still not fully normalized among the citizens of the DPRK. Although some of the bellicose nationalist rhetoric is well integrated in the micro-world of family, wider kinship and locality, as already illustrated by various examples, the absence of non-state social organizations, movements and associations means that the development of any alternative articulations of nationalist ideology is stifled. Since civil society networks are generally proscribed and the state authorities have no organizational means to penetrate the private realm fully, in order to maintain an ideological monopoly they have to foster and direct continuous nationalist mobilization. In other words, to prevent the emergence of alternative civil society networks, which would ultimately challenge the state authorities, the rulers rely on the incessant nationalist mobilization. For this purpose the entire apparatus of the state, the ruling party, educational system, mass media, courts, sporting events, military, police, publishing etc. become saturated with government-formulated nationalist rhetoric. Crucially, as long as the state authorities have an ideological monopoly they are in a position to control the direction and intensity of this rhetoric and use nationalist mobilization to counter external pressure and internal dissent. Nonetheless, as nationalism is not an autonomous force but a solely state-regulated phenomenon it is much weaker than it appears. To use Mark Beissinger's (1998) distinction between nationalisms that bark and nationalisms that bite, North Korean nationalism is much more of the barking than the biting type. Instead of being a relatively independent and habitual force that infuses the everyday life of individuals in the DPRK, North Korean nationalism remains highly dependent on the actions of the party and military elites. In this sense, despite the micro-level nationalist offshoots present in the family and communal life, North Korean nationalism is essentially a top-down affair. The absence of civil society networks, combined with the permanent mobilization where nationalism is subsumed under the dominant normative (communist) ideology, means that North Korean citizens do not embrace nationalism as something obvious, as a second nature. Instead, nationalist ideology is generally understood as a defensive mechanism generated from above and collectively enacted in recurring, emotionally intense, ritual practices.

In direct contrast, Danish nationalism seems very timid but in fact is much more forceful. This strength comes from the advanced bureaucratization of coercive power and popular ideologization and the processes through which these two link up with the pockets of micro-solidarity. Nevertheless, the success of this long-term historical process also owes a great deal to the vibrancy of civil society networks, which have articulated alternative nationalist narratives and in this way have fostered the penetration of nationalist ideas and practices into the pores of Danish society.

There is no question that Denmark is one of the most liberal states in the world. Yet this liberalism is built on the contours of an extremely powerful state. To use Mann's (2012; 1993) terminology, Denmark is characterized by highly advanced infrastructural organizational powers: the state is very efficient in collecting taxes at source without consent; it enforces its laws quickly over the entire territory; it operates an exceptionally efficient and complex welfare regime that includes the entire population; it has a significant impact on the economy; it maintains a sophisticated military fully integrated into the high-tech NATO programmes; and it also has state-of-the-art police forces. In addition, as Jenkins (2010: 160–71) demonstrates, the state successfully gathers and can instantly recall all vital information on all its citizens and residents. Everybody is issued with an official personal number by the Central Person Register (CPR) and through this system the state can monitor births, deaths, marriages, divorces, changes in address (which have to be reported immediately), health insurance status, GP allocation, bank accounts, criminal record, house and car ownership, driving and hunting licence details and so on. Furthermore, the state regulates which names can be given to children: the Name Law, no. 193 of 29 April 1981, together with the official name lists and official legal commentary, determine that 'one cannot choose a name which is not *egentligt* – i.e. "real" or "proper"' (Jenkins 2010: 166).

Hence, despite the popular image of North Korea as an omnipotent state machine and Denmark as a soft, freewheeling state, it is Denmark that has an infrastructurally more forceful state apparatus. And it is this complex state apparatus that, in tandem with the vibrant civil society, makes the maintenance of habitual nationalism possible.

Unlike North Korea, where one encounters a single version of an integral nationalism, recent Danish history generated two competing but complementary forms of nationalist experience: state and popular nationalisms.[13] Although both rely on the same symbolism (*Dannebrog*, royal family, *dannelse*, etc.), popular nationalism is regularly juxtaposed to official nationalism. For example, every Danish commune uses its own version of the national flag and many ordinary individuals insist on popular ownership of this symbol: 'It is simply joy. We are happy about our flag ... It is the people's flag, it is not the state's flag!' (Jenkins 2010: 137–8). In a similar way, the royal family is understood as a quintessential national symbol where the individual royals are criticized but the institution of the monarchy is consecrated. In this context the 'ordinariness' of Danish monarchs is symbolically opposed to the extravagance of other European monarchs: 'Exaggerated ordinariness is an important part of the Danish national self-image and Queen Margrethe's "ordinariness" is part of what makes her so special' (Jenkins 2010: 128). In this way popular nationalism often outbids the state articulation of nationalist ideology, as many individuals perceive it not as a product of top-down engineering but as a genuine expression of popular sentiment. The fact that both the state and civil society are very strong helps reinforce the nationalist understanding of the world. The attempt to reclaim popularly the flag, royal family or any other national symbol will not weaken but can only strengthen the nationalist feelings. This is best expressed in the popularly shared view that Denmark is an egalitarian and culturally homogeneous society, 'a little country' where 'we are all the same, we are all equal' (Østergaard 2006). Moreover, this internal egalitarianism, reinforced in both official and popular nationalism, is often combined with a sense of superiority to the rest of the world. In his numerous interviews in the small Danish town of Skive, Jenkins (2010: 169, 265) captures these sentiments well: 'People have always thought that in Denmark they lived in the most free and best country in the world'; 'There is a way of thinking, I was brought up in it, that we are special, that this is a special country, compared to other places.' Hence the combination of strong state and strong civil society helps to normalize and naturalize nation-ness as a habitual daily practice.

However, for nationalism to become an integral, unquestioned, taken-for-granted set of values and practices it also has to penetrate the micro-world of family, friendships, neighbourhoods, local communes, church parishes and kinship networks. In the Danish context the state, civil society and the universe of micro-solidarities are all tightly bound together, helping to reinforce the popularly shared view that all Danes are similar, are equal and belong together. These sentiments stem from several ideological and organizational sources. The ideology of *dannelse*, with its focus on the cultivation of children's characters and an emphasis on proper behaviour, self-discipline and fitting in with others, stimulates a shared belief that modesty, equality and cultural similarity are prime virtues. This is clearly acknowledged by state officials. As the municipal director of education in Skive states: 'In Denmark we don't like sub-cultures. We like to be united . . . We have something called Jante Law . . . Nobody must be different. And this can be a bad thing. But it is also a positive thing. We are watching you. We are looking after you. We will not leave you alone' (Jenkins 2010: 189). The principles of *dannelse* are organizationally grounded in micro-groups, as children stay together in small cohorts throughout their primary and secondary education, thus developing deep and long-lasting friendships. Such friendships and close relationships are later often reinforced in shared neighbourhoods, places of work, church parishes and local communes. Together with the family networks they are the primary source of *hygge*: a time spent together in intimate, close groups where one experiences warmth, security and inclusion. As Hansen (1980: 59) defines it, *hygge* is 'a state one achieves most often with close members of one's family, extended family and friends. Although it is by no means tied to a specific setting, it is strongly associated with one: home. . . . It is a many-layered concept with strong personal associations.' *Hygge* is perceived as a uniquely Danish experience not accessible to foreigners; a sense of deep micro-solidarity that is fully and unproblematically integrated into a broader nationalist narrative.[14]

Hence the Danish case demonstrates that nationalism thrives best when it is least hostile and visible. The combination of the infrastructurally strong state and vibrant civil society that are able to penetrate pockets of micro-solidarity successfully creates conditions for the development and expansion of well-entrenched, widespread, routine, habitual nationalism. And it is this everyday triviality that regularly trumps virulence. While on the surface North Korea might seem much more nationalist than Denmark, the opposite is the case. The hostility of North Korean nationalism is also a sign of its weakness. This is nationalism that is more grounded in the despotic than in infrastructural powers. In contrast, as Danish nationalism is fully integrated into the institutions of the state, civil society and the micro-world of family, locality and friendships, it does not require permanent mass mobilization. There is no need to shout against 'the American bastards' when you have warm and cosy *hyggelig* time with your close friends and family.

Conclusion

The study of everyday life has a long history in the social sciences. Bourdieu (1977), Lefebvre (1971) and others have made clear not only that human beings are creatures of habit but also that habitual dispositions and judgements are built into the practices and routines of everyday conduct. Once something becomes fully ingrained into the habitus, such dispositions and judgements become almost automatic, and human beings view their world through the prism of such habitual experience. Although Bourdieu, Lefebvre and other scholars have focused on class as the central category of analysis that captures habitual reproduction, it is really nationhood that has proved to be the most significant category of practice in the modern era. While class is a contested category, both within specific societies and in the global arena, nationhood is nearly universally understood to be an indispensable ingredient of social life. The view that every individual is a member of a particular nation is not only shared by most individuals on this planet but is also codified in the constitutions, laws and regulations of most states as well as the leading international organizations. Moreover, this ubiquity and normality of national designations is reinforced by a plethora of everyday triviality – from sporting competitions, international song contests, festivals, cuisine, children's toys and games to the mass consumption of national brands. Although all of these events and practices are generally perceived as either irrelevant, innocent or feeble, they are in fact highly significant ways through which nation-centric images are constantly reproduced and reinforced. Despite popular views that associate nationalism with aggressive emotional outbursts, it is the low-intensity institutional routine that keeps nationalist ideology alive and well. The strength of nationalism does not rest on the barrel of the gun or in permanent violent mobilization. Instead its omnipotence comes from organizational and ideologically articulated habit and triviality. In this sense, everyday nationalism is not a historical exception confined to post-World War II Western Europe, Australia or North America. This is not only a prerogative of what Billig (1995) terms 'the established states'. Triviality is and has always been the dominant form of nationalist experience. What has changed in late modernity is only that the long-term processes of cumulative bureaucratization of coercion and centrifugal ideologization have gradually fostered the emergence of a much larger nationalist audience. Whereas in the late eighteenth and nineteenth centuries only small groups of elites were responsive to the nationalist messages, by the end of the twentieth and the beginning of this century nationalist ideology had enveloped nearly all social strata throughout the globe. Whether we like it or not, in many important respects, we are all nationalists now.

6

Beyond National Identity

Introduction

There is little, if any, doubt that most contemporary individuals subscribe to the view that national identities are something factual, self-evident and pervasive.[1] Such images as a soldier dying to protect his homeland, children commemorating a national holiday, a poet composing and performing an elegy to celebrate a specific national tragedy, or a politician unveiling a new statue of national importance are often invoked as poignant expressions of shared national identity. Moreover, as numerous surveys indicate, at least eight out of ten Europeans see their national identities as important or very important (Medrano 2009; Antonsich 2009: 285–90; Fligstein 2008). However, the fact that something is widely believed and highly valued does not necessarily make it true. The claim of possessing a national identity is still only a claim, not proof of its existence. More importantly, taking such popular claims at face value and summoning 'national identity' as a conceptual or even explanatory device only obscures what really requires a proper sociological explanation: why and when such claims acquire strong popular resonance.

One of the central arguments of this chapter is that 'national identity' is a conceptual chimera not worthy of serious analytical pursuit. It is a concept that is theoretically vapid while also lacking clear empirical referents. Rather than acting as a useful analytical tool able to untangle different and often contradictory processes at work in the formation, maintenance and reproduction of nationhood and nation-states, the idiom of national identity often operates as a populist umbrella term that helps reproduce what Bourdieu (1990) calls doxic experience. In other words, 'national identity' is a residual concept often utilized by social actors to make objective material order consistent with their subjective experience of that order. In this way the existing categorizations of the social world tend to be taken for granted as obvious and natural. Simply put, appeals for the preservation, maintenance and strengthening of 'authentic national identities' are often nothing more than expressions of particular ideological discourses (Malešević 2006). Hence any attempt to explain social action effectively entails moving away from looking at what human beings allegedly are, towards how they act and who they think they are. That is, to understand the phenomena of nationhood and nation-states one needs to move away from the fashionable but largely metaphoric and hazy, and hence futile, concept of 'identity' towards the well-established but generally neglected processual idioms that are 'ideology', 'solidarity' and 'social organizations'.

The first part of this chapter critically engages with some representative theoretical and empirical attempts to study and gauge 'national identities', while the second part outlines an alternative interpretation that refocuses the study of nation-ness through the prism of the relationships between micro-solidarity and two long-term historical macro-processes; coercive bureaucratization and ideologization.

What is Wrong with 'National Identity'?

We live in a world where nationhood is taken for granted and where not having a formal and emotional attachment to a particular nation is generally perceived as unusual if not abnormal. When asked at any international meeting where you are from, the expectation is that you will name a recognizable, distinct geographic and political entity such as 'Russia', 'Pakistan', 'Ghana' or 'Paraguay'. If you were to say 'I have no nation' your answer would not be taken as a serious response. Instead you would be seen as either a joker, a naïve utopian or a nuisance. Alternatively you would be asked further questions to clarify your 'real' origin. As this planet is divided into more than 200 distinct politically defined entities,[2] it is practically impossible (with the partial exception of the polar caps and the non-territorial waters of the oceans) to be born outside the jurisdiction of a particular territorially defined political entity, most of which are referred to as nation-states. Hence by locating one's place of birth it is supposedly easy to determine one's 'national origin'. While there is no doubt that tracing the 'nationhood' of some individuals such as those born in Western Sahara, Ache, Puntland or South Ossetia might be more complicated and contested, for most this is allegedly a simple and straightforward procedure: you are born in France, you speak French, you possess a French passport, you attended French schools, you vote in French elections, therefore you are French. Even if you do not feel particularly attached to France or if you belong to a distinct minority you are still perceived as belonging to a clearly defined group (e.g. Corsicans, Bretons, Basques, Algerians, Berbers etc.). If you are not French you must be something else, but you cannot opt out of nationhood.

Hence the existence of nations as real, factual entities composed of numerous individuals is rarely questioned. What is questioned and seen as a relevant area of study is only the intensity of one's attachment to a respective nation, a phenomenon regularly referred to as 'national identity'. Thus most researchers have been preoccupied with the changing intensity of national identification. This usually has taken two forms: (1) macro-level-based research that focuses on the origins, development and strength of national identity through time; and (2) micro-level studies that aim to gauge the intensity of one's personal feeling of attachment to a particular nation in a specific place.

Among the macro-level analyses two approaches have dominated recent research: modernism and ethno-symbolism. Although, as discussed in chapter 4, these two leading perspectives disagree on many issues (e.g. the dating of the origins of nations, the importance of collective myths, the decisive role of politics, culture or economics in the development and spread of nations etc.), they both see national identity as a key epistemological and ontological category of modern life. For ethno-symbolists (Smith 2009; 1999; 1986; Hutchinson 2004; 1994) contemporary national identities are for the most part rooted in pre-modern ethnic and religious attachments, whereas for modernists (Breuilly 1993; Mann 1993; Gellner 1997) national identities are essentially a product of modernity. To corroborate their claims both schools of thought rely on historiographic methods, case studies and secondary research. While the ethno-symbolists focus on tracing cultural continuity between traditional and modern forms of identification, modernists aim to emphasize the structural discontinuity between the two, insisting that there was little if any national identity before the modern era.

The micro-level analyses consist of empiricist and interpretative models that aim to capture snapshots of 'national identity' in specific spatial contexts. While the empiricists (Moreno 1988; McCrone et al. 1998; Smith and Kim 2006; Coakley 2007) regularly rely on large-scale surveys with a view to assessing the attitudes of various populations, the interpretativists use participant observation, ethnographic and other qualitative research techniques to grasp the workings of 'national identity' in everyday life (Fox and Miller-Idriss 2008; Edensor 2002; Reicher and Hopkins 2001; Mackey 1999).

Despite immense differences between these two traditions of research (including all four approaches), they all start from the same assumption that human beings possess national identities. In contrast to these views I argue that there is little empirical evidence to attest the existence of national identity either before or after modernity. While there is no doubt that many individuals show great affinity for abstract political entities such as nations, states and ethnicities, and on special occasions express sincere devotion to a 'national cause', none of these is a reliable proof for the existence of a durable, stable and monolithic entity called 'national identity'.

To make this point clearer, let us take a close look at the way the concept of 'national identity' is utilized in both of these traditions. In many of the macro-level analyses there is a linguistic confusion whereby idioms such as 'nation', 'nationality', 'nationhood', 'nationalism', 'national character', 'national consciousness', 'national psyche' or 'state' are often used as synonyms for 'national identity'. For example, Kumar (2003: 34) writes that 'one kind of national identity is the imperial type I called imperial nationalism', while for both Miller (1995) and Williams (1999) nationality is a synonym for national identity: Williams (1999: 7) writes about 'nationality or national identity' whereas for Miller 'nationality is an identity that embodies historical continuity' (Miller 1995: 23). However, this is highly problematic, as using the concept of national identity as a semantic substitute for 'nation', 'nation-state', 'nationalism', 'nationality' or 'national character' wrongly implies that sharing a same collective name (e.g. German, Bulgarian) or inhabiting the same 'national space' automatically means a shared sense of belonging and an almost innate proclivity for joint social action. However, simple group designation is not national identity. The mere fact of birth in a particular place is never a reliable indicator of one's inner feelings, values or interests. Although most human beings find security, comfort and warmth in their immediate family and kinship relations, and develop and often maintain a sense of attachment to the place of their birth and upbringing, this in itself cannot tell us much or anything about their attitudes towards more abstract entities that envelop these micro-places. In other words, the fact that we live in a nation-centric time and space colours our understanding and categorization of individuals in such a way that highly complex and contradictory processes, such as belonging to a particular abstract entity that is a nation-state, are often simply deduced from one's place of birth. More importantly, this nonchalant usage does not distinguish between formal membership in a particular political or cultural entity (nationality, nation-state), a personal sense of belonging (self-identity, consciousness and psyche) and ideological processes at work (violent and trivial or ethnic and civic articulations of nationalism).

Furthermore, this approach is often prone to reifying groups, essentializing collective relations and anthropomorphizing political institutions and social organizations. For example, David Miller

(1995: 20) distinguishes between a nation and an ethnic group on the basis of an anthropomorphized identity claim and argues that: 'where an ethnic group finds its identity being threatened . . . [it] begin[s] to think of itself as a nation', or 'a nation emerges from an ethnic community that furnishes it its distinct identity', as if collective entities of this size can acquire the attributes of individual human beings. Rather than treating millions of people as a single undifferentiated agent, it is vital to distinguish the concrete individual and social actors organized in social movements, political parties, armed forces, civil society groupings etc. who are able to pursue a particular course of action and who make specific identity claims. Furthermore, rather than tautologically arguing, as Miller does, that 'national identity requires that the people who share it should have something in common' and that 'national identity connects a group of people to a particular geographic place' (Miller 1995: 24), one needs to explore how such claims are made and when and why they publicly resonate. 'National identities' are neither things nor living beings that can impose requirements, make connections or feel threatened. In a similar vein other scholars write about how 'national identity makes one group believe its members share common features' (Fawn 2003: 13); how 'national identities shape national languages' (Joseph 2004: 13), how 'Turkish national identity which had been held back by the persistence of the Ottoman regime began to assert itself with a vengeance' (Glenny 2000: 328), how Spain 'has dramatically transformed its identity' and how Canada is able 'to reinforce its national identity' (Guibernau 2007: 1, 4), or how 'once [national identities] were formed and had an opportunity to consolidate themselves, their chances of survival were good even if they lost their political autonomy' (Llobera 1994: 5). Nevertheless, it is not Canada, Spain, Turkey or national identities that shape, transform, consolidate, reinforce or make individuals do things; it is only specific individuals and organized collectivities that are capable of social action.

However, even when one encounters clearly articulated concepts of national identity, as in Smith (2009; 2001; 1991) or Guibernau (2007), such definitions remain too vague, static or tautological to be of much empirical use. For example, Smith (2001: 30) defines national identity 'as maintenance and continuous reproduction of the patterns of values, symbols, memories, myths and traditions that compose the distinctive heritage of nations, and the identifications of individuals with that particular heritage and those values, symbols, memories, myths and traditions'. This is for the most part a tautological definition that, apart from stressing the importance of the reproduction of cultural heritage, defines identity circularly as a process of self-identification with that cultural heritage. For example, if one were to attempt to operationalize this definition to find out what constitutes 'French national identity' one would not go very far. Not only are there no universally accepted parameters on what constitutes 'patterns of values, symbols, myths and traditions' that compose 'French heritage', but even if one knew with absolute certainty what that heritage is, this definition gives no clue to how one is to assess an individual's sense of attachment to that heritage. For example, the idea of *laïcité* (the strict separation between the church and state) might be pinpointed as one of the key components of the national heritage inspired by the philosophy of the Enlightenment and the ideals of the 1789 Revolution. However, for many individuals and groups who have lived in France and have seen themselves as French, from religious conservatives and monarchists to representatives of minority religious associations, this idea is deeply contested and seen as something that is not integral to being French (Joppke 2009; Brubaker 1992). Nevertheless, even if there were near-absolute unanimity on *laïcité* as an 'essential' component of Frenchness, it is not clear how one can distinguish between French and other 'national identities' using Smith's definition. While I, as a person who has no connection to France, might share this ideal and might work on continuous reproduction of this heritage outside of France (e.g. advocating separation of church and state in Ireland), that would not make me French. In other words I, and many other non-residents of France, might know about and identify strongly with the cultural heritage of France (the Enlightenment, the arts, philosophy, history etc.) but that in itself would not indicate that I have 'French national identity'.

Guibernau's (2007: 11) definition of national identity as 'a collective sentiment based upon the belief of belonging to the same nation and of sharing most attributes that make it distinct from other nations' is just as problematic. This overly psychologistic understanding reduces the complex processes at work in making individuals and groups express attachment to distinctly abstract entities, such as nation, to a mere feeling. However, since emotions are changeable and many of them are of a highly temporary nature it is very difficult, if not impossible, to maintain a durable and stable 'national identity' over several centuries based on a simple feeling of belonging together (i.e. 'collective sentiment'). How is this 'collective sentiment' any different from that expressed by committed Liverpool football fans? They share a very strong emotion based on the belief of belonging to the same collectivity and they also share 'most attributes that make' them distinct from the supporters of other football clubs (i.e. different jersey colours, different chants, club anthems, different symbols, etc.). Furthermore, the Liverpool supporters also share collective myths and memories built around tragic and glorious events. These include the Haysel Stadium (1985) and Hillsborough disasters (1989) as well as the dramatic victories in European competitions. Does all of this mean that once a simple majority stops expressing such an emotion the 'national identity' automatically ceases to exist? In addition, the phrase 'sharing most attributes that make it distinct from other nations' is empirically futile, as it is far from clear which are the attributes that need to be shared, who decides what these attributes are and how many of them have to be shared. For example, if an Austrian living in Upper Austria, who shares many customs and practices with a fellow Bavarian across the border and speaks similar German in a similar dialect, feels during a football match between Germany and Italy a strong 'collective sentiment of belonging' does that qualify him as having a 'German national identity'? Probably not.

The micro-level analyses are no better. In fact, as they usually lack the robust theoretical frameworks that characterize many macro-level approaches, they either tend to assume unproblematically the existence of multiple identities (interpretativists) or operate with a highly simplified, colloquial understanding of 'national identity' (empiricists). Despite the fact that many researchers who utilize interpretativist approaches, such as Edensor (2002) or Reicher and Hopkins (2001), insist on the dynamic and reflexive quality of national identities per se, they are far from being immune to objectifying and anthropomorphizing identity claims. While for Reicher and Hopkins (2001: 3) one of the key research questions is 'how people come to assume and inhabit . . . identities, and how the identity then shapes what they do', for Edensor (2002: 34, 169) national identities are able to 'territorialize and assume recognizable characteristics' and 'merge, squabble and ignore each other'. Such stark attribution of human characteristics to abstract entities is in part grounded in an epistemology that posits identity as a central concept of social analysis, and in part stems from a casual methodology that relies heavily on literary and metaphoric language to make substantive analytical claims (Malešević 2006: 50–6). It is not enough to deconstruct essentialism and show the highly arbitrary character of claims to singular, primordial national identities. The more comprehensive understanding of nation-ness demands going beyond the indolent mantra of 'multiple identities' in the direction of contextualizing and deconstructing the very concept of identity (Brubaker and Cooper 2000; Brubaker 2004; Malešević 2006).[3]

Nevertheless, interpretativism is by and large a new, developing model of empirical analysis in the study of nationhood and nation-states. A much more prominent, and publicly recognizable, tradition of social research has been empiricism. Relying on large-scale data sets such as the European Values Study (EVS), World Values Survey (WVS), International Social Survey Programme (ISSP) and Eurobarometer, empiricists attempt to measure the intensity of 'national identity' for specific countries. According to Sinnott (2005), who has evaluated the character of these surveys, most of them gauge the intensity of one's 'national identity' by focusing either on the relationship of proximity (with questions about one's feeling of closeness to the respective group) or on the relationship of identification (with questions that centre on one's sense of attachment to, belonging to or identifying with a particular collective). That is, most such surveys provide rankings or ratings for one's individual sense of belonging that range from the local and regional through the national to the global entities. Hence the respondents are usually asked questions about their primary group attachment or sense of pride in belonging to the various groups. The surveys focus on the measurement of 'national pride' and see this measure as a reliable indicator of the strength or weaknesses of one's national identity. In the (tautological) words of authors working in this tradition of research: 'National pride is the positive affect that the public feels towards their country as a result of their national identity' (Smith and Kim 2006: 127). Hence most studies compile comparative scales that rank national populations in terms of the intensity of 'national pride'. For example, according to ISSP's surveys conducted on twenty-four countries in 1995/6, Austria and the USA topped the rankings, with Germany and Slovakia the bottom two. In the surveys conducted in 2003/4, the USA and Australia were on top and Sweden and Latvia were at the bottom on general 'national pride' (Smith and Kim 2006; see also Theiss-Morse 2009; Tyler and Blader 2000).

Nevertheless, despite the statistical sophistication utilized in sampling procedures and data analysis, most of these large-scale surveys operate with conceptually and theoretically deficient models which provide very crude measures of something that is a highly complex and multifaceted phenomenon.[4] Not only do many surveys conflate concepts as different as nationality, nationalism, national attachment and national pride (Smith and Kim 2006: 127; Sinnott 2005: 219; Antonsich 2009) but they also tend to reduce complex processes of self-identification to a single emotion of pride or shame. However, using 'pride' as a proxy for 'identity' is flawed on at least two methodological accounts. As Sinnott (2005: 214) shows in the analysis of EVS and WVS data sets, the correlations between two questions that attempt to measure 'national pride' and one's feeling of belonging to a specific nation, referred to as 'national identity', are very low. Being proud of one's nation-state is not necessarily linked with one's feeling of attachment to that nation-state. In various EVS, WVS and Eurobarometer surveys one encounters a discrepancy between 'national attachment' and 'national pride'. For example, the survey results for Denmark show that the 'high degree of national attachment does not find an equivalent in terms of national pride', whereas in the case of Spain the 'high degree of national pride does not find an equivalent in terms of national attachment' (Antonsich 2009: 288). Hence it is clear that 'national pride' and 'national attachment' are perceived differently and these attitude scales obviously measure two different phenomena. Sinnott (2005: 214) concludes that such a weak correlation is the result of 'measurement error involved in the attempt to capture feelings of national identity by means of a truncated ranking question. The findings suggest that identity is not well captured by the WVS/EVS measure.' More importantly, since pride and shame are variable, changeable and contextual emotions that convey temporary expressions of feelings, they are not reliable indicators of the long-term processes that involve the construction and reproduction of nation-ness.

The survey results also demonstrate that there are immense oscillations in scores for national pride over the years for some countries. For example, while 56 per cent of German respondents in 1994 felt very or quite proud to be German, in 2002 this figure rose to 76 per cent. Similarly, whereas in 1997 only 46 per cent of Belgian respondents felt proud of being Belgian, in 2003 this figure jumped to a staggering 86 per cent (Antonsich 2009: 286). In the case of Scotland this is even more pronounced as, according to two surveys conducted on 'national identity' in 1991 and 1992, the category 'being Scottish not British' suddenly deflated from 40 per cent of respondents in September 1991 to 19 per cent in 1992 (McCrone et al. 1998: 631). Such dramatic fluctuations suggest either that there is no durable, stable and monolithic national identity, as popular attitudes simply follow the situational context and so change quickly and spectacularly, or that empiricism cannot capture this phenomenon through the attitude scales. Reducing 'national identity' to simple dichotomous variables such as 'Are you Scottish or British? More Scottish than British? Equally Scottish and British?' and so on (Moreno 1988; McCrone 1997) just reinforces the stereotypical, simplified and essentialist categories created and maintained in the everyday discourse of social organizations and public institutions. Rather than revealing the social reality, this approach creates and props up this reality. As surveys are being conducted in a historically specific time and place, their results cannot be simply taken as given, as a matter of individual choice. Instead they are also a reflection of the dominant normative and operative ideologies of their time and place (Malešević 2006; 2002). In other words, just as in Heisenberg's uncertainty principle, by asking questions in a particular way the empiricists create 'national identities' where they do not necessarily exist. If there is a thing called 'national identity' its complexity cannot be captured through a single question; the researcher has to look at the cognitive, emotional, motivational and other psychological dimensions as well as economic, cultural, political, coercive, ideological and other sociological aspects through which this process is developed and articulated.

The key problem with the attitude measurements is that they infer the existence of national identity on the basis of a narrow, decontextualized snapshot of popular views captured in a specific moment in time and at a specific place. Nevertheless, such an approach is unable to differentiate between the dominant popular beliefs and the sociological reality: the fact that an overwhelming majority of our respondents believe that every individual holds an ingrained and indisputable 'national identity' does not mean that the researcher should take this belief at face value. As Collins (2004: 96) rightly points out: 'It is a fallacy to take symbols at face value, as if we can read their meanings from what participants say they mean. It is as naïve as a child who thinks that "How are you?" means a request for information about their health . . . We are in much the same position if we treat religious [and national] symbols as if they were a self-sufficient explanation of what people who invoke them do.' In this sense and from the researcher's point of view there is not much difference between the popularly widespread beliefs in the magical power of witchcraft, in dances that bring rain, in faith healers and in the existence of monolithic national identities. Rather than taking such claims as given, our job as researchers is to probe, contextualize, deconstruct and generally problematize them. Why in 2005 did more than 95 per cent of people in Finland and Greece say that they felt very or fairly attached to their nation (Antonsich 2009: 289), whereas in the late eighteenth and early nineteenth centuries (for which unfortunately we have no surveys) such affection for the nation probably would not have spread beyond the narrow circles of cultural enthusiasts, political elites and a few merchants? The point is that the fact that more individuals believe in the existence of something does not make it any more real than when this belief was shared by a very small minority.

Moreover, the very fact that in most of these surveys on national pride, national attachment and national identity respondents agree with the statements to an unprecedentedly high degree is in itself a symptom of the methodological weakness. For example, when 99 per cent of respondents say that they are very or fairly proud to be Irish or Greek or that they are strongly attached to their countries, and the scores for the other European populations range between the high 80s and 90 per cent (Antonsich 2009: 286), then this is a sign of simplified and poor measurement unable to differentiate between several processes involved. No attitude measurement which generates such a high degree of acceptance is particularly useful for sociological or even statistical analyses.

What one really needs to address is when, why and how such beliefs spread and start to dominate. In other words, all claims of national identity reflect the historical, political and social context in which they are made. Since human beings are ideological creatures, no identity claim is free of ideology. Popular attitudes, just like the attitudes and research designs of empiricists, are heavily coloured by the taken-for-granted, normalized and naturalized idioms of everyday life and, as argued in chapter 5, ideologies work best when tacit and invisible. The very fact that few if any individuals question the existence of national identity is a potent indicator of how naturalized and normalized such beliefs have become.

From Social Organizations and Ideology to Solidarity

The concept of 'national identity' is a sweeping conceptual chimera that is often simply used as a description of assumed social reality or invoked as a short-cut explanation for particular forms of collective behaviour. For example, one regularly encounters statements such as '[it is] this sense of national identity under threat that gives rise to the demand for devolution' (Bogdanor 1996: 197) or 'national identity gives us a much more ambitious account of our place in the world. It assigns us to a large collective unit, and tells us a great deal about the historic achievements and failures of that unit' (Miller 1995: 164). Nevertheless, it is not only that, as some researchers start now to realize, 'national identities have no obvious empirical referents' (Laitin 2007: 31) and 'there simply is no way of showing incontrovertibly that such a thing exists' (Kumar 2003: 53) but, more importantly, by deploying uncritically and unproblematically the notion of 'national identity' the researchers themselves contribute to the perpetuation of this conceptual monstrosity. Rather than simply assuming the existence of national identities or using this concept as an explanation of social behaviour, it is crucial to unpack carefully the different and often contradictory processes hidden beneath this giant, loose umbrella term (Malešević 2006: 13–57). Instead of presuming that 'national identities' are able to do things, there is a need to analyse, dissect and explain what such blunt statements conceal and to investigate and capture the variety of individual and collective motives, thoughts, emotions and actions that the sweeping concept of 'national identity' obscures.

I will focus here only on two such processes: the relationships between micro-level solidarity and more macro-based processes of bureaucratization and ideologization. In his more recent work, Smith (2009: 123) argues that '"identity" as distinctive "essence" and difference is something that many people have felt they need to find and have sought to create and pursue, and even die for'. While there is no doubt that many individuals throughout modern history have made (and still do make) grand pronouncements about the importance of finding, creating and pursuing 'lost identities', and some have also expressed their willingness to die for such abstract entities, it is important to probe, contextualize and analyse all such claims before making a hasty judgement about their self-explanatory force. There is no denying the fact that human beings need other human beings to feel safe, comfortable, loved, honoured, recognized, fulfilled and for so many other reasons, but it is not so self-evident that we need nationhood or nation-states for that at all. Whereas feeling emotionally close to one's family and finding comfort in the intimate surroundings of people one grew up with seem a spontaneous and expected form of social solidarity, there is nothing obvious in one's attachment to millions of people that one will never meet and get to know in person. Bearing in mind that for 99 per cent of its existence *Homo sapiens* lived in small, egalitarian, nomadic, kinship-based hunting and gathering bands that rarely exceeded 50 people (Fry 2007; Service 1978), there is no simple rationale for maintaining a strong and continuous sense of attachment to such large and anonymous entities as a nation-state and nationhood (see chapter 2).

To get to grips with the phenomenon whereby many modern-day human beings express intense affinity for such an abstract entity as a nation, it is necessary to explore the processes through which group attachments become politicized and popularly mobilized. As elaborated in chapter 4, the seminal theorists of nations and nationalism (such as Gellner 1983; Smith 1986; Mann 1993; Anderson 1983; Hobsbawm 1990; Breuilly 1993) have successfully explained the historical origins of this phenomenon, which owes a great deal to state centralization, protracted warfare, the introduction of universal conscription, standardization of vernacular languages, the proliferation of mass literacy, the establishment of state-sponsored education systems, print capitalism, intensified division of labour, and the emergence of institutions of 'high culture', all of which have contributed to transforming peasants into loyal and often enthusiastic members of their nation-states. It was these gigantic structural alterations that created the modern universe, a universe susceptible to and dependent on nation-centric understandings of social reality. Nevertheless, while we now know a great deal about these structural forces that gave birth to the age of nation-states and nationalisms, we still do not know much about the changing character of group solidarity. In other words, it is far from being self-evident how and why human beings are able to shift their loyalties from small, local, family- and kinship-based groupings to the large-scale abstract entities that are nation-states. To put it simply, how is it possible to make a person feel so attached to an abstract entity that he or she allegedly expresses willingness to treat and cherish this entity in the same way one cherishes his or her close family or friends?

I argue that to understand this phenomenon fully we need to refocus our attention from vague, fuzzy, metaphoric, often static and inward-looking concepts such as 'identity', 'consciousness' or 'psyche' towards the multilayered processes that are social organization, ideology and solidarity. As I have argued elsewhere (Malešević 2011b; 2010; 2006; 2002), by 'ideology' I do not mean the closed, dogmatic and inflexible political or sanctimonious doctrines or the Marxist-inspired notions of 'false consciousness' and 'hegemonic manipulation'. Instead I understand ideology as a relatively universal and complex social process through which human actors articulate their actions and beliefs. Since social and political events and social facts are unable to speak for themselves, there is a need to decode, understand and contextualize them. Hence human beings rely on existing ideological maps and concepts to decipher meaningful interpretations of these events and facts. In this way ideological narratives impose structure and provide coherence to what otherwise would be incoherent and utterly contingent images, events and acts. So ideology is a process that incorporates thinking and action, whereby our behaviour is dependent on (but not determined by) ideologically articulated cognitive maps. As the contents of ideological discourses are infused with the transcendent grand vistas of a specific imagined social order that invokes advanced ethical claims, collective interests and emotions or calls upon the possession of superior knowledge, most ideologies surpass everyday experience and evade testability. As such, ideological discourses are very efficient in justifying a particular course of social action and in legitimizing or contesting existing power relations (Malešević 2010: 8–12; 2006: 69–79).

More specifically, when dealing with nation-states attention should focus on the ideological processes through which nation-ness becomes our second nature, through which human beings naturalize and normalize nationhood as the self-evident and only legitimate way of comprehending the world we live in. Hence, rather than taking the existence of 'national identity' as given and unproblematic, the idea is to explore how this ideological process of making nation-states emotionally equivalent to families operates. If one starts from the classical sociological research on social ties (Simmel 1950 [1908]; Tönnies 1955 [1887]), it becomes apparent that group solidarity is a precious commodity difficult to sustain over long periods of time. Even more importantly, genuine solidarity entails regular face-to-face interaction. It is a fragile social relation that requires constant work in a similar way to love. Just as two people in love need constant reaffirmation of their mutual and deep affection for each other, so do individuals caught in the bond of solidarity. Those held by solidarity ties are similar to lovers who, despite saying 'I love you' a thousand times, find themselves in situations where if one lover is hesitant to utter this statement for a thousand and first time, this itself might be a sign that the strong emotional bond is starting to break.

To account for this inherent fragility of solidarity, it is neces-sary to distinguish clearly between the micro-interactional social mechanisms at work in small, mostly kinship- and locality-based groups and the macro-, organizationally produced social cohe-sion that characterizes large-scale entities such as nation-states, political parties, social movements and business corporations (Malešević 2010: 191–201, 219–32). In other words, rather than treating group bonds at the micro- and macro-level as being the same phenomenon originating in the same psychological, his-torical, political or cultural processes, it is epistemologically more beneficial to decouple the two and analyse them separately as two different phenomena. While it seems that Durkheim (1997 [1893]) does this too by distinguishing between mechanical and organic solidarity, I would argue that since his developmentalist and functionalist model is too focused on the time dimension, it does not capture well the range and the spatial aspect of social cohesion. For Durkheim, mechanical solidarity stands for the traditional, segmental types of primitive social orders characterized by mere group resemblance, and organic solidarity is seen as a feature of the advanced division of labour and functional interdependence of modern societies. However, what is really distinctive about solidarity is the scope and size of groups involved. Rather than just distinguishing between traditional and modern, it is of paramount importance to explore the character and processes of social bonding in small-scale collectivities such as families, peer groups, neighbourhoods and kinship-based networks and those created in vast social organizations such as nation-states, empires, large corporations or social movements. Contra Durkheim I would argue that genuine, deeply felt emotional solidarity is only possible on the micro-, face-to-face level where individuals are familiar and physically interact with other individuals. Since Simmel's early works (1955 [1917]; 1950 [1908]) it has become apparent that, as he puts it, 'solidarity decreases in the measure in which numerical increase involves the admission of heterogeneous individual elements' (Simmel 1950: 95). As recent sociological studies indicate (Wohlstein and McPhail 1979; McClelland 1985; Collins 2008; 2004), long-term intensive solidarity entails physical contact. Sometimes this involves high-intensity interaction rituals where one achieves pleasure 'from being fully and bodily absorbed in deeply synchronised social interaction' (Collins 2004: 66), while on other occasions this entails a sense of trust, security and the serenity of familiar, family surroundings.[5]

The ethno-symbolists, such as Smith (2009; 2004; 1991), argue that the strength of national identities is well evidenced in the widespread popular mobilization that periodically occurs in times of crisis and in particular in warlike situations. Thus ethno-symbolists share the assumption that national identities operate as a single, all-embracing and for the most part synchronized collective feeling present throughout the entire society. Smith has argued on numerous occasions that an individual's willingness to die for her or his nation is a reliable indicator of the intensity of national solidarity and the vigour of national identities. Nevertheless, studies on individual behaviour in wars and particularly on the performance of soldiers in combat have shown that, for the majority of those who have taken part in actual battles, the primary motive was not the preservation or protection of national identity but solidarity with their regimental or platoon comrades (Marshall 1947; Holmes 1985; Gabriel 1987; Bourke 1999). As Neitzel and Welzer (2012) and Shils and Janowitz (1948) have demonstrated, the stubborn resistance of Wermacht soldiers at the end of World War II was not simple, blind loyalty to Nazi Germany but a direct product of small-group cohesion, where individual squads operated as kinship-like groups. Similarly, for many Japanese kamikaze pilots the loyalty expressed in the idea of *Gi* (righteousness, duty) was a sense of devotion not so much to the emperor and Japan as to the pilot's comrades and family (Hill 2006: 24). It is in these small-scale, face-to-face groups that individuals build a sense of collective attachment, a dependency on others and a strong sense of responsibility to their fellow members. In the words of an American soldier who in World War II left his hospital bed to rejoin his platoon on the battlefield: 'Those men on the line were my family, my home. They were closer to me than I can say, closer than any friends had been or ever would be. They never let me down, and I couldn't do it to them . . . Any man in combat who lacks comrades who will die for him, or for whom he is willing to die, is not a man at all' (Holmes 1985: 300).[6]

The willingness to die for others increases with, and in most respects is dependent on, the intensity of group integration. Since very large groups of individuals, popularly conceptualized as ethnic collectivities or nations, usually consist of millions of people, it is very unlikely that such entities would ever be able to attain and maintain group integration of such a level and intensity as to motivate mass-scale self-sacrifice. Despite official proclamations to the contrary, this genuine feeling of solidarity requires a small group exposed to prolonged and life-threatening situations. Even among the military units on the front line this solidarity remains fragile, an almost sacred object that invites the envy of other units. The regular squads and platoons would usually look up to the special, commando units whose attachment to their micro-group was even stronger. In the words of one American Vietnam War veteran:

> When [this] . . . unit came in the bar, everybody else in the joint would shift out of the way. . . . They were all crazy, but I respected them. They were [human] ear collectors. They lay their ears on the bar. The guy who had the most ears that didn't match up in pairs, had to buy rounds for all the rest the whole night. . . . I was fascinated with this group of men. They were all on their second or third tour of Nam. . . . Their kinship was even stronger than ours . . . They didn't even think of anyone else around. (Baker 1982: 121)

There is a clear emphasis here on the kinship-like quality of the small group bond; a micro-unit of merciless individuals who have crossed the boundary of universal morality and who show little hesitation to kill or die for their micro-group. Being exposed to violence and the possibility of instant death on an everyday basis, their reliance on small-group solidarity becomes an essential precondition of their existence. Hence it is such small, selected groups, not large-scale entities such as nation-states, that truly operate as a 'chosen people'.

While large-scale organizations such as nation-states, social movements or political parties rely on similar rhetoric to invoke feelings of solidarity, there is a very different process at work here. Following the research and arguments of leading national-ism studies scholars, it becomes apparent that in the modern era the nation-state acquires a central ontological role in the lives of most people. However, this rampant pervasiveness of nationhood in everyday life does not automatically signal the existence of uniform and durable national identities. Instead it is a symptom of the prevalence of a particular meta-ideology that is nationalism. It is the dominant (operative) ideology of national-ism that colours and infuses the thoughts, beliefs and actions of modern human beings (Malešević 2006; 2002). Not only do we live in a world of nation-states but many of our cognitive, emo-tional, conative, cultural, political and economic categories are heavily saturated with nation-centric discourses (Brubaker 1996;

Billig 1995). In other words, what really is worth exploring is not 'national identity' but the ideology of nationalism, and unlike 'national identities' nationalism has clear empirical referents. It is an ideological doctrine and practice whose presence, intensity and prevalence can be empirically corroborated. Kedourie (1993 [1960]: 1), Smith (1998: 187) and Breuilly (1993: 2) among others have identified the core, relatively universal, principles of nationalist ideology. According to Smith (1998: 187) these are:

1. The world is naturally divided into nations, each of which has its peculiar character and destiny; 2. The nation is the source of all political power, and loyalty to it overrides all other loyalties; 3. If they wish to be free, and to realize themselves, men must identify with and belong to a nation; 4. Global freedom and peace are functions of the liberation and security of all nations; 5. Nations can only be liberated and fulfilled in their own sovereign states.

In contrast to 'national identity', these statements do not have a chimerical quality but allow for transparent operationalization and steadfast empirical validation. Rather than assuming the existence of 'national identity', one can empirically assess the presence, intensity and transformation of nationalist discourses. In other words, unlike 'identity', concepts such as 'ideology', 'social organization' and 'solidarity' are analytically sound, operationally effective and empirically potent while also maintaining a dynamic, processual and non-essentialist quality (Malešević 2010; 2006). Instead of treating 'national identity' as an analytical or, even worse, explanatory category, the focus on ideology, social organization and solidarity helps us historically unpack its origin and present-day nearly hegemonic potential. Hence rather than understanding national identities as given, normal and unproblematic, and nationalism as some sort of ideological perversion or pathology, the focus would shift towards the social organizations and ideological discourses that transform micro-solidarities into 'virtuous' national identities. To historicize this development briefly, it is enough to look at the late nineteenth century, when most respectable individuals were firmly convinced that the development of civilization is premised on continuous race wars (Banton 1997). In this context the technological successes, imperial conquests and scientific advancements of the 'white race' were interpreted as a reliable sign of its natural dominance. The then-dominant view that the 'white race' was unique, authentic and superior to other 'races' was at that time understood to be a self-evident reality. However, with the hindsight of a century or more it is commonplace to describe such views not as natural reflections of 'racial identity' but simply as 'racism'. It is very clear to us that such beliefs were not spontaneous expressions of one's identity, but were in fact a direct product of a specific ideology – racism. Nevertheless, there is a reluctance to use similar tools of historic analysis to decontextualize the concept of national identity. Instead of looking at nationhood and nation-states as a direct by-product of nationalism, there is a tendency to assume that national identities are objective, durable and sincere expressions of one's identity.

Nevertheless, regardless of the images projected by nationalists themselves, nationalism is not a synonym for group solidarity. Rather than originating and functioning as an all-embracing (Durkheimian) *conscience collective* able to galvanize automatic popular support, nationalist ideology is heavily dependent on the work of concrete social organizations: the states, social movements, educational systems, military, mass media, local authorities etc. As most theorists of nationalism recognize, it is these social organizations that have contributed to making nationalism a dominant (operative) ideology of modernity. However, despite the official pronouncements about the 'formation of stable and established national identities', this process is never complete. Instead the pervasiveness of nationalist ideology is rooted in the continuous production and maintenance of imagery, practices, discourses and institutions that sustain this ideology. This is a process that works in both directions: on the one hand, the existence of large nationalist meta-narratives is often utilized by local actors and various small-scale groups that map their own individual or collective grievances and discords by articulating them in staunchly nationalist terms. For example, in his comparative studies on civil wars Kalyvas (2006) demonstrates convincingly how ideological labels such as 'communist', 'monarchist', 'democrat' and most of all 'nationalist' are regularly used by individual and social actors to cover up their own instrumental, personal, micro-political and other non-ideological motives. As he puts it: 'rather than reflecting the politicization of private life, civil war violence often privatizes politics' (Kalyvas 2006: 14). On the other hand, to mobilize popular support successfully, the social organizations adopt the guise and rhetoric of micro-solidarity. They speak in the language of close family and friendship ties: they describe the territory one inhabits as 'our motherland' or 'our fatherland', inhabited by close-knit friends and family; they depict mobilized soldiers as 'our brothers who are sacrificing their lives on the battlefields'; and they portray citizens who remain behind the front lines as 'our sisters, daughters and mothers who need to be saved and protected' from the opposing social organization, often referred to as 'the merciless enemy'. Even though social organizations embrace the discourse of kinship in an attempt to project solidarity beyond the micro-groups, this is not a straightforward process that guarantees success. Instead this ideologization of solidarity requires long-term work: it relies on the existing atoms of genuine micro-solidarity that is generated on the local level. When successful, ideologization operates as a giant fishing net that catches highly diverse and heterogeneous forms of micro-solidarity generated by a variety of small-scale social networks, and in the process articulates its catch as a singular, homogeneous 'national identity'. Ideologization appears as a structural replacement for genuine solidarity; it is a process through which social organizations attempt to forge something that resembles real kinship bonds.

Anderson (1983: 6) made clear that 'all communities larger than primordial villages of face-to-face contact ... are imagined', and the nation-state is no exception here. However, regardless of our appreciation of and nominal attachment to such 'imagined communities', the fact remains that what is imagined is not real. The 'image of their communion' (Anderson 1983: 6) is something quite different from actual face-to-face interaction. We all can and often do embrace the rhetoric of national(ist) identitarianism and might in extraordinary circumstances proclaim our willingness to die for our nation, but even when individuals make the ultimate sacrifice and shout 'Viva la patria!' their reasons for sacrifice often, if not always, remain personal. Rather than addressing the entire nation of millions of anonymous and unknown individuals, their act of sacrifice is addressed to those they know and whose approval they seek: their family, friends, lovers and peers, the micro-cosmos where they truly belong.

Conclusion

To argue that one can analytically gain much more by shifting the focus of research from 'identity' towards 'solidarity', 'ideology' and 'social organization' does not mean to deny the fact that human beings are profoundly social creatures who seek attachment and emotional support from group membership. On the contrary, precisely because we are social beings who thrive in the presence of others, we invoke national identity as an anchor that provides emotional stability, historical durability and a strong sense of ontological security. The point is not to deny the obvious truth that for an overwhelming majority of individuals the existence of national identities is beyond question – and in fact national identity is seen as one of the key pillars of selfhood – but to move our attention towards the socio-historical processes that generate and reproduce such beliefs and practices. In other words, by simply taking social actors at their word and assuming that social action is driven by strong national identities, we might lose sight of the wider sociological processes that are responsible for the organizational and ideological production of such claims and that also help maintain their popularity. It is only through tracing the social origins, probing, contextualizing and deconstructing all claims of national identity, that one will be in a position to explain why, when and how 'national identity' becomes so important to most individuals that it assumes an unproblematic, normal and habitual character. And as decades of sociological research show only too well, whenever a particular social practice and belief are deemed to be normal, natural and obvious, this in itself is an instant warning sign which signals the organizational pervasiveness of a particular ideology. Rather than being an autonomous and self-evident factual reality, 'national identity' is only a symptom of a more complex, multifaceted and highly variable sociological phenomenon that requires a careful diagnosis and explanation: nationalist ideology.

7

The Future of Nationalisms

Introduction

The view that the nation-state is the dominant form of power organization and that nationalism remains the principal source of political legitimacy in the contemporary world has been vigorously challenged by many scholars. Some argue that globalization has undermined the potency of the nation-state and that nationalism has been replaced by neo-liberal, consumerist, capitalist and other economic-centred ideological projects. In this view, as economic globalization advances, the economic sovereignty of nation-states diminishes, which has a profound impact on their autonomy in the domestic arena and in foreign policy. The contention is that new technologies lower transport and communication costs, open new markets and intensify the mobility of global capital, material goods, services and people, which all enhance the power transfer from the elected governments of nation-states to the CEOs of global corporations, banking moguls and omnipotent financial institutions such as the IMF or World Bank. Furthermore, these structural transformations are linked to changing belief systems and patterns of behaviour. The general argument is that globalization promotes ever-increasing individualism, cosmopolitanism and the tendency for most human beings to identify as individualized consumers rather than members of distinct nation-states (Harvey 2009; Bauman 2006; 2000; Beck 2007; 2006; 2002; Kaldor 2004; Castells 1998). It seems that in such a globalized and ever-changing world there is no place for nationalism. In Beck's (2007) view, the nation-state has become irrelevant as globalization and what he calls cosmopolitanization have eroded distinct state boundaries; in this way the unhampered flow of capital and information has led to internalized cosmopolitanism and an 'internal globalization' that 'alters the conditions for the construction of social identity' and ultimately abolishes the 'us vs. them' polarizations. Thus, any attempt to conceptualize the contemporary world through the prism of nation-states and nationalisms is outdated, wrong and counterproductive: 'Anyone who adheres to the old, national dogmatism (to the fetish of sovereignty, for instance, and to the unilateral policies derived from it) will be skipped over, rolled over, and won't even be in position to complain about it' (Beck 2007: 1). For Beck (2000: 85) we live in a world where 'the cosmopolitan project contradicts and replaces the nation-state project'. In a similar vein, Bauman (2002: 84) argues that 'nation-building coupled with patriotic mobilization has ceased to be the principal instrument of social integration and states' self-assertion'.

Other critics have identified a resurgence of religion, which is seen as having a greater world-wide popular appeal and capability for mass mobilization than its nationalist counterparts (Ram 2008; Reader 2000; Burleigh 2009). The focus here is on the global religious revival stretching from the rise of Evangelical Protestantism in North America and Africa, radical Hinduist teachings in South-East Asia and Orthodox Judaism in Israel to the reinvigoration of Islam in the Middle East, North Africa and Asia and among immigrant populations in Western Europe. Most of these studies have focused on Islam and have argued that throughout the Muslim world and further afield, religious identity regularly trumps national attachments: when people have to choose between national and religious loyalties, it is the *umma* or universal community of believers that has the upper hand. Moreover, some argue that since religious-inspired belief systems are often rooted in the uncompromising vistas of sacred and profane, good and evil, are bent on establishing a better and purer world and see other belief systems as sinful or evil, they are more likely to be dismissive of the essentially secular ideology that is nationalism. This is confirmed in the writings of Islamist and Salafist scholars and political figures who express a preference for the establishment of an Islamic caliphate over what they deem to be the Western-imposed institution of the nation-state. In addition, the radicalism of suicide bombers and other forms of terrorism is attributed to strong and uncompromising religious commitments which allegedly overpower national and other allegiances (Thomas 2005; Burleigh 2009; Reader 2000; Juergensmeyer 2003).

Leaving aside the question of how pervasive and novel the processes of globalization and religious resurgence are,[1] there is no reliable evidence that these two processes have undermined the strength of nation-states or nationalisms. On the contrary, it seems that globalization has in fact strengthened most nation-states, fostering the proliferation of nationalist ideology and the popularity of national self-identification (Mann 2013; Sutherland 2012; Breuilly 2011; Hearn 2011). Similarly the apparent religious revival did not arise at the expense of nationalism: instead, most religious rhetoric and practice tends to be highly syncretic not only in blending nationalist and religious discourses but also in articulating alternative visions of the desirable social and political orders (Brubaker 2012; Lapidus 2001). Let us briefly discuss both of these developments.

Globalization and the Nation-State

The view that globalization inevitably leads to a weakening of the state, individualism and the demise of nationalism is largely built on misperceptions of past eras. Such interpretations take the proclamations of politicians, administrators and nationalist historiography at face value and assume that in contrast to present-day polities, the nineteenth- and early twentieth-century nation-states were isolated, self-sufficient and self-reliant, centralized entities in full control of their territories and population. Nevertheless, as the historical record shows, most nineteenth- and early twentieth-century nation-states did not possess the fully developed organizational and ideological means to control their territory and population fully. While their organizational abilities were certainly much better than those of polities from previous periods, it was really in the second half of the twentieth century that nation-states and nationalisms managed to penetrate, organizationally and ideologically, all social strata and almost every nook and corner of the territory under their nominal control. The notion of full sovereignty and administrative control of the entire territory, including the ability to tax at source, police their borders comprehensively or collect information on their citizens (from official statistics, birth certificates, conscription lists etc.), substantially developed only in the twentieth century (Mann 2012; 1993; 1986; Calhoun 2007). In addition, over the last several decades nation-states have gained more not less control over their citizens, as their influence has substantially expanded in such areas as public education, health, environmental planning, immigration, mass media, sports, culture, employment and labour, fiscal policy and urban surveillance (Smith 2010: 134; Meyer et al. 1997). In this sense, when compared to their contemporary counterparts, the nineteenth- and early twentieth-century nation-states were puny, weak leviathans. For example, before World War I, passports and identity cards were rarely used, were completely unstandardized, and had no personalized photographs but only included a vague description of the holder. However, as the infrastructural powers of European states substantially increased during and after the war, the authorities were in a position to make the use of such documents, including passports with standardized photographs, compulsory (Torpey 2000; Marrus 1985).[2] In contrast to nineteenth- and early twentieth-century polities, most contemporary nation-states have at their disposal highly sophisticated surveillance technologies that allow them to police their borders and control their population with relative ease.

Furthermore, the globalization theorists insist that the weakness of the institution of the nation-state is particularly pronounced in foreign policy as, they allege, most polities have lost their sovereign powers. However, as Smith (2010: 133) rightly emphasizes, apart from the handful of Great Powers, most nation-states never had much autonomy in the conduct of their foreign policy: 'few national states in the last two centuries have exercised untrammelled sovereignty; states were bound by various treaties and understandings, and their capacities for effecting changes in general were limited by the relatively undeveloped technologies and communications at their disposal'. Hence globalization could not undermine something that was not there in the first place.

Secondly, the idea that the proliferation of economic liberalization and capitalism is bound to weaken the nation-state and nationalisms is also premised on an incorrect assumption. Since Weber's early studies (1968 [1921]), it has become clear that the birth of the nation-state owes a great deal to the emergence of autonomous trading towns in pre-modern Europe, and that this particular development was also linked to the formation and expansion of capitalism. Rather than denting the state's power, capitalism fostered instrumental rationality, efficiency, predictability, transparent hierarchies and formalized contractual arrangements, all of which are at the heart of nation-state building too. In other words, the spread of capitalism and economic liberalization regularly went hand in hand with the development of the bureaucratic and ideological apparatuses of nation-states. It is the combined forces of international trade and military competition that gave the impetus for the development of nation-states and nationalisms. The international networks of trade and financial exchange have generally fostered the expansion of state power, the rulers of nation-states utilized the changing geo-political conditions to establish greater fiscal control, and in the process they were often forced to grant greater citizenship rights to their populations (Conrad 2006; Tilly 1975; Downing 1992; Ertman 1997; Mann 1993; 1986). Nationalism did not emerge in opposition to capitalism; instead, the two phenomena were regularly interdependent.

Although the recent wave of globalization might have added another layer of complexity by fostering an environment where one encounters large financial and trading markets and much faster exchange of goods, services, transport and communication, such a change did not dampen the organizational and ideological powers of nation-states. Moreover, globalization is not necessarily an enemy of nationalism or a friend of world-wide cultural uni-formity. As Sutherland (2012: 167) puts it, 'Globalization does not necessarily encourage homogeneity . . . Quite the opposite: it literally brings diversity home, as nationalists and nation-states are faced with increasingly heterogeneous communities due to migration and diaspora.' More importantly, as Hall (2006), Vogel (1996), Sen (1984) and others have demonstrated, rather than being mutually opposing processes, economic liberalization and bureaucratization generally tend to reinforce each other. Economic liberalization entails a substantial degree of administra-tive regulation: privatization of large-scale assets, opening up of markets, providing an environment for the rise of financial capital exchange. These necessitate the existence of an infrastructur-ally strong state. It is no accident that neo-liberal policies were pioneered by the most powerful states, such as the USA and the UK, whereas the very weak states (e.g. in sub-Saharan Africa) have traditionally opted for protectionist economic models. For example, Vogel's (1996) comparative study of reform policies in finance, transport, utilities, telecommunications and broadcasting industries in the UK, the USA, Japan, France and Germany has shown how economic liberalization was in most instances prem-ised on greater bureaucratization. In his own words: 'a movement aimed at reducing regulation has only increased it; a movement propelled by global forces has reinforced national differences; and a movement purported to push back the state has been led by the state itself' (Vogel 1996: 5). The key point here is that economic globalization and marketization require very strong nation-states. Economic liberalization entails a stable geo-political environment with powerful state structures in place. Since the economic crisis of 2008, it has become apparent that the economic policies of powerful individual states such as the USA, China or Germany still determine the direction of globalization processes. Even in the most tightly organized supranational association in the world, the European Union, the key decision-making processes remain dependent on deals made by leaders of the largest nation-states (Hall 2011; 2006).

Finally, the perception that nationalism is on the wane and

that its place has been filled by alternative ideological discourses such as consumerism, cosmopolitanism, or globalism is also misplaced. As elaborated in chapters 5 and 6, most surveys indicate that for an overwhelming majority of European citizens, nationhood remains one of the most important forms of identification, and longitudinal studies show that a sense of attachment to one's nation-state has continued to increase over recent years (Medrano 2009; Antonsich 2009; Fligstein 2008). Cosmopolitanism is not a new ideological discourse but it was always integral to various elite projects, including imperial doctrines, civilizing missions and the more recent humanitarian discourses of human rights. As Calhoun (2007: 24–5) convincingly argues, the theorists of cosmopolitanism such as Beck, Kaldor, Held (2003) or Nussbaum (2006) remain blind to the sociological conditions for cosmopolitanism: 'No one lives outside particularist solidarities. Some cosmopolitan theorists may believe they do, but this is an illusion made possible by positions of relative privilege and the dominant place of some cultural orientations in the world at large.' Beck's view that cosmopolitanism will eventually overcome the 'us vs. them' divide is not only naïve but also profoundly unsociological. Since Weber (1968), Schmitt (1996) and Mouffe (2005), it has become apparent that there is no politics without antagonism. All unifying group solidarities are 'achieved in struggle and at the expense of others. This makes them neither artificial nor erroneous, but products of history' (Calhoun 2007: 21).

In a similar vein, Bauman's insistence that consumerism has replaced nationalism is equally flawed. As argued in chapter 5, not only has consumerism always been an integral part of nationalist experience, but the two have rarely been mutually opposing forces. As Yu (2009), Aronczyk (2007), Gerth (2003) and Yoshino (1999) demonstrate, consumerism is often an important aspect of nationalist projects. Nationalist movements in less developed parts of the world have often made links between economic development, which is defined not only by mass production but also by mass consumption, and the political power of one's nation-state. Third world nationalist ideologues, politicians and business elites have often engaged in propaganda campaigns that encourage their citizens to buy 'the national products'. The calls to buy Irish, Chilean, Philippine, Croatian or other 'national' goods and to spend money at 'national' hotel resorts are still highly prevalent throughout the world. This link between nationalism and consumerism is even more pronounced in the economically powerful states. The American, Japanese or German nationalisms were often rooted in popular consumerist images that enhance the national prestige of those nation-states. Although Coca-Cola, Toyota or BMW have become universal symbols of consumerism, they are also univocally recognized as the national symbols of the economic power of the USA, Japan and Germany. As Yu (2009) shows, the recent resurgence of Chinese nationalism is intimately linked with the ability of ordinary Chinese to consume goods and services that they could not afford in previous times. The booming economy has also contributed to the gradual expansion of the new middle classes, which strongly identify with the economic success of their nation-state. The more affluent among these groups have also become obsessed with buying artefacts of traditional Chinese culture. Yoshino (1999) and his collaborators have studied such diverse consumption practices as the national lottery, theme parks, museums, cross-cultural handbooks, popular song and audio-visual media to show how consumerism reinforces nationalism and vice versa.

Consumerism is in fact an ideal social device for the proliferation of nationalist practice. Since most forms of dominant nationalist experience are trivial and routine, they rely on mass consumption. National images often accompany advertising campaigns for a variety of products: Neutrogena hand cream with an imprinted Norwegian flag, Guinness beer as a symbol of Irishness, the 'American Eagle' clothing chain, 1990s Cool Britannia marketing campaigns and so many others. The currencies used in commercial transactions all over the world contain and thus reinforce the reproduction of national symbols. Large-scale global sporting events such as the Olympics and football world cups thrive on the mass production and sale of 'national' merchandise. Hence, instead of diminishing the influence of nationalism and nation-states, globalization, economic liberalization, capitalism and consumerism foster even greater expansion of nationalist ideology all over this planet.

Religious Revival and Nationalisms

If globalization is not a serious obstacle to the expansion of nationalism, what about the ideological force that had a profound impact on human history for thousands of years and which seems to be experiencing a visible resurgence – religion? However, the argument that the religious revival is likely to overpower or lessen nationalism is also built on the wrong assumptions.

Firstly, religious revivals are not particularly new phenomena, nor are they necessarily incompatible with nationalist ideologies. Most religious traditions have periodically experienced revivals. For example, there were notable Christian 'awakenings' throughout eighteenth- and nineteenth-century Europe (in 1727, 1792, 1830, 1857 and 1882) as well as significant revivalist practices in the early twentieth century, including the Pentecostal Azusa Street revival in 1906 California, the Chile Revival in 1909, and the 1930s East African Balokole revival. The best known and most highly influential were the Second (1800–30s) and the Third (1857–1900) Great Awakening in the USA, which witnessed a dramatic increase in church attendances and religious practice in the everyday life of many Protestant groupings (Wolffe 2007; Hankins 2004). However, none of these nineteenth- and early twentieth-century revivals hampered the development and expansion of nationalism. On the contrary, as McKenna (2007) and O'Leary (2000) show, the Third Great Awakening successfully combined religious and nationalist rhetoric and practice: it emphasized the egalitarian ethos, national solidarity and responsibility to other Christian Americans. Evangelical groups believed that 'their nation had been providentially set apart for a special purpose and they condemned the flaws that kept it from realizing that purpose' (McKenna 2007: 206).

Other religious traditions have also experienced periodic revivalist movements. For example, there were several revivalist peaks in Islam, the most notable being those of the Almoravids in Spain and North Africa in the tenth and eleventh centuries, the Indian revivalist movements (including Naqshbandi and Ahl-i Hadith) in the sixteenth and nineteenth centuries, and most recently a 1970s revival throughout much of the Middle East. The 1970s revival was defined by an increasing mass observance of five religious pillars in everyday life and by huge increases in the annual pilgrimage to Mecca: attendance at the Hajj, which in 1926 was under 90,000, by 1979 had sprung to over two million (Kepel 2002: 75). Here too nationalist ideology was not perceived as an obstacle to religious resurgence. Instead the 1970s saw a proliferation of nationalist ideas and movements throughout the Islamic world, many of which attempted to blend Islamic teachings with nationalist aspirations (Zubaida 2004).

Although recent revivalist trends have raised questions about the plausibility of the secularization paradigm in its classical form (Taylor 2007; Spohn 2003), the resurgence of religion in the world generally did not come at the expense of nationalism. On the contrary, many such movements have successfully combined religious and nationalist narratives and very few have challenged the institution of the nation-state. For example, the Hindutva movements in India have proved to be highly sympathetic to the cause of Hindu-centred Indian nationalism as articulated by the Bharatiya Janata Party (BJP) and other nationalist movements (Gould 2004; van der Veer 1999). Shinto has always been and remains a state religion deeply infused with Japanese nationalism (Fukase-Indergaard and Indergaard 2008). Although some strands of Orthodox Judaism are fiercely opposed to Zionist ideas, an overwhelming majority of Judaist religious organizations are highly supportive of Israeli nationalism. Similarly, all mainstream Eastern Orthodox Christian churches are autocephalous, state-supporting religious institutions that generally tend to reaffirm their nationalist credentials and are seen by the nationalist ideologues as the backbone of their respective nationalist ideologies (Roudometof 2001). Although Roman Catholicism is established as a universalist institution, as the Irish and Polish cases illustrate well it historically played a significant role as a beacon of nationalist ideas (Zubrzycki 2006;

Coakley 2012). There is no evidence that this 'nationalization of religion' has changed much recently (Brubaker 2012; Haupt and Langewiesche 2004). Although some Protestant churches and groups are lukewarm towards or ignore the nation-state, most Protestant denominations are either integral to official nationalist discourses (as in Scandinavia or the USA) or at the forefront of the nationalist projects (Gorski 2003; Greenfeld 1992).

It seems that the Islamic revival is the only one that has challenged nation-states and nationalism directly. There is indeed a long tradition among some Islamic scholars of denouncing both the institution of the nation-state, as an attempt to fragment the *umma*, and nationalism as a secular belief system that is seen to be antithetic to Islamic teachings. For example, Sayid Qutb, the founding father of modern radical Islamism and Salafism, described the relationship between Islam and nationalism in the following terms: 'I believe that the bonds of ideology and belief are more sturdy than those of patriotism based upon region and that this false distinction among Muslims on a regional basis is but one consequence of crusading and Zionist imperialism which must be eradicated' (Zubaida 2004: 407).[3] Such sentiments are echoed in the writings of several influential Islamic scholars, the Friday sermons of prominent imams, popular Islamist websites and individual prayers. For example, Sivan (1997) analysed taped sermons of radical preachers in the 1970s and 1980s and found most of them profoundly hostile to nationalism and pan-Arabism. The typical view was that 'Arab nationalism was conceived in sin and born in corruption and dissolution' (Sivan 1997: 211). These views are echoed today on many popular Islamic and Islamist websites. Hence the highly influential, Shia-leaning Ahlul Bayt Digital Islamic Library Project emphasizes the intrinsic incompatibility of Islam and nationalism:

> conflict between Islam and nationalism is inevitable. The Islamic ideology is not compatible with any other ideology on the question of sovereignty over the private and social life of Muslims. A Muslim cannot at the same time be a Muslim and a polytheist, or a Muslim and communist. In Islam, there is no room for one to be a loyal and

genuine nationalist . . . Nationalism is incompatible with Islam, both schools having two opposite ideologies. These two assume two totally opposite poles in their spirit, essence, direction and goal. (Al-Islam 2012)

Notwithstanding this officially proclaimed, elite-based animosity to nation-states and nationalism, the attitudes of most ordinary Muslims are much more complex. As several empirical studies indicate, most practising Muslims do not differ significantly from non-Muslims in their sense of attachment to their respective nation-states (Berggren 2007; Zubaida 2004; Joppke 2009). Berggren's (2007) analysis of WVS data sets has found that 'most Muslims have strong national feelings and are willing to fight for their country, even if it is a non-Muslim country and a non-Islamic state'. Furthermore, despite more than a decade of anti-Islamic rhetoric in Europe, most European Muslims tend to identify strongly with the institution of the nation-state (whether that means their host country or their country of origin). For example, in 2007, at the height of the headscarf debate, 42 per cent of Muslims in France considered themselves 'French first, Muslim second' and 70 per cent supported *laïcité* (Joppke 2009: 28; Giry 2006: 4). As Zubaida (2004: 417) emphasizes,

> most Muslims in the West see themselves in terms of nationality of origin and are often distant from or even contemptuous of other nationalities. Iranians have definite views of Arabs, and Egyptian and Levantine Arabs see themselves as culturally superior to their Gulf brethren, and all consider themselves distinct from Pakistanis and Bangladeshis, who, in turn, have little time for one another.

Thus, despite the highly publicized events and speeches of Islamists and Salafists who fiercely oppose the nation-state, such views are not representative of the majority, who remain just as committed to nationalism as the rest of the world.

However, even the most radical denunciations of the nation-state cannot escape the rhetoric of nationalism. Nominally anti-nationalist movements such as Hizb ut-Tahrir or Al-Qaida that advocate the replacement of nation-states with a pan-Islamic caliphate tend to conceptualize the future caliphate as a super-state that in many important respects resembles the existing large nation-states. For example, the caliphate would be organized as a unitary state headed by a popularly elected caliph, and it would be comprised of the standard institutions associated with the nation-state: policing, military, law, education, health etc. In addition, the speeches and sermons of leading Islamists are filled with a rhetoric that appears very similar to nationalist discourse: what once was a universal *umma* now becomes the particularist identity of a 'Muslim nation'. In the words of a prominent Al-Qaida member, in the Bosnian war 'we realised we were a nation [*umma*] that had a distinguished place among nations' (Midlarsky 2011: 165–6). This discursive similarity and the religious appropriation of nationalist rhetoric have prompted several scholars to argue that Islamism is only a particular kind of nationalism (Aburaiya 2009; Anderson 2003). Nonetheless, such pan-Islamic aspirations to create a unified, territorially continuous state that would stretch from Indonesia to southern Spain have not attracted a large following among ordinary Muslim believers, most of whom remain deeply loyal to their respective nation-states.

The recent spectacular expansion of suicide terrorism has led some commentators to advocate that such resolute commitment is a reliable indicator that religious identification has the upper hand over national and other allegiances. Nevertheless, as much of the latest research clearly shows, the motivations of jihadist bombers are not so simple and straightforward. Rather than being driven by religious zealotry, the behavioural patterns and motivations of most suicide bombers resemble those of other small groups involved in direct, face-to-face violence, including soldiers on the battlefield, gang members, violent demonstrators or riot police. In all of these instances, ideology, whether religious or secular, has proved a significant motivator of one's action only when embedded in the personal networks of family and friendship (Hassan 2011; Collins 2008; Kalyvas 2006; Ricolfi 2006; Sageman 2004). In this context, most suicide attack missions combine religious with nationalist rhetoric. In Palestine, Chechnya, Afghanistan,

Iraq and until recently Sri Lanka, martyrdom was primarily celebrated through the prism of one's dedication to and sacrifice for the national cause. As Gambetta (2006: 261–2) shows, from their inception in the current form in 1981 until the Iraq War in 2003, the clear majority of suicide bombing missions were carried out by secular, nationalist groups (52.8 per cent) while Islamists were responsible for just 34.6 per cent of such attacks.

To sum up, religious revivals have not replaced the dominance of nation-states and nationalism in the contemporary world. An overwhelming majority of religious denominations show no interest in establishing alternative forms of polity, and very few are ill-disposed towards nationalism. Even when there is a pronounced nominal hostility to nationalism, as in some Islamic circles, this rarely translates into popularly supported attempts to abolish the institution of the nation-state. The absolute organizational and ideological dominance of the nation-state model in today's world means that is nearly impossible to conduct a successful large-scale political action outside of this mighty social organization.

Nation-States and Nationalisms: Organization, Ideology and Solidarity

Despite the predictions, made by many social scientists over the last 200 years, that nationalism is a transient phenomenon which will eventually fade away, the historical record and contemporary events show otherwise. At the beginning of the nineteenth century only small sections of political, cultural, administrative, military and economic elites were preoccupied with advocating ideas of popular sovereignty, national homogeneity or the political independence of culturally defined states; however, at the beginning of the twenty-first century the nation-state has become the dominant form of social organization, and nationalism has established itself as a principal source of state legitimacy worldwide. More importantly, nationalism has revealed its resilient and protean character – its ability to change and adapt to a variety of political and social orders. In the modern age, no ruler can stay long in power if she or he is willing seriously to compromise the political autonomy, territorial integrity or principal cultural symbols of her or his nation-state. In the modern era, nearly all social orders, whether nominally defined as liberal-democratic, communist, theocratic or militarist, tend to legitimize their existence in nationalist terms.

However, this is not to say that a nationalist habitus is somehow a 'given' or 'natural condition' of human beings. On the contrary, as emphasized throughout this book, both nation-states and nationalisms emerge accidentally and fairly late on the historical stage. For 99.99 per cent of their existence on this planet, human beings have lived in entities that were either much smaller (bands, clans, tribes, chiefdoms and city-states) or much larger (empires) than nation-states. Moreover, unlike the nation-state, these entities did not have the interest, organizational means or will to forge cultural homogeneity. That is, nationalism as a coherent, society-wide form of mass politics and ideology could not emerge before modernity. Nevertheless, this classical modernist argument requires a significant qualification. Neither nation-states nor nationalisms have sprung out of historical thin air. Although nation-states are profoundly modern social organizations and nationalism is an ideological doctrine which generally would make no sense in the pre-modern world, their historical arrival was not only accidental but also deeply rooted in the structures of past eras.

In one of his last debates, Gellner (1996: 367) posed the question whether nations have navels – meaning whether one's cultural past matters – and answered that some 'have it and some don't and in any case it's inessential'. This view was directly counterposed to Smith's (1996; 1986) argument about the ethnic origins of nations and the importance of cultural continuity for the emergence of nationalist ideology. One of the key ambitions of this book is to move this debate in a different direction: to look for the elements of historical continuity which are neither cultural nor biological but principally organizational and, to some extent, ideological. Although navels are necessary for simple self-reproduction, once the child leaves the womb they serve no purpose. What matters much more for one's future development is the quality of internal organs and, most of all, the spine. Hence, nation-states can function with relative ease without navels – that is, the cultural heritage, shared myths and memories – but they cannot exist without the spine – that is, the organizational structure. Although the institution of the nation-state has no historical precedent, its existence is embedded in the organizational know-how which was pioneered and perfected in other forms of polity over thousands of years. Even though it is difficult to recognize any substantial similarities between the present-day Federal Republic of Germany and various polities that once occupied the same territory, such as the Hanseatic League, the Frankish and Holy Roman empires, the Alemannic confederation of Suebian tribes or the Personal Union of Brandenburg and the Duchy of Prussia, there is a significant element of organizational continuity present, without which there would be no modern-day Germany as we know it. To understand fully the emergence of the nation-state, it is of paramount importance to look into its organizational past. Despite all the enormous differences between the present-day bureaucratic polity and its patrimonial, tribal and other pre-modern counterparts, they all share some important organizational underpinnings. What once, with the first sedentary hunter-gatherers, was a rudimentary form of territorialized social organization has over thousands of years developed into a complex, sophisticated, bureaucratic vessel able to provide for, service, protect, control and manage millions of individuals, most of whom perceive that social organization as the most natural form of group solidarity. Thus, it is only when one looks at the gradual transformation of social organizations through history that it is possible to identify what is so distinct about the nation-state and the dominant ideology that justifies its very existence – nationalism.

As repeatedly emphasized throughout this book, a nation-state is first and foremost a bureaucratic unit, a social organization that gradually and strenuously grew out of the previous organizational forms – foraging bands, chiefdoms, tribal confederacies, city-states, composite kingdoms and empires. There is no question that the nation-state is a very different form of organization from any of its predecessors, yet it is important to stress the elements of organizational continuity too. In this context, long-term historical processes such as the cumulative bureaucratization of coercion stand out. Although the last two and a half centuries have witnessed its unprecedented acceleration, it is a process that has been in motion for thousands of years.

Similarly, unlike any other pre-modern polity, a nation-state generates its legitimacy from the ideas of popular sovereignty, territorial autonomy and a substantial degree of cultural homogeneity – the key pillars of any nationalist discourse. However, despite its unquestionable modernity, nationalism also owes much to long-term historical processes, not least the centrifugal ideologization that, too, has dramatically intensified over the last two and half centuries. Nevertheless, despite the lack of society-wide, cross-strata, ideological congruency before modernity, nationalism could not have emerged without some grounding in the pre-modern, proto-ideological doctrines: from totemism, mythology and religion to imperial doctrines and civilizing missions. This, of course, is not to say that nationalism had pre-modern equivalents but only that this ideology developed relying on the existing organizational and proto-ideological social devices that were present in the pre-modern world.

One of the key such social devices is the nearly universal human propensity to thrive in small, face-to-face, groups. Although the classics of sociology from Tönnies and Durkheim to Marx and Weber have made much of the distinction between *Gemeinschaft* and *Gesellschaft*, with the former describing the kinship-based world of our ancestors and the latter the contractual character of modernity, there is as much *Gemeinschaft* in modernity as there was in the pre-modern world. Nevertheless, this is usually a different kind of *Gemeinschaft*, which combines individual choice with necessity and where one feels comfortable in the company of one's friends, peers, lovers, close family and many additional significant others. Unlike Durkheim's mechanical solidarity, these forms of micro-solidarity are based not necessarily on physical and cultural resemblance but on strong emotional and value-rational ties. In this sense, micro-solidarity is a precondition of all sociality and ultimately helps secure our survival as species. As human beings we all tend to find comfort, ontological security, meaning, warmth and emotional solace through interaction with the individuals that we value and care about. In this important sense, micro-solidarity is at the heart of all solidarity.

However, what is distinct about the age of nationalism is the unparalleled ability of nation-states to penetrate the networks of micro-solidarity and make themselves the centre of emotional and value-rational attachments for millions of individuals. Unlike any other ideology, nationalism when successful is capable of tapping into our everyday micro-universes and appears as close to us as our daughters, brothers and mothers, husbands, lovers and best friends. This is not to say that nation-states are giant brainwashing machines or that nationalism is a sophisticated lie. Far from it: although nation-states are coercive bureaucratic organizations, they are also considered by their own citizens as the most legitimate form of rule. No other polity in history could claim that level of popular legitimacy. In a similar vein, although nationalism springs from the organizational scaffolding of coercive cumulative bureaucratization and centrifugal ideologization, it fully reflects the genuine individual and collective feelings and desires of most contemporary men, women and children. In the era of the nation-state, not being a national is hardly an option any more.

Hence, to understand fully how nationalism became such a powerful worldview and the nation-state such a dominant form of polity, one has to take stock of the *longue durée* organizational and ideological build-up: the emergence and gradual increase in the cumulative strength of social organizations and the steady diffusion of ideological power in time and space. However, before modernity, social organizations were still too weak and the proto-ideologies too stratified, factionalized and unable to penetrate the pockets of kinship-based micro-solidarity. It is only in modernity that social organizations acquire the substantial degree of organizational sophistication and territorial omnipresence necessary to allow for the shift to nation-state formation. It is only in this era that ideological penetration can become so widespread, institutionally entrenched and capable of interweaving the hubs of micro-solidarity into a society-wide nationalist narrative. As long as these processes are fully in motion, the future of nationalism is not in doubt.

Notes

Chapter 1 The Salience of Nationalism

1 My understanding of social organization closely resembles that of Jenkins (2008: 167), who defines organizations as particular kinds of institutions where: 'there are always members ... [who] combine in pursuit of explicit objectives, which serve to identify the organization; there are criteria for identifying, and processes for recruiting, members; there is a division of labour in the specification of the specialised tasks and functions performed by individual members; and there is a recognised pattern of decision-making and task allocation'. I would just emphasize that membership in social organizations does not have to be voluntary or active: we are all born into a particular nation-state which confers membership on us even though we do not have to embrace, or identify with, that social organization.

2 For my definition of ideology see Malešević (2011a; 2010: 8–12; 2006: 69–79) and chapter 6 in this book, pp. 170–2.

Chapter 2 Group Solidarities before the Nation-State

1 As Maryanski and Turner (1996) emphasize, among surviving species of higher apes such as gorillas, chimpanzees or orang-utans most social ties among adults are weak and the only strong ties are those between a mother and its immature offspring.

2 But as the very small number of surviving apes demonstrates, it was close to happening!

3 It is important to emphasize that hunting and gathering is significantly older than *Homo sapiens*, who originated *c.*200,000 years ago and took the present form *c.*50,000 years ago.

4 The concept of 'tribe' is often criticized by anthropologists as a latter-day modernist/colonial invention that projected cultural homogeneity onto groups of individuals where often there was none (see Fried 1975). For an

alternative view which rehabilitates the concept of tribe see Crone (1986). In this study I use the term 'tribe' simply as shorthand for sedentary, complex hunter-gatherers and simple horticulturalists.

5 For an extensive criticism of the socio-biological approach in the study of ethnicity and nationalism see Malešević (2004: 86–93; 2010: 180–4).

6 As Geary (1988: 41–2) demonstrates, in Roman ethnography 'barbarians' were often described 'with almost monotonous similarity: all barbarians resembled each other and animals more than Romans in both their virtues and in their vices. They were generally tall, blond, and foul-smelling; they lived not according to fixed, written laws but according to senseless and unpredictable customs. They were fierce and dangerous in war, but sloth-ful, easily distracted, and quarrelsome in peace. Their faithlessness to those outside their tribe was proverbial; their love of drinking and fighting with each other the cause of their own destruction. Their language was more like animal cries than true human speech.'

7 In direct contrast to the line taken by ethno-symbolist approaches (Smith 2009; 1986; Hutchinson 2005), it seems that shared language was not of major importance for early tribal associations. Rather the focus was on 'clothing, styles of hair, ornamentation, types of weapons, material culture, religious cult, and a shared oral history'. However, these were not necessar-ily tribal in-group markers, as they have also served 'for social distinctions within a tribe' (Geary 1988: 54).

8 In Geary's (2002: 118) words: 'Whatever a Goth was in the third-century kingdom of Cniva, the reality of a Goth in sixth-century Spain was far differ-ent, in language, religion, political and social organization, even ancestry. . . . With the constant shifting of allegiances, intermarriages, transformations, and appropriations, it appears that all that remained constant were names, and these were vessels that could hold different contents at different times.'

9 Roshwald's (2006: 14–22) evidence is extremely slim, as he utilizes standard biblical references and relies almost exclusively on a single piece of archaeo-logical evidence – a coin minted in the 130s CE (the Bar Kokhba rebellion coin).

10 As Smith (2004: 132) and Hall (1997: 53) insist, Athenian culture was just a variation of the broader Ionian Hellenic culture, and as the Solonian fragments indicate, 'the Athenians considered themselves Ionian by at least 600 BC'.

11 At the outset of the thirteenth century there were up to 300 autonomous cities in the north and central part of the Apennine peninsula (Burke 1986: 140; Waley 1969: 11).

12 It is important to accentuate the fact that, unlike most other city-states through history, many European city-states were characterized by three features: (1) republican ideas of citizenship, (2) the rise of an independent middle class and (3) the emergence of non-kinship-based confraternities (Parker 2004; Spruyt 1994).

13 Snyder (1968: 17) argues that 'modern nationalism was an extension of the city-state idea on a greater scale. The same bonds of common language, religion, customs, and heroes, the same patriotism, the same xenophobia – all these were combined to form the stuff of nationalism.'

14 Even though Athens was more inclusive, as it incorporated free peasantry into the governing process, 'yet even in the fifth century, Athenian policy was largely determined by one man, like Pericles, for years at a time' (Griffeth and Thomas 1981: 187).

15 Even in the case of Japan the use of the title 'imperial' is exclusively reserved for the monarch, who according to the 1947 Constitution is 'the symbol of the state and of the unity of the people', whereas the state itself is understood in non-imperial terms. More specifically, in Japanese the emperor is called *Tennō*, that is, 'the heavenly sovereign'. In the previous, Meiji constitution, which lasted until 1947, the emperor was tightly linked with the imperial character of the state. The opening line of that constitution spells out this relationship clearly: 'The Empire of Japan shall be reigned over and governed by a line of Emperors unbroken for ages eternal' (Mann 2012: 104).

16 In the time of the Emperor Augustus (63 BCE to 14 CE) Rome was by far the most populous city on the planet (even ahead of the Chinese capital Chang'an), but out of its million inhabitants only a quarter were citizens (Burbank and Cooper 2010: 35).

17 Neither Roman nor Chinese imperial elites knew, or were interested in finding out, about the other.

18 For example, both Maya and Aztec empires did not use bronze but relied exclusively on tool technology that was equivalent to that of the Eurasian Neolithic Age.

19 This transition is nicely illustrated by Poggi (1978: 68–9) with the example of Louis XIV, who was a public figure in every sense: 'His mother gave birth to him in public . . . He ate in public, went to bed in public, woke up and was clothed and groomed in public, urinated and defecated in public . . . when he died (in public), his body was promptly and messily chopped up in public'.

20 The centrality of the monarch in absolutism was often emphasized by the ruler's claim that he was the father of the nation (e.g. Peter the Great in Russia). On the theoretical and juridical underpinnings of this principle that nation is to be identified with the person of the king see Foucault (2003: 215–37). He emphasizes that 'it is the body of the king, in his physico-juridical relationship with each of his subjects, that creates the body of the nation' (p. 217).

21 Schulze (1996: 36) shows that in Europe there was no systematic tax collection before the sixteenth century, when revenues 'began to be collected on a regular basis', as taxes 'had originally been levied only in emergencies or on special occasions'.

22 For alternative interpretations which argue that the nascent form of British/

English nationalism that included commoners was already present in the sixteenth or eighteenth century respectively, see Greenfeld (1992) and Colley (2009).

23 The idea of 'Poland' was preserved not because there was a widespread recognition that there was a 'Polish nation' but exclusively because there was an exceptionally large conglomerate of nobles, *szlachta*, who were able to pursue their individual interest under the guise of 'shared Polish origins'. As Schulze (1996: 65) argues: 'the Polish state was totally subordinated to the interests of the nobility ... by 1700 Poland was in effect no more than a confederation of some 60,000 magnates, who took their lead in foreign policy from Russia, Prussia or Austria'.

24 Obviously there were important structural differences between these three empires. For example, strong traditions of parliamentary rule, citizenship rights and local administration were substantially more developed in the British and Dutch cases than in that of France (or Prussia/Germany). The consequence of this was a much greater bureaucratization of coercion in the latter two cases.

25 The treaty acknowledged the *cuius regio, eius religio* principle, already adopted in Augsburg (1555), and went a step further by guaranteeing freedom of worship and belief for various Protestant groups.

Chapter 3 The Birth and Expansion of Nationalisms

1 There are several very good critical overviews of these classic studies, including Smith (1998), Özkırımlı (2010), Hearn (2006) and Coakley (2012).

2 Despite the popular perception of the USA as having an exceptionally weak welfare state, it too was a pioneer of some welfare provisions such as old age pensions. In the American case just as in Prussia welfare was tightly linked to warfare, as only the soldiers (and their widows) who fought on the Union side in the American Civil War were recipients of pensions (Lachmann 2013; 2010; Mennell 2007). As Skocpol (1992) shows, after the Civil War more than a third of all federal spending was used to pay pensions to war veterans or their widows – more than a million recipients.

3 For an extensive criticism of neo-Durkheimian approaches in nationalism studies see Malešević (2011b; 2011c; 2006), and for replies to my criticisms see Smith (2011; 2010; 2009). For a powerful critique of the neo-Durkheimian idea that national ceremonies preserve 'collective memory' see Uzelac (2011).

4 For various explanations of the origins and causes of modernity see Gellner (1988), Mann (1993; 1986) and Hall (1985).

5 This practice of turning republics into empires was present in the twentieth century, the prominent example being that of Jean-Bédel Bokassa, who in 1976 renamed the Central African Republic an empire.

6 This pre-nationalist, local sense of belonging was well illustrated by the

self-description of peasantry. For example, the population of what is today Estonia, Latvia and Eastern Poland did not see themselves as Estonians, Latvians or Poles but as *tutejszy* (local people) or *maarahvas* (country people)' (Coakley 2012: 163).

7 At the time of Italian unification only 2.5 per cent of its population were fully literate (Schulze 1996: 161).

8 As recent archival research indicates, it was a former education minister, Ferdinando Martini, who in 1896 uttered this sentence for the first time (Koenig-Archibugi 2003: 108).

9 Clark (1998) demonstrates that at the time of unification only a tiny minority of the inhabitants of the Apennine peninsula saw themselves as 'Italians' and only 3 per cent spoke Italian. Hence most peasant rebellions and uprisings throughout the nineteenth century, including those leading to 'national unification', were really expressions of local grievances and had little or nothing to do with nationalism.

10 For an extensive critical analysis of this one-directional change see Malešević (2011c).

Chapter 4 Nationalist Ideologies and Violence

1 Hassan (2011) and Pape (2005) have identified a stereotypical version of this model, popular among psychologists and psychiatrists, who tend to treat political extremism as a form of disease. Hence when studying suicide bombers they resort to a clichéd methodology: 'Typically, the writer begins by interviewing the suicide bomber's immediate family, friends, and other close associates, asking detailed questions about the personal history and psychological conditions of the individual. From these interviews, the suicide attacker's life history is stitched together, often with painstaking effort to identify the key moments of transition that "caused" the person to wish to die and so to willingly accept a suicide terrorist mission. Finally, there is a summary of the statement – often to the effect that, much to the writer's surprise, no clear "moment of transition" could be found' (Hassan 2011: 38–9, quoting Pape 2005: 171). A very similar strategy is often used to explain the development of nationalist leaders and their pathway to violence.

2 For an extensive critical analysis of all these different perspectives see Malešević (2004).

3 The 'great men' approach is still popular in perceiving scientific inventions and artistic achievements as the work of individual geniuses. However, both Collins (2000) and Merton (1952) have demonstrated the importance of historical contexts, social circumstances and collective networks in the creation and recognition of a 'genius'. Thus rather than being solely an inborn quality, artistic and scientific genius is also for the most part a social product. Furthermore, the importance of social and historical context is

well illustrated in the cases of many discoveries such as those of nitrogen, photography, calculus, the telegraph or the phonograph (Sztompka 1994; Merton 1952).

4 The title of Horowitz's (1985) book is highly indicative of this approach: *Ethnic Groups in Conflict.*

5 Brubaker (2004) is very convincing in his criticism of the groupist discourse that permeates much of nationalism and ethnic relations studies. For a similar criticism see also Malešević (2011b; 2006; 2002).

6 On the complexity of Rwandan ethno-national relations see Lemarchand (2013), Gourevitch (2000) and Mamdani (2001).

7 This is not to say that once the nation-state emerges, empires vanish, as it is obvious that for much of the nineteenth and early twentieth centuries many European nation-states continued to be overseas empires as well. The focus is on the different sources of legitimacy in modernity, where even the imperial nation-states have to justify their existence to their 'homeland' populations in national terms.

8 In most twentieth-century wars, recruitment policies have depended on the local organizational context, which helps merge macro-ideology with micro-solidarity: 'Volunteers signed on in local units, for example in the British "Pals' battalions", and their commitment was to people they knew ... Peer-group pressure to enlist urged not being a shirker' (Mann 2012: 146).

9 The second part of this argument, which states that national movements have brought about the collapse of empires, is also problematic, as it is premised on the idea that imperial breakdown was a singular and irreversible event rather than a slow, protracted and reversible process. On this see Kumar (2010), Mann (2012), Malešević (2013a; 2012a; 2011a) and Burbank and Cooper (2010).

Chapter 5 The Omnipotence of Triviality

1 This is not to say that the British imperial project was benign. On the contrary, in the early periods the imperial expansion relied on the pervasive use of violence: 'when it was liberalizing into informal empire in earlier zones of expansion, bloody conquest and direct empire dominated new colonies' (Mann 2012: 40).

2 Empirical research has found that there is a strong positive correlation between the expansion of a welfare state and a sense of personal attachment to one's nation-state. See Suszycki (2011) and Alesina et al. (1999).

3 Although cartography was institutionalized in the wake of the Napoleonic Wars, its mass use became prominent only at the end of the nineteenth century. This was 'facilitated not least by falling production and printing costs' (Conrad 2006: 60).

4 For example, political mural painting in Northern Ireland began only in the

nineteenth century when a new industrial paint, one that would not wash off external walls, was imported for use in Belfast shipyards and was then gradually appropriated by loyalist workers (Rolston 1987).

5 As Smith (2008: 565) rightly points out, the notion of 'ordinary people' as employed by many representatives of this 'everyday' approach is highly problematic and requires unpacking: 'One might question the assumption of an undifferentiated "ordinary people" at the heart of the enterprise. Either "the people" (folk) is a construct of nationalism itself, as in "We, the people . . ."; or it is an unsociological category that needs to be broken down into its constituent parts, be they individuals, or various organised groups of people.'

6 However, I would certainly question Billig's epistemological idealism. It is not so much that nationalism reproduces institutions as it is institutions (and the social action of individual human beings) that help reproduce nationalism.

7 On flag burning in the USA see Marvin and Ingle (1999).

8 Mann (2012: 7, 282) sees nineteenth- and early twentieth-century patriarchy, nationalism and racism as the prime examples of what he calls 'the institutionalized ideologies', with nationalism maintaining this position throughout the twentieth and early twenty-first centuries.

9 It is very interesting that despite their defection many of these refugees remain enchanted by North Korean nationalism: 'I still think of us, the group, and country first rather than myself . . . I will not abandon such ideology until I die', or 'I defected in 2007, but I still support the North Korean regime . . . I am proud of our nuclear weapons. I have always believed that we would win a war and if we lost it, I would die after breaking up America with a nuclear bomb' (Kang 2012: 17–22).

10 In addition to *Juche*, other nationalist-grounded North Korean concepts include *Ilmin Chuui* ('one peoplehood') and 'the modernization of the fatherland' (Shin 2006).

11 Although initially *dannelse* was similar to the German concept of *bildung*, indicating self-cultivation, from the nineteenth century onwards its meaning was transformed.

12 According to Østergaard (2006: 76) the influence of Grundtvig on Danish nationalism was critical, as from then on Danish nationalism was 'less chauvinistic than most in the nineteenth century'. Korsgaard (2008: 65) writes about Grundtvigian influence on 'a standard formulation in Denmark of an anti-essentialist definition of national identity'.

13 The origins of this divide can be traced back to the military defeat by Prussia in 1864, which resulted not only in large territorial losses (Holstein, Schleswig and Lauenburg) but also in the delegitimization of the nationalism articulated by the state elite (see Korsgaard 2008).

14 There are clear resonances here with the Irish concept of *craic* (see Keohane 1997).

Chapter 6 Beyond National Identity

1 This is a revised and expanded version of the paper originally published in *Nations and Nationalism* 17 (1): 272–90 under the title 'The Chimera of National Identity'. I would like to thank the publishers for allowing me to reproduce this revised version.

2 The UN has 193 members and one observer state (the Holy See), but there are at least thirteen non-member states which are granted full or partial recognition by other UN member states (the Republic of China/Taiwan, Abkhazia, the Turkish Republic of Northern Cyprus, Kosovo etc.).

3 For a more extensive critique of the interpretativist and anti-foundationalist approaches in the study of ethnic and national identity see Malešević (2006: 46–57; 2004: 143–59).

4 As Paasi (2009: 139) emphasizes, the Eurobarometer and similar surveys simply force unrealistic choices on respondents in having to 'identify' with mutually exclusive nations, regions or ethnic groups.

5 Collins (2008) provides illustrative examples of small-scale group settings such as football hooliganism, street gang violence, mosh pits and mock fights where one's feelings are intensified through the rhythm of bodies caught in the coordinated joint action.

6 This intense feeling of attachment to one's squad or platoon is nicely captured by Remarque (1984 [1929]: 186): 'I am no longer a shuddering speck of existence, alone in the darkness; – I belong to them and they to me; we all share the same fear and the same life, we are nearer than lovers, in a simple, a harder way; I could bury my face in them, in these voices, these words that have saved me and will stand by me.'

Chapter 7 The Future of Nationalisms

1 There is a large literature that questions the novelty and prevalence of globalization and religious revival (Breuilly 2011; Hutchinson 2011; Conrad 2006; Hirst et al. 2009; Mann 2003; 1997; Hall 2002; 2000). For example, Conrad (2006: 4–9) convincingly demonstrates that the globalizing processes of the late nineteenth century were vital in making nationalism a mass phenomenon, as the creation of global labour markets stimulated the spread of nationalist ideas: 'Globalization contributed, around 1900, to the popularity of ideas about distinct national characteristics . . . during the nineteenth century some 60 million people emigrated from Europe alone, mainly to the New World . . . from 1834 to 1937, between thirty and 45 million people left the Indian subcontinent; almost 50 million moved from Russia and north-eastern Asia to Siberia and Manchuria; over 19 million Chinese emigrated to south-eastern Asia.'

2 The standardized policing of borders, including the compulsory checking

of documentation and the hygiene-related rules for immigration, developed only in the early twentieth century (Conrad 2006: 385–6).

3 However, as Zubaida (2004: 411) shows, late nineteenth- and early twentieth-century Islamists were generally sympathetic to Arab nationalism. Even the founder of the Muslim Brotherhood, Hassan al-Banna, attempted to reconcile Islam and Arabism: 'The Arabs are [the] mainstay of Islam and its guardians . . . and it is a duty of every Muslim to work for the revival and support for Arab unity.'

Bibliography

Aburaiya, Issam 2009. Islamism, nationalism, and Western modernity: the case of Iran and Palestine, *International Journal of Politics, Culture, and Society* 22 (1): 57–68.

Alesina, Alberto, Reza Baqir and William Easterly 1999. Public goods and ethnic divisions, *Quarterly Journal of Economics* 114 (4): 1243–84.

Al-Islam 2012. Part Seven: Islam and nationalism. Al-Islam.org (http://www.al-islam.org/islamandnationalism/9.htm).

Anderson, Benedict 2012. Nationalism and time. Manuscript of the lecture delivered at UCD School of Sociology, Dublin, 19 September.

Anderson, Benedict 1998. *The Spectre of Comparisons: Nationalism, Southeast Asia, and the World*. London: Verso.

Anderson, Benedict 1983. *Imagined Communities: Reflections on the Origin and Spread of Nationalism*. London: Verso.

Anderson, Jon W. 2003. The internet and Islam's new interpreters, in J. W. Anderson and D. F. Eickelman (eds.), *New Media in the Muslim World*, 2nd edition. Bloomington: Indiana University Press.

Anderson, Fred and Andrew Cayton 2005. *The Dominion of War: Empire and Liberty in North America, 1500–2000*. New York: Viking.

Antonsich, Marco 2009. National identities in the age of globalization: The case of Western Europe, *National Identities* 11 (3): 281–99.

Armstrong, John 2004. Definitions, periodization, and prospects for the *longue durée*, *Nations and Nationalism* 10 (1–2): 9–18.

Armstrong, John 1982. *Nations before Nationalism*. Chapel Hill: University of North Carolina Press.

Aronczyk, Melissa 2007. New and improved nations: Branding national identity, in C. Calhoun and R. Sennett (eds.), *Practicing Culture*. London: Routledge.

Azaryahu, Maoz and Rebecca Kook 2002. Mapping the nation: Street names and Arab-Palestinian identity: The three case studies, *Nations and Nationalism* 8 (2): 195–213.

Bibliography

Baert, Patrick 1998. *Social Theory in the Twentieth Century*. Cambridge: Polity.

Baker, Mark 1982. *Nam: The Vietnam War in the Words of the Men and Women Who Fought There*. New York: Morrow.

Banton, Michael 1997. *Ethnic and Racial Consciousness*. New York: Prentice Hall.

Barthes, Roland 1993. *Mythologies*. London: Vintage.

Bartov, Omer 1992. *Hitler's Army: Soldiers, Nazis, and War in the Third Reich*. Oxford: Oxford University Press.

Bauman, Zygmunt 2006. *Liquid Fear*. Cambridge: Polity.

Bauman, Zygmunt 2002. *Society under Siege*. Cambridge: Polity.

Bauman, Zygmunt 2000. *Liquid Modernity*. Cambridge: Polity.

Bauman, Zygmunt 1989. *Modernity and the Holocaust*. Cambridge: Polity.

Beck, Hermann 1995. *The Origins of the Authoritarian Welfare State in Prussia*. Ann Arbor: University of Michigan Press.

Beck, Ulrich 2007. A new cosmopolitanism is in the air. Signandsight.com (http://www.signandsight.com/features/1603.html).

Beck, Ulrich 2006. *Cosmopolitan Vision*. Cambridge: Polity.

Beck, Ulrich 2002. The cosmopolitan society and its enemies, *Theory, Culture and Society* 19 (1–2): 17–44.

Beck, Ulrich 2000. The cosmopolitan perspective: Sociology of the second age of modernity, *British Journal of Sociology* 51 (1): 79–105.

Beissinger, Mark 1998. Nationalisms that bark and nationalisms that bite: Ernest Gellner and the substantiation of nations, in J. A. Hall (ed.), *The State of the Nation*. Cambridge: Cambridge University Press.

Bell, David 2007. *The First Total War: Napoleon's Europe and the Birth of Warfare as we Know it*. Boston: Houghton Mifflin.

Berggren, Jason 2007. More than the Ummah: Religious and national identity in the Muslim world, *American Journal of Islamic Social Science* 24 (2): 71–93.

Billig, Michael 2002. Ideology, language and discursive psychology, in S. Malešević and I. Mackenzie (eds.), *Ideology after Poststructuralism*. London: Pluto.

Billig, Michael 1995. *Banal Nationalism*. London: Sage.

Bogdanor, Vernon 1996. *Politics and the Constitution; Essays on British Government*. Aldershot: Dartmouth.

Boli, John and George Thomas 1997. *World Culture in the World Polity: A Century of International Non-Governmental Organizations*. Stanford: Stanford University Press.

Bourdieu, Pierre 1990. *The Logic of Practice*. Cambridge: Polity.

Bourdieu, Pierre 1977. *Outline of a Theory of Practice*. Cambridge: Cambridge University Press.

Bourke, Joan 1999. *An Intimate History of Killing*. London: Granta.

Boyce, David 1999. *Decolonization and the British Empire, 1775–1997*. New York: Palgrave.

Breuilly, John 2011. Nationalism as global history, in D. Halikiopoulou and S. Vasilopoulou (eds.), *Nationalism and Globalization: Conflicting or Complementary?* London: Routledge.

Breuilly, John 1993. *Nationalism and the State*. Manchester: Manchester University Press.

Bromberg, Norbert and Verna Volz Small 1983. *Hitler's Psychopathology*. Ann Arbor: University of Michigan Press.

Browning, Christopher 1993. *Ordinary Men: Reserve Police Battalion 101 and the Final Solution in Poland*. New York: HarperCollins.

Brubaker, Rogers 2012. Religion and nationalism: Four approaches, *Nations and Nationalism* 18 (1): 2–20.

Brubaker, Rogers 2004. *Ethnicity without Groups*. Cambridge, MA: Harvard University Press.

Brubaker, Rogers 1996. *Nationalism Reframed*. Cambridge: Cambridge University Press.

Brubaker, Rogers 1992. *Citizenship and Nationhood in France and Germany*. Cambridge, MA: Harvard University Press.

Brubaker, Rogers and Frederic Cooper 2000. Beyond 'identity', *Theory and Society* 29 (1): 1–37.

Brubaker, Rogers, Margit Feischmidt, Jon Fox and Liana Grancea 2006. *Nationalist Politics and Everyday Ethnicity in a Transylvanian Town*. Princeton: Princeton University Press.

Burbank, Jane and Frederick Cooper 2010. *Empires in World History: Power and Politics of Difference*. Princeton: Princeton University Press.

Burke, Peter 1986. City-states, in J. A. Hall (ed.), *States in History*. Oxford: Blackwell.

Burleigh, Michael 2009. *Blood and Rage: A Cultural History of Terrorism*. New York: HarperCollins.

Calhoun, Craig 2007. *Nations Matter: Culture, History and the Cosmopolitan Dream*. London: Routledge.

Calvert, Peter 1970. *Revolution*. Oxford: Clarendon.

Cannadine, David 1983. The context, performance and meaning of ritual: The British monarchy and the 'invention of tradition', *c.*1820–1977, in E. Hobsbawm and T. Ranger (eds.), *The Invention of Tradition*. Cambridge: Cambridge University Press.

Carlyle, Thomas 1963 [1857]. *On Heroes, Hero-Worship, and the Heroic in History*. London: Doubleday.

Carroll, Rory and Jonathan Franklin 2010. Chile miners: Rescued foreman Luis Urzúa's first interview, *Guardian* 14 October.

Castells, Manuel 1998. *End of Millennium. Vol. III: The Information Age: Economy, Society and Culture*. Malden, MA: Wiley-Blackwell.

Centeno, Miguel Angel, Jose Miguel Cruz, René Flores and Gustavo Silva Cano 2013. Internal wars and Latin American Nationalism, in J. A. Hall and

Bibliography

S. Malešević (eds.), *Nationalism and War*. Cambridge: Cambridge University Press.

Chavez, John R. 2009. *Beyond Nations: Evolving Homelands in the North Atlantic World 1400–2000*. Cambridge: Cambridge University Press.

Cicero, Marcus Tullius 2009. *The Republic and The Laws*. New York: Digireads.

Cigar, Norman 1995. *Genocide in Bosnia: The Policy of 'Ethnic Cleansing'*. College Station: Texas A&M.

Clark, Martin 1998. *The Italian Risorgimento*. Harlow: Longman.

Coakley, John 2012. *Nationalism, Ethnicity and the State*. London: Sage.

Coakley, John 2007. National identity in Northern Ireland: Stability or change?, *Nations and Nationalism* 13 (4): 573–98.

Cohen, Anthony P. 1996. Personal nationalism: A Scottish view of some rites, rights, and wrongs, *American Ethnologist* 23 (4): 802–15.

Cohen, Edward 2000. *The Athenian Nation*. Princeton: Princeton University Press.

Colas, Alejandro 2007. *Empire*. Cambridge: Polity.

Colley, Linda 2009. *Britons: Forging the Nation 1707–1837*. New Haven: Yale University Press.

Collins, Randall 2012. Time-bubbles of nationalism: Dynamics of solidarity ritual in lived time, *Nations and Nationalism* 18 (3): 383–97.

Collins, Randall 2008. *Violence: Micro-Sociological Theory*. Princeton: Princeton University Press.

Collins, Randall 2004. *Interaction Ritual Chains*. Princeton; Princeton University Press.

Collins, Randall 2000. *The Sociology of Philosophies: A Global Theory of Intellectual Change*. Cambridge, MA: Harvard University Press.

Collins, Randall 1999. *Macrohistory: Essays in Sociology of the Long Run*. Stanford: Stanford University.

Collins, Randall 1989. Sociological theory, disaster research and war, in G. Krebs (ed.), *Social Structure and Disaster*. Newark: University of Delaware Press.

Confino, Alon 1997. *Nation as a Local Metaphor: Württemberg, Imperial Germany, and National Memory, 1871–1918*. Chapel Hill: University of North Carolina Press.

Confucius 2007. *The Analectics*. New York: Columbia University Press.

Connor, Walker 2005. The dawning of nations, in A. Ichijo and G. Uzelac (eds.), *When is the Nation?* London: Routledge.

Connor, Walker 1994. *Ethno-Nationalism: The Quest for Understanding*. Princeton: Princeton University Press.

Conrad, Sebastian 2006. *Globalization and the Nation in Imperial Germany*. Cambridge: Cambridge University Press.

Cordell, Karl and Stefan Wolff 2010. *Ethnic Conflict*. Cambridge: Polity.

Crone, Patricia 1989. *Pre-Industrial Societies*. Oxford: Blackwell.

Bibliography

Crone, Patricia 1986. The tribe and the state, in J. A. Hall (ed.), *States in History*. Oxford: Oxford University Press.

Cushman, Thomas and Stjepan Meštrović 1996. *This Time We Knew: Western Responses to Genocide in Bosnia*. New York: New York University Press.

Dadrian, Vahkan 1995. *The History of the Armenian Genocide: Ethnic Conflict from the Balkans to Anatolia to the Caucasus*. Providence, RI, and Oxford: Berghahn Books.

Damasio, Antonio 2003. *The Feeling Of What Happens: Body, Emotion and the Making of Consciousness*. New York: Vintage.

Damasio, Antonio 1994. *Descartes' Error: Emotion, Reason, and the Human Brain*. New York: Putnam.

Darwin, John 2009. *The Empire Project: The Rise and Fall of the British World-System, 1830–1970*. Cambridge: Cambridge University Press.

Darwin, John 2007. *After Tamerlane: The Rise and Fall of Global Empires, 1400–2000*. London: Penguin.

David, Ann R. 1982. *The Ancient Egyptians: Religious Beliefs and Practices*. London: Routledge & Kegan Paul.

Davidson, Eugene 1977. *The Making of Adolf Hitler*. London: Macmillan.

Davis, H. W. C. 1915. *The Political Thought of H. von Treitschke*. New York: Charles Scribner's Sons.

de Romilly, Jacqueline 1963. *Thucydides and Athenian Imperialism*. Oxford: Blackwell.

De Votta, Neil 2004. *Blowback: Linguistic Nationalism, Institutional Decay, and Ethnic Conflict in Sri Lanka*. Stanford: Stanford University Press.

Deutsch, Karl 1966. *Nationalism and Social Communication: An Inquiry into the Foundations of Nationality*. New York: MIT Press.

Diamond, Jared 2005. *Guns, Germs, and Steel: The Fates of Human Societies*. New York: W. W. Norton.

Djukić, Slavoljub 1994. *Izmedju Slave i Anateme: Politička Biografija Slobodana Miloševića*. Belgrade: Filip Višnjić.

Downing, Brian 1992. *The Military Revolution and Political Change*. Princeton: Princeton University Press.

Drori, Gili S., John W. Meyer, Francisco O. Ramirez and Evan Schofer 2003. *Science in the Modern World Polity: Institutionalization and Globalization*. Stanford: Stanford University Press.

Duran, Diego 1964. *The Aztecs: The History of the Indies of New Spain*. New York: Orion Press.

Durkheim, Emile 1997 [1893]. *The Division of Labour in Society*. New York: Free Press.

Durkheim, Emile 1995 [1915]. *The Elementary Forms of Religious Life*. New York: Free Press.

Eatwell, Roger 2003. *Fascism: A History*. London: Pimlico.

Bibliography

Eckhardt, William 1992. *Civilizations, Empires and Wars: A Quantitative History of War*. Jefferson: McFarland.

Edensor, Tim 2002. *National Identity, Popular Culture and Everyday Life*. Oxford: Berg.

Eriksen, Thomas Hylland 1993. Formal and informal nationalism, *Ethnic and Racial Studies* 16 (1): 1–25.

Ertman, Thomas 1997. *Birth of the Leviathan*. Cambridge: Cambridge University Press.

Falkenstein, Adam 1974. *The Summerian Temple City*. Malibu: Udena.

Fawn, Rick 2003. Ideology and national identity in post-communist foreign policies, in R. Fawn (ed.), *Ideology and National Identity in Post-Communist Foreign Policies*. London: Routledge.

Feld, Werner 1972. *Non-Governmental Forces and World Politics*. New York: Praeger.

Figes, Orlando 2011. *Crimea*. London: Penguin.

Fligstein, Neil 2008. *Euroclash: The EU, European Identity and the Future of Europe*. Oxford: Oxford University Press.

Foster, Ann 2010. *Projections of Power: The United States and Europe in Colonial Southeast Asia, 1919–1945*. Durham, NC: Duke University Press.

Foster, Greg 2008. *The Contested Public Square: The Crisis of Christianity and Politics*. Downers Grov: InterVarsity Press.

Foucault, Michel 2003. *Society Must Be Defended: Lectures at the College de France 1975–1976*. New York: Picador.

Foucault, Michel 1975. *Discipline and Punish: The Birth of the Prison*. London: Penguin.

Fox, Jon E. and Cynthia Miller-Idriss 2008. Everyday nationhood, *Ethnicities* 8 (4), 536–63.

Freeden, Michael 1998. Is nationalism a distinct ideology?, *Political Studies* 46, 748–50.

Freeden, Michael 1996. *Ideologies and Political Theory: A Conceptual Approach*. Oxford: Clarendon.

Fried, Morton 1975. *The Notion of Tribe*. Menlo Park: Cummings.

Friedrichs, Christopher 1981. The Swiss and German city-states, in R. Griffeth and C. G. Thomas (eds.), *The City-State in Five Cultures*. Santa Barbara and Oxford: ABC-Clio.

Fry, Douglas 2007. *Beyond War*. Oxford: Oxford University Press.

Fry, Douglas 2005. *The Human Potential for Peace*. Oxford: Oxford University Press.

Fukase-Indergaard, Fumiko and Michael Indergaard 2008. Religious nationalism and the making of the modern Japanese state, *Theory and Society* 37 (4): 343–74.

Gabriel, Richard 1987. *No More Heroes: Madness and Psychiatry in War*. New York: Hill and Wang.

Gambetta, Diego 2006. Can we make sense of suicide missions?, in D. Gambetta (ed.), *Making Sense of Suicide Missions*. Oxford: Oxford University Press.

Gat, Azar 2006. *War in Human Civilization*. Oxford: Oxford University Press.

Geary, Patrick. J. 2002. *The Myth of Nations*. Princeton: Princeton University Press.

Geary, Patrick, J. 1988. *Before France and Germany: The Creation and Transformation of the Merovingian World*. Oxford: Oxford University Press.

Geisler, Michael E. 2009. The calendar conundrum: National days as unstable signifiers, in D. McCrone and G. McPherson (eds.), *National Days: Constructing and Mobilising National Identity*. Basingstoke: Palgrave.

Gellner, Ernest 1997. *Nationalism*. London: Phoenix.

Gellner, Ernest 1996. Do nations have navels?, *Nations and Nationalism* (2) 2: 366–70.

Gellner, Ernest 1988. *Plough, Sword and the Book: The Structure of Human History*. London: Collins Harvill.

Gellner, Ernest 1983. *Nations and Nationalism*. Oxford: Blackwell.

Gellner, Ernest 1964. *Thought and Change*. London: Weidenfeld and Nicolson.

Gerstle, Gery 2002. *American Crucible: Race and Nation in the Twentieth Century*. Princeton: Princeton University Press.

Gerth, Karl 2003. *China Made: Consumer Culture and the Creation of the Nation*. London: Routledge.

Giddens, Anthony 1985. *The Nation-State and Violence*. Cambridge: Polity.

Giry, Stéphanie 2006. France and its Muslims, *Foreign Affairs* 85 (5): 87–105.

Glenny, Misha 2000. *The Balkans 1804–1999: Nationalism, War and the Great Powers*. London: Granta.

Goffman, Erving 1961. *Encounters: Two Studies in the Sociology of Interaction*. London: Macmillan.

Goldhagen, Daniel 1996. *Hitler's Willing Executioners: Ordinary Germans and the Holocaust*. New York: Alfred A. Knopf.

Goldstein, Ivo 1999. *Croatia: A History*. London: Hurst.

Goldstone, Jack 1991. *Revolutions and Rebellions in the Early Modern World*. Berkeley: University of California Press.

Gorski, Philip 2003. *The Disciplinary Revolution: Calvinism and the Rise of the State in Early Modern Europe*. Chicago: University of Chicago Press.

Gould, William 2004. *Hindu Nationalism and the Language of Politics in Late Colonial India*. Cambridge: Cambridge University Press.

Gourevitch, Philip 2000. *We Wish to Inform You That Tomorrow We Will Be Killed with Our Families: Stories from Rwanda*. London: Picador.

Greenfeld, Liah 1992. *Nationalism: Five Roads to Modernity*. Cambridge, MA: Harvard University Press.

Griffeth, Robert and Carol Thomas 1981. Five city-state cultures compared, in R. Griffeth and C. G. Thomas (eds.), *The City-State in Five Cultures*. Santa Barbara and Oxford: ABC-Clio.

Bibliography

Griffin, Roger 2007. *Modernism and Fascism: The Sense of a Beginning under Mussolini and Hitler*. Basingstoke: Palgrave.

Griffith, Paddy 1989. *Battle Tactics of the Civil War*. New Haven: Yale University Press.

Grosby, Steven 2006. *Nationalism: A Very Short Introduction*. Oxford: Oxford University Press.

Grossman, Dave 1996. *On Killing: The Psychological Cost of Learning to Kill in War and Society*. Boston: Little, Brown.

Grossman, Dave and Loren W. Christensen 2008. *On Combat: The Psychology and Physiology of Deadly Conflict in War and in Peace*. Millstadt, IL: Warrior Science.

Gruen, Erich 1992. *Culture and National Identity in Republican Rome*. Ithaca: Cornell University Press.

Guibernau, Montserrat 2007. *The Identity of Nations*. Cambridge: Polity.

Gurr, Ted 2000. *Peoples versus States: Minorities at Risk in the New Century*. Washington, DC: U.S. Institute of Peace Press.

Gurr, Ted 1993. *Minorities and Risk: A Global View of Ethnopolitical Conflicts*. Washington, DC: U.S. Institute of Peace Press.

Gurr, Ted and Barbara Harff 1994. *Ethnic Conflict in World Politics*. Boulder: Westview Press.

Hall, John A. 2011. Nationalism might change its character, again, in D. Halikiopoulou and S. Vasilopoulou (eds.), *Nationalism and Globalization: Conflicting or Complementary?* London: Routledge.

Hall, John A. 2010. *Ernest Gellner: An Intellectual Biography*. London: Verso.

Hall, John A. 2006. Plaidoyer pour l'Europe des patries, in R. Rogowski and C. Turner (eds.), *The Shape of the New Europe*. Cambridge: Cambridge University Press.

Hall, John A. 2002. A disagreement about difference, in S. Malešević and M. Haugaard (eds.), *Making Sense of Collectivity: Ethnicity, Nationalism and Globalization*. London: Pluto.

Hall, John A. 2000. Globalization and nationalism, *Thesis Eleven* 63: 63–79.

Hall, John A. 1988. States and societies: The miracle in comparative perspective, in J. Baechler, J. A. Hall and M. Mann (eds.), *Europe and the Rise of Capitalism*. Oxford: Blackwell.

Hall, John A. 1985. *Powers and Liberties*. Oxford: Blackwell.

Hall, John A. and Siniša Malešević 2013. Introduction: Wars and nationalisms, in J. A. Hall and S. Malešević (eds.), *Nationalism and War*. Cambridge: Cambridge University Press.

Hall, Jonathan 1997. *Ethnic Identity in Greek Antiquity*. Cambridge: Cambridge University Press.

Hankins, Barry 2004. *The Second Great Awakening and the Transcendentalists*. Westport: Greenwood.

Hansen, Judith 1980. *We Are a Little Land: Cultural Assumptions in Danish Everyday Life*. Williamsville: Ayer.

Harvey, David 2009. *Cosmopolitanism and the Geographies of Freedom*. New York: Columbia University Press.

Hassan, Riaz 2011. *Suicide Bombings*. London: Routledge.

Hastings, Adrian 1997. *The Construction of Nationhood*. Cambridge: Cambridge University Press.

Haupt, Heinz-Gerhard and Dieter Langewiesche (eds.) 2004. *Nation und Religion in Europa*. Frankfurt: Campus.

Hearn, Jonathan 2011. Global crisis, national blame, in D. Halikiopoulou and S. Vasilopoulou (eds.), *Nations and Globalization: Conflicting or Complementary?* London: Routledge.

Hearn, Jonathan 2007. National identity: Banal, personal, and embedded, *Nations and Nationalism* 13 (4): 657–74.

Hearn, Jonathan 2006. *Rethinking Nationalism: A Critical Introduction*. New York: Palgrave.

Held, David 2003. *Cosmopolitanism: A Defence*. Cambridge: Polity.

Hill, Peter 2006. Kamikaze, 1943–5, in D. Gambetta (ed.), *Making Sense of Suicide Missions*. Oxford: Oxford University Press.

Himmelfarb, Milton 1984. No Hitler, no Holocaust, *Commentary* 77 (3): 37–43.

Hinsley, Frances H. 1967. *Hitler's Strategy*. Cambridge: Cambridge University Press.

Hintze, Otto 1975. *The Historical Essays of Otto Hintze*. New York: Oxford University Press.

Hippler, Thomas 2008. *Citizens, Soldiers and National Armies: Military Service in France and Germany, 1789–1830*. London: Routledge.

Hirst, Paul, Grahame Thompson and Simon Bromley 2009. *Globalization in Question*, 3rd edition. Cambridge: Polity.

Hobsbawm, Eric 1990. *Nations and Nationalism since 1780*. Cambridge: Cambridge University Press.

Hobsbawm, Eric 1983. Mass producing traditions: Europe, 1870–1914, in E. Hobsbawm and T. Ranger (eds.), *The Invention of Tradition*. Cambridge: Cambridge University Press.

Hoffmann, Claudia 2007. *Learning in Modern International Society*. New York: Springer.

Holmes, Richard 1985. *Acts of War*. New York: Free Press.

Hopgood, Steven 2006. Tamil Tigers 1987–2002, in D. Gambetta (ed.), *Making Sense of Suicide Missions*. Oxford: Oxford University Press.

Horowitz, Donald 2001. *The Deadly Ethnic Riot*. Berkeley: University of California Press.

Horowitz, Donald 1985. *Ethnic Groups in Conflict*. Berkeley: University of California Press.

Bibliography

Hroch, Miroslav 1985. *Social Preconditions of a National Revival in Europe.* Cambridge: Cambridge University Press.

Hutchinson, John 2011. Globalization and nation formation in the longue durée, in D. Halikiopoulou and S. Vasilopoulou (eds.), *Nationalism and Globalization: Conflicting or Complementary?* London: Routledge.

Hutchinson, John 2006. Hot and banal nationalism: The nationalization of 'the masses', in G. Delanty and K. Kumar (eds.), *The Sage Handbook of Nations and Nationalism.* London: Sage.

Hutchinson, John 2005. *Nations as Zones of Conflict.* London: Sage.

Hutchinson, John 2004. Myth against myth: The nation as ethnic overlay, *Nations and Nationalism* 10 (1–2): 109–24.

Hutchinson, John 1994. *Modern Nationalism.* London: Fontana Press.

Hutchinson, John 1987. *The Dynamics of Cultural Nationalism: The Gaelic Revival and the Creation of the Irish Nation State.* London: Allen & Unwin.

İnalcık, Halil and Donald Quataert (eds.) 1994. *An Economic and Social History of the Ottoman Empire, 1600–1914. Vol. 2.* Cambridge: Cambridge University Press.

Jenkins, Richard 2010. *Being Danish: Paradoxes of Identity in Everyday Life.* Copenhagen: Museum Tusculanum Press.

Jenkins, Richard 2008. *Social Identity*, 3rd edition. London: Routledge.

Jones, Barbara and Bill Howell 1972. *Popular Arts of the First World War.* New York: McGraw-Hill.

Jones, Rhys and Peter Merriman 2009. Hot, banal and everyday nationalism: Bilingual road signs in Wales, *Political Geography* 28 (3): 164–73.

Jones, Robert Edward 1973. *The Emancipation of the Russian Nobility 1762–1785.* Princeton: Princeton University Press.

Joppke, Christian 2009. *Veil: Mirror of Identity.* Cambridge: Polity.

Joseph, John 2004. *Language and Identity: National, Ethnic, Religious.* New York: Palgrave.

Juergensmeyer, Mark 2003. *Terror in the Mind of God: The Global Rise of Religious Violence.* Berkeley: University of California Press.

Kaldor, Mary 2004. Nationalism and globalization, *Nations and Nationalism* 10 (1–2): 161–77.

Kalyvas, Sthatys 2006. *The Logic of Violence in Civil War.* Cambridge: Cambridge University Press.

Kang, Jin Woong 2012. North Korea's militant nationalism and people's everyday lives: Past and present, *Journal of Historical Sociology* 25 (1): 1–30.

Kant, Immanuel 1990 [1784]. *Foundations of the Metaphysics of Morals and What is Enlightenment?* London: Macmillan.

Kaufman, Stewart 2001. *Modern Hatreds: The Symbolic Politics of Ethnic War.* Ithaca: Cornell University Press.

Kedourie, Elie 1993 [1960]. *Nationalism.* Oxford: Blackwell.

Keegan, John 1994. *A History of Warfare.* New York: Vintage.

Kelly, Raymond 2000. *Warless Societies and the Origin of War*. Ann Arbor: University of Michigan Press.

Keohane, Kieran 1997. *Symptoms of Canada*. Toronto: University of Toronto Press.

Kepel, Gilles 2002. *Jihad: On the Trail of Political Islam*. Cambridge, MA: Harvard University Press.

Kiernan, Ben 2007. *Blood and Soil: A World History of Genocide and Extermination from Sparta to Darfur*. New Haven: Yale University Press.

Kitromilides, Paschalis 2010. The Orthodox Church in modern state formation in South-East Europe, in W. Van Meurs and A. Mungiu-Pippidi (eds.), *Ottomans into Europeans: State and Institution Building in South Eastern Europe*. London: Hurst.

Koenig-Archibugi, Mathias 2003. National and European citizenship: the Italian case in historical perspective, *Citizenship Studies* 7 (1): 85–109.

Korsgaard, Uve 2008. *The Struggle for the People: Five Hundred Years of Danish History in Short*. Copenhagen: Danish School of Education Press.

Kumar, Krishan 2010. Nation-States as empires, empires as nation-states: Two principles, one practice?, *Theory and Society* 39 (2): 119–43.

Kumar, Krishan 2003. *The Making of English National Identity*. Cambridge: Cambridge University Press.

Lachmann, Richard 2013. Mercenary, citizen, victim: The evolution of the Western soldier, in J. A. Hall and S. Malešević (eds.), *Nationalism and War*. Cambridge: Cambridge University Press.

Lachmann, Richard 2010. *States and Power*. Cambridge: Polity.

Laitin, David 2007. *Nations, States, and Violence*. Oxford: Oxford University Press.

Lapidus, Ira 2001. Between universalism and particularism: The historic basis of Muslim communal, national and global identities, *Global Networks* (1) 1: 37–55.

Leerssen, Joep 2006. *National Thought in Europe*. Amsterdam: Amsterdam University Press.

Lefebvre, Henri 1971. *Everyday Life in the Modern World*, trans. Sacha Rabinovitch. New York: Harper and Row.

Lemarchand, René 2013. War and nationalism: The view from Central Africa. In J. A. Hall and S. Malešević (eds.), *Nationalism and War*. Cambridge: Cambridge University Press.

Lieven, Dominic 2003. *Empire: the Russian Empire and its Rivals*. New York: Random House.

Lim, Jae-Cheon 2009. *Kim Jong Il's Leadership of North Korea*. London: Routledge.

Llobera, Josep 1994. *The God of Modernity: The Development of Nationalism in Western Europe*. Oxford: Berg.

Löfgren, Orvar 1993. Materializing the nation in Sweden and America, *Ethnos* 3–4: 161–97.

Mackey, Eva 1999. *The House of Difference: Cultural Politics and National Identity in Canada*. London: Routledge.

Magaš, Branka 2007. *Croatia Through History: The Making of a European State*. London: Saqi Books.

Malešević, Siniša (in preparation) Where does solidarity come from? The case of Bosnian Serb soldiers (1992–1995). Dublin: UCD School of Sociology.

Malešević, Siniša 2013a. Obliterating heterogeneity through peace: Nationalisms, wars and states in the Balkans, in J. A. Hall and S. Malešević (eds.), *Nationalism and War*. Cambridge: Cambridge University Press.

Malešević, Siniša 2013b. Is nationalism intrinsically violent?, *Nationalism and Ethnic Politics* 19 (1): 12–37.

Malešević, Siniša 2012a. Wars that make states and wars that make nations: Organised violence, nationalism and state formation in the Balkans, *European Journal of Sociology* 53 (1): 31–63.

Malešević, Siniša 2012b. Did wars make nation-states in the Balkans? Nationalisms, wars and states in the 19th and early 20th century South East Europe, *Journal of Historical Sociology* 25 (3): 299–330.

Malešević, Siniša 2011a. Ideology, in K. Dowding (ed.), *Encyclopedia of Power*. London: Sage.

Malešević, Siniša 2011b. Nationalism, war and social cohesion, *Ethnic and Racial Studies* 34 (1): 142–61.

Malešević, Siniša 2011c. Ethnicity in time and space: A conceptual analysis, *Critical Sociology* 37 (1): 67–82.

Malešević, Siniša 2010. *The Sociology of War and Violence*. Cambridge: Cambridge University Press.

Malešević, Siniša 2007. Between the book and the new sword: Gellner, violence and ideology, in S. Malešević and M. Haugaard (eds.), *Ernest Gellner and Contemporary Social Thought*. Cambridge: Cambridge University Press.

Malešević, Siniša 2006. *Identity as Ideology: Understanding Ethnicity and Nationalism*. New York: Palgrave Macmillan.

Malešević, Siniša 2004. *The Sociology of Ethnicity*. London: Sage.

Malešević, Siniša 2002. *Ideology, Legitimacy and the New State*. London: Routledge.

Mamdani, Mahmood 2001. *When Victims Become Killers: Colonialism, Nativism and the Genocide in Rwanda*. Princeton: Princeton University Press.

Mann, Michael 2013. The role of nationalism in the two world wars, in J. A. Hall and S. Malešević (eds.), *Nationalism and War*. Cambridge: Cambridge University Press.

Mann, Michael 2012. *The Sources of Social Power III: Global Empires and Revolution, 1890–1945*. Cambridge: Cambridge University Press.

Mann, Michael 2006a. The sources of social power revisited: A response to criticism, in J. A. Hall and R. Schroeder (eds.), *An Anatomy of Power: The Social Theory of Michael Mann*. Cambridge: Cambridge University Press.

Bibliography

Mann, Michael 2006b. Reply: Is democracy, and was fascism, sacred?, *Political Studies Review* 4 (3): 290–7.

Mann, Michael 2005. *The Dark Side of Democracy: Explaining Ethnic Cleansing.* Cambridge: Cambridge University Press.

Mann, Michael 2004. *Fascists.* Cambridge: Cambridge University Press.

Mann, Michael 2003. *Incoherent Empire.* London: Verso.

Mann, Michael 1997. Has globalization ended the rise and rise of the nation-state?, *Review of International Political Economy* 4 (3): 472–96.

Mann, Michael 1995. A political theory of nationalism and its excesses, in S. Periwal (ed.), *Notions of Nationalism.* Budapest: CEU Press.

Mann, Michael 1993. *The Sources of Social Power II: The Rise of Classes and Nation States 1760–1914.* Cambridge: Cambridge University Press.

Mann, Michael 1988. *States, War and Capitalism: Studies in Political Sociology.* Oxford: Blackwell.

Mann, Michael 1986. *The Sources of Social Power I: A History of Power from the Beginning to AD 1760.* Cambridge: Cambridge University Press.

Marrus, Michael 1985. *The Unwanted: European Refugees in the Twentieth Century.* New York: Oxford University Press.

Marshall, Samuel L. A. 1947. *Men against Fire: The Problem of Battle Command.* New York: Morrow.

Martines, Lauro 1983. *Power and Imagination: City-States in Renaissance Italy.* Harmondsworth: Penguin.

Marvin, Carolyn and David Ingle 1999. *Blood Sacrifice and the Nation: Totem Rituals and the American Flag.* Cambridge: Cambridge University Press.

Marx, Anthony 2003. *Faith in the Nation: Exclusionary Origins of Nationalism.* Oxford: Oxford University Press.

Marx, Karl and Friedrich Engels 1977. *Collected Works.* London: Lawrence and Wishart.

Maryanski, Alexandra and Jonathan Turner 1996. *The Social Cage.* Stanford: Stanford University Press.

Mazower, Mark 2000. *Dark Continent: Europe's Twentieth Century.* Harmondsworth: Penguin.

McClelland, Kent 1985. On the social significance of interactional synchrony. Unpublished paper, Department of Sociology, Grinnell College.

McCrone, David 1997. Unmasking Britannia: The rise and fall of British national identity, *Nations and Nationalism* 3 (4): 579–96.

McCrone, David and Gayle McPherson 2009. Introduction, in D. McCrone and G. McPherson (eds.), *National Days: Constructing and Mobilising National Identity.* Basingstoke: Palgrave.

McCrone, David, Robert Stewart, Richard Kiely and Frank Bechhofer 1998. Who are we? Problematising national identity, *Sociological Review* 46 (4): 629–52.

Bibliography

McDougal, James 2006. *History and the Culture of Nationalism in Algeria.* Cambridge: Cambridge University Press.

McKenna, George 2007. *The Puritan Origins of American Patriotism.* Ithaca: Yale University Press.

Medrano, Juan Díez 2009. *Framing Europe: Attitudes to European Integration in Germany, Spain and the United Kingdom.* Princeton: Princeton University Press.

Mennell, Stephen 2007. *The American Civilizing Process.* Cambridge: Polity.

Meriage, Lawrence P. 1977. The first Serbian uprising (1804–1813): National revival or a search for regional security?, *Canadian Review of Studies in Nationalism* 4 (2): 187–205.

Merton, Robert 1952. Bureaucratic personality and structure, in R. Merton, A. Gray, B. Hockey and H. Selvin (eds.), *Reader in Bureaucracy.* Glencoe, IL: Free Press.

Meyer, John W., John Boli, George M. Thomas and Francisco O. Ramirez 1997. World society and the nation-state, *American Journal of Sociology* 103 (1): 144–81.

Meyer, John W., David H. Kamens and Aaron Benavot, with Yun-Kyung Cha and Suk-Ying Wong 1992. *School Knowledge for the Masses: World Models and National Primary Curricular Categories in the Twentieth Century.* London: Falmer Press.

Midlarsky, Manus 2011. *Origins of Political Extremism: Mass Violence in the Twentieth Century and Beyond.* Cambridge: Cambridge University Press.

Miller, Alice 1983. *For Your Own Good: Hidden Cruelty in Child-Rearing and the Roots of Violence.* New York: Farrar, Straus & Giroux.

Miller, David 1995. *On Nationality.* Oxford: Oxford University Press.

Miller, William Ian 2000. *The Mystery of Courage.* Cambridge, MA: Harvard University Press.

Miller-Idriss, Cynthia 2009. *Blood and Culture: Youth, Right-Wing Extremism, and National Belonging in Contemporary Germany.* Durham, NC: Duke University Press.

Minogue, Kenneth 2003. 'Managing' nationalism, *New Left Review* 23: 46–67.

Moreno, Luis 1988. Scotland and Catalonia: The path to home rule, in D. McCrone and A. Brown (eds.), *The Scottish Government Yearbook.* Edinburgh: Unit for the Study of Government in Scotland.

Mosse, George 1991. *Fallen Soldiers: Reshaping the Memory of the World Wars.* Oxford: Oxford University Press.

Mosse, George 1975. *Nationalization of the Masses: Political Symbolism and Mass Movements in Germany from the Napoleonic Wars through the Third Reich.* New York: Howard Fertig.

Mouffe, Chantal 2005. *On the Political.* New York: Routledge.

Mouzelis, Nicos 2007. Nationalism: Restructuring Gellner's theory, in

Bibliography

S. Malešević and M. Haugaard (eds.), *Ernest Gellner and Contemporary Social Thought*. Cambridge: Cambridge University Press.

Muller, John 2007. *Remnants of War*. Ithaca: Cornell University Press.

Munkler, Herfried 2007. *Empire*. Cambridge: Polity.

Musil, Robert 1986. *Selected Writings*. London: Continuum.

Nairn, Tom 1981. *The Break-Up of Britain: Crisis and Neo-Nationalism*. London: Verso.

Nanjira, Daniel 2010. *African Foreign Policy and Diplomacy from Antiquity to the 21st Century*. Santa Barbara and Oxford: ABC-Clio.

Neitzel, Sönke and Harald Welzer 2012. *Soldaten: On Fighting, Killing and Dying*. New York: Simon and Schuster.

Neurberger, Benjamin 2006. Genocide in Rwanda: The dark side of democracy?, *Nations and Nationalism* 12 (3): 402–7.

Nimni, Ephraim 1991. *Marxism and Nationalism*. London: Verso.

Nussbaum, Martha C. 2006. *Frontiers of Justice: Disability, Nationality, Species Membership*. Cambridge, MA: Belknap Press.

O'Leary, Brendan 1998. Ernest Gellner's diagnosis of nationalism: A critical overview, or, What is living and what is dead in Ernest Gellner's philosophy of nationalism?, in J. A. Hall (ed.), *The State of the Nation: Ernest Gellner and the Theory of Nationalism*. Cambridge: Cambridge University Press.

O'Leary, Cecilia 2000. *To Die for: The Paradox of American Patriotism*. Princeton: Princeton University Press.

Opello, Walter and Steven Rosow 2004. *The Nation-State and Global Order: A Historical Introduction to Contemporary Politics*. Boulder and London: Lynne Rienner.

Opie, Robert F. 2006. *Guillotine: Timbers of Justice*. Stroud: Sutton.

Orridge, Andrew W. 1981. Uneven development and nationalism, *Political Studies* 29 (1): 1–15.

Østergaard, Uffe 2006. Denmark: A big small state – the peasant roots of Danish modernity, in J. L. Campbell, J. A. Hall and O. K. Pedersen (eds.), *National Identity and the Varieties of Capitalism: The Danish Experience*. Montreal: McGill-Queen's University Press.

Özkırımlı, Umut 2010. *Theories of Nationalism: A Critical Introduction*. New York: Palgrave.

Paasi, Anssi 2009. The resurgence of the 'region' and 'regional identity': Theoretical perspectives and empirical observations on regional dynamics in Europe, *Review of International Studies* 35 (1): 121–46.

Padget, Tim 2010. How the miners have won respect for Chile's workers, *Time* 14 October.

Pape, Robert 2005. *Dying to Win: The Strategic Logic of Suicide Terrorism*. New York: Random House.

Pareto, Vilfredo 1963 [1902]. *Mind and Society: A Treatise on General Sociology*. New York: Dover.

Bibliography

Parker, Geoffrey 2004. *Sovereign City: City-States through History*. London: Reaktion Books.

Pavlowitch, Stefan 1999. *A History of the Balkans 1804–1945*. London: Longman.

Pinker, Steven 2011. *The Better Angels of Our Nature: Why Violence has Declined*. New York: Viking.

Poggi, Gianfranco 1978. *The Development of the Modern State*. Stanford: Stanford University Press.

Pomeranz, Kenneth 2000. *The Great Divergence: China, Europe, and the Making of the Modern World Economy*. Princeton: Princeton University Press.

Proust, Marcel 2004 [1913]. *Swann's Way*. London: Penguin.

Raento, Pauliina and Stanley D. Brunn 2005. Visualizing Finland: Postage stamps as political messengers, *Geografiska Annaler: Series B, Human Geography* 87 (2): 145–64.

Ram, Uri 2008. Why secularism fails? Secular nationalism and religious revivalism in Israel, *International Journal of Politics, Culture and Society* 21 (1–4): 57–73.

Ramet, Sabrina P. 2004. Explaining the Yugoslav meltdown, *Nationalities Papers* 32 (4): 731–63, 765–79.

Reader, Ian 2000. *Religious Violence in Contemporary Japan*. Honolulu: University of Hawai'i Press.

Reicher, Steve and Nick Hopkins 2001. *Self and Nation*. London: Sage.

Remarque, Erich Maria 1984 [1929]. *All Quiet on the Western Front*. New York: Ballantine Books.

Renan, Ernest 1990 [1882]. What is a Nation?, in H. Bhaba (ed.), *Nation and Narration*. London: Routledge.

Rhee, Song Nai 1981. Sumerian city-states, in R. Griffeth and C. G. Thomas (eds.), *The City-State in Five Cultures*. Santa Barbara and Oxford: ABC-Clio.

Ricolfi, Luca 2006. Palestinians, 1981–2003, in D. Gambetta (ed.), *Making Sense of Suicide Missions*. Oxford; Oxford University Press.

Roeder, Philip G. 2007. *Where Nation-States Come From: Institutional Change in the Age of Nationalism*. Princeton: Princeton University Press.

Rolston, Bill 1987. Politics, painting and popular culture: The political wall murals of Northern Ireland, *Media, Culture and Society* 9 (1): 5–28.

Roshwald, Aviel 2006. *The Endurance of Nationalism: Ancient Roots and Modern Dilemmas*. Cambridge: Cambridge University Press.

Roudometof, Victor 2001. *Nationalism, Globalization, and Orthodoxy: The Social Origins of Ethnic Conflict in the Balkans*. Westport: Greenwood.

Sageman, Marc 2004. *Understanding Terror Networks*. Philadelphia: University of Pennsylvania Press.

Sand, Shlomo 2010. *The Invention of the Jewish People*. London: Verso.

Scheff, Thomas 1994. *Bloody Revenge: Emotions, Nationalism, and War*. Boulder: Westview Press.

Bibliography

Schmitt, Carl 1996. *The Concept of the Political*. Chicago: Chicago University Press.

Schulze, Hagen 1996. *States, Nations and Nationalism: From the Middle Ages to the Present*. Oxford: Blackwell.

Sell, Louis 2002. *Slobodan Milosevic and the Destruction of Yugoslavia*. Durham, NC: Duke University Press.

Sen, Gautam 1984. *The Military Origins of Industrialisation and International Trade Rivalry*. London: Pinter.

Service, Elman 1978. *Profiles in Ethnology*. New York: Harper and Row.

Seth, Michael 2010. *A History of Korea: From Antiquity to the Present*. New York: Rowman and Littlefield.

Shaw, Ian 2004. *Ancient Egypt: A Very Short Introduction*. Oxford: Oxford University Press.

Shils, Edward and Morris Janowitz 1948. Cohesion and disintegration in the Wehrmacht in World War II, *Public Opinion Quarterly* 12: 280–315.

Shimazu, Naoko 2009. *Japanese Society at War: Death, Memory and the Russo-Japanese War*. Cambridge: Cambridge University Press.

Shin, Gi-Wook 2006. *Ethnic Nationalism in Korea: Genealogy, Politics, and Legacy*. Stanford: Stanford University Press.

Simmel, Georg 1955 [1917]. *Conflict and the Web of Group Affiliations*. New York: Free Press.

Simmel, Georg 1950 [1908]. *The Sociology of Georg Simmel, translated and edited by Kurt Wolff*. New York: Free Press.

Sinnott, Richard 2005. An evaluation of the measurement of national, sub-national and supranational identity in cross-national surveys, *International Journal of Public Opinion Research* 18 (2): 211–23.

Siskind, Janet 1992. The invention of Thanksgiving, *Critique of Anthropology* 12: 167–91.

Sivan, Emmanuel 1997. Arab nationalism in the age of Islamic resurgence, in J. P. Jankowski and I. Gershoni (eds.), *Rethinking Nationalism in the Arab Middle East*. New York: Columbia University Press.

Skey, Michael 2009. The national in everyday life: A critical engagement with Michael Billig's thesis of banal nationalism, *Sociological Review* 58 (2): 331–64.

Skocpol, Theda 1992. *Protecting Soldiers and Mothers: The Political Origins of Social Policy in the United States*. Cambridge, MA: Harvard University Press.

Skocpol, Theda 1979. *States and Social Revolutions: A Comparative Analysis of France, Russia, and China*. Cambridge: Cambridge University Press.

Smith, Anthony D. 2011. National identity and vernacular mobilization in Europe, *Nations and Nationalism* 17: 223–56.

Smith, Anthony D. 2010. *Nationalism*, 2nd edition. Cambridge: Polity.

Smith, Anthony D. 2009. *Ethno-Symbolism and Nationalism: A Cultural Approach*. London: Routledge.

Bibliography

Smith, Anthony D. 2008. The limits of everyday nationhood, *Ethnicities* 8 (4): 563–73.

Smith, Anthony D. 2005. The genealogy of nations: An ethno-symbolic approach, in A. Ichijo and G. Uzelac (eds.), *When is the Nation?* London: Routledge.

Smith, Anthony D. 2004. *The Antiquity of Nations.* Cambridge: Polity.

Smith, Anthony D. 2003. *Chosen Peoples: Sacred Sources of National Identity.* New York: Oxford University Press.

Smith, Anthony D. 2001. Interpretations of national identity, in A. Dieckhoff and N. Gutierrez (eds.), *Modern Roots: Studies of National Identities.* Aldershot: Ashgate Press.

Smith, Anthony D. 1999. *Myths and Memories of the Nation.* Oxford: Oxford University Press.

Smith, Anthony D. 1998. *Nationalism and Modernism.* London: Routledge.

Smith, Anthony D. 1996. The nation: Real or imagined?, *Nations and Nationalism,* 2 (3): 357–70.

Smith, Anthony D. 1995. *Nations and Nationalism in a Global Era.* Cambridge: Polity.

Smith, Anthony D. 1991. *National Identity.* London: Penguin.

Smith, Anthony D. 1986. *The Ethnic Origins of Nations.* Oxford: Blackwell.

Smith, Anthony D. 1971. *Theories of Nationalism.* London: Duckworth.

Smith, Tom and Seokho Kim 2006. National pride in cross-national and temporal perspective, *International Journal of Public Opinion Research* 18 (1): 127–36.

Snyder, Jack 2000. *From Voting to Violence: Democratization and Nationalist Conflict.* New York: W. W. Norton.

Snyder, Louis 1968. *New Nationalism.* Ithaca: Cornell University Press.

Sombart, Werner 1913. *Krieg und Kapitalismus.* Munich: Duncker & Humblot.

Soustelle, Jacques 1995. *The Daily Life of the Aztecs on the Eve of the Spanish Conquest.* Stanford: Stanford University Press.

Spillman, Lyn 1997. *Nation and Commemoration: Creating National Identities in the United States and Australia.* Cambridge: Cambridge University Press.

Spohn, Willfried 2003. Multiple modernity, nationalism, and religion: A global perspective, *Current Sociology* 51 (3/4): 265–87.

Spruyt, Hendrik 1994. *The Sovereign State and its Competitors.* Princeton: Princeton University Press.

Steuer, Heiko 2006. Warrior bands, war lords and the birth of tribes and states in the first millennium AD in Middle Europe, in T. Otto, H. Thrane and H. Vandkilde (eds.), *Warfare and Society: Archaeological and Social Anthropological Perspectives.* Aarhus: Aarhus University Press.

Stoakes, Geoffrey 1986. *Hitler and the Quest for World Dominion.* Oxford: Berg.

Surak, Kristin 2012. Nation-work: A praxeology of making and maintaining nations, *European Journal of Sociology* 53 (2): 171–204.

Bibliography

Suszycki, Marcin (ed.) 2011. *Welfare Citizenship and Welfare Nationalism.* Helsinki: NordWel.

Sutherland, Claire 2012. *Nationalism in the Twenty-First Century: Challenges and Responses.* Basingstoke: Palgrave.

Sutherland, Claire 2010. *Soldered States: Nation-Building in Germany and Vietnam.* Basingstoke: Palgrave.

Sztompka, Piotr 1994. *The Sociology of Social Change.* Oxford: Blackwell.

Taylor, Charles 2007. *Secular Age.* Cambridge, MA: Harvard University Press.

Taylor, Charles 1993. *Reconciling the Solitudes: Essays on Canadian Federalism and Nationalism.* Montreal: McGill-Queens University Press.

Theiss-Morse, Elizabeth 2009. *Who Counts as an American? The Boundaries of National Identity.* Cambridge: Cambridge University Press.

Thomas, Carol 1981. The Greek polis, in R. Griffeth and C. G. Thomas (eds.), *The City-State in Five Cultures.* Santa Barbara and Oxford: ABC-Clio.

Thomas, Scott 2005. *The Global Resurgence of Religion and the Transformation of International Relations.* Basingstoke: Palgrave.

Thompson, Andrew 2001. Nations, national identities and human agency: Putting people back into nations, *Sociological Review* 49 (1): 18–33.

Thompson, Andrew and Graham Day 1999. Situating Welshness: 'Local' experience and national identity, in R. Fevre and A. Thompson (eds.), *Nation, Identity and Social Theory: Perspectives from Wales.* Cardiff: University of Wales Press.

Tilly, Charles 1992. *Coercion, Capital and European States.* Oxford: Blackwell.

Tilly, Charles 1985. War making and state making as organized crime, in P. Evans, D. Rueschemeyer and T. Skocpol (eds.), *Bringing the State Back In.* Cambridge: Cambridge University Press.

Tilly, Charles 1978. *From Mobilization to Revolution.* Reading, MA: Addison-Wesley.

Tilly, Charles 1975. *The Formation of National States in Western Europe.* Princeton, NJ: Princeton University Press.

Tönnies, Ferdinand 1955 [1887]. *Community and Association.* London: Routledge & Kegan Paul.

Torpey, John 2000. *The Invention of the Passport: Surveillance, Citizenship and the State.* Cambridge: Cambridge University Press.

Trigger, Bruce, Barry Kemp, David O'Connor and Alan B. Lloyd 1983. *Ancient Egypt: A Social History.* Cambridge: Cambridge University Press.

Tsouras, Peter 2005. *Montezuma: Warlord of the Aztecs.* Washington, DC: Potomac Books.

Turner, Jonathan 2007. *Human Emotions: A Sociological Theory.* London: Routledge.

Turner, Jonathan and Alexandra Maryanski 2005. *Incest: Origins of the Taboo.* Boulder: Paradigm.

Tyler, Tom R. and Steven Blader 2000. *Cooperation in Groups: Procedural*

Bibliography

Justice, Social Identity, and Behavioral Engagement. Philadelphia: Psychology Press.

Uzelac, Gordana 2011. National ceremonies: The pursuit of authenticity, *Ethnic and Racial Studies* 33 (10): 1718–36.

van den Berghe, Pierre 1995. Does race matter?, *Nations and Nationalism* 1 (3): 357–68.

van den Berghe, Pierre 1990. Introduction, in P. van den Berghe (ed.), *State Violence and Ethnicity*. Niwot: University Press of Colorado.

van den Berghe, Pierre 1981. *The Ethnic Phenomenon*. New York: Elsevier.

van der Dennen, Johan 1999. Of badges, bonds and boundaries: In-group/out-group differentiation and ethnocentrism revisited, in K. Thienpont and R. Cliquet (eds.), *In-Group/Out-Group Behaviour in Modern Societies: An Evolutionary Perspective*. Brussels: NIDI CBGS.

van der Veer, Peter 1999. Hindus: A superior race, *Nations and Nationalism* 5 (3): 419–30.

Viroli, Maurizio 1997. *For Love of Country: An Essay on Patriotism and Nationalism*. Oxford: Clarendon Press.

Vogel, Steven 1996. *Freer Markets, More Rules: Regulatory Reform in Advanced Industrial Countries*. Ithaca: Cornell University Press.

Waley, Daniel 1969. *The Italian City-Republics*. London: World University Library.

Wallerstein, Immanuel 1974. *The Modern World-System: Capitalist Agriculture and the Origins of the European World-Economy in the Sixteenth Century*. New York: Academic Press.

Weber, Eugen 1978. *Peasants into Frenchmen: The Modernization of Rural France, 1870–1914*. Stanford: Stanford University Press.

Weber, Max 1968 [1921]. *Economy and Society*. New York: Bedminster Press.

Whitmeyer, Joseph M. 2002. Elites and popular nationalism, *British Journal of Sociology* 53 (3): 321–41.

Wilk, Richard 1993. Beauty and the feast: Official and visceral nationalism in Belize, *Ethnos* 53 (3–4): 1–25.

Williams, Lynn 1999. National identity and the nation state: Construction, reconstruction and contradiction, in K. Cameron (ed.), *National Identity*. Exeter: Intellect.

Wimmer, Andreas 2012. *Waves of War: Nationalism, State Formation and Ethnic Exclusion in the Modern World*. Cambridge: Cambridge University Press.

Wimmer, Andreas and Yuval Feinstein 2010. The rise of the nation-state across the world, 1816–2001, *American Sociological Review* 75 (5): 764–90.

Wimmer, Andreas and Wesley Heirs 2013. Is nationalism the cause or consequence of the end of empire?, in J. A. Hall and S. Malešević (eds.), *Nationalism and War*. Cambridge: Cambridge University Press.

Bibliography

Wimmer, Andreas and Brian Min 2006. From empire to nation-state: Explaining wars in the modern world, 1816–2001, *American Sociological Review* 71 (6): 867–97.

Wodak, Ruth, Rudolf de Cillia, Martin Reisigl and Karin Liebhart 1999. *The Discursive Construction of National Identity*. Edinburgh: Edinburgh University Press.

Wohlstein, Ronald and Clark McPhail 1979. Judging the presence and extent of collective behaviour from film records, *Social Psychology Quarterly* 42: 76–81.

Wolffe, John 2007. *The Expansion of Evangelicalism: The Age of Wilberforce, More, Chalmers and Finney*. Downers Grove: InterVarsity Press.

Yoshino, Kosaku (ed.) 1999. *Consuming Ethnicity and Nationalism*. Honolulu: University of Hawai'i Press.

Yu, Haiqing 2009. *Media and Cultural Transformation in China*. London: Routledge.

Zhao, Dingxin 2006. *The Rise of the Qin Empire and Patterns of Chinese History*. Shanghai: Sanlian.

Zielonka, Jan 2006. *Europe as Empire: The Nature of the Enlarged European Union*. Oxford: Oxford University Press.

Zubaida, Sami 2004. Islam and nationalism: Continuities and contradictions, *Nations and Nationalism* 10 (4): 407–20.

Zubrzycki, Geneviève 2006. *The Crosses of Auschwitz: Nationalism and Religion in Post-Communist Poland*. Chicago: University of Chicago Press.

Index

Index

Index

Index

Index

Index